Anna Bartlett Warner

My Brother's Keeper

Anna Bartlett Warner

My Brother's Keeper

ISBN/EAN: 9783743301467

Manufactured in Europe, USA, Canada, Australia, Japa

Cover: Foto ©ninafisch / pixelio.de

Manufactured and distributed by brebook publishing software (www.brebook.com)

Anna Bartlett Warner

My Brother's Keeper

MY BROTHER'S KEEPER.

BY

A. B. WARNER,

AUTHOR OF "DOLLARS AND CENTS," "MR. RUTHERFORD'S CHILDREN," &C.

'He that hath light within his own clear breast,
May sit i' the centre and enjoy bright day.'—MILTON.

NEW YORK:
D. APPLETON & COMPANY,
443 & 445 BROADWAY.
LONDON: 16 LITTLE BRITAIN.
1866.

ENTERED according to Act of Congress, in the year 1855, by
D. APPLETON & COMPANY,
In the Clerk's Office of the District Court for the Southern District of New York.

CONTENTS.

Chap.		Page
I.—A Voluntary from the Wind,		5
II.—Gold Stick in Waiting,		8
III.—Love in the Market,		17
IV.—Quaker Lilies,		26
V.—The Last Day of December,		36
VI.—The First of January,		44
VII.—A Night View,		52
VIII.—Miss Morsel's Second Breakfast,		63
IX.—The Butterflies of 1812,		72
X.—From the War Hawk,		82
XI.—Little Kindnesses,		91
XII.—Confusion,		107
XIII.—'Into the Shadow—Out of the Sun,'		121
XIV.—What Sort of Sunshine it was,		132
XV.—Lady Hume's Blush,		144
XVI.—This Gentleman's Cousin, Sir,		153
XVII.—Yankees abroad,		166
XVIII.—Patriotic Candles,		174
XIX.—The Secret Society of Medicine,		187
XX.—Work by Firelight,		202
XXI.—The Morning's Fresh Breath,		215

CONTENTS.

Chap.	Page
XXII.—A Day at the Quakerage,	227
XXIII.—Of Peace,	239
XXIV.—The Burden of the Spring Winds,	249
XXV.—The Old Thirteen,	258
XXVI.—Meadow-Sweet,	270
XXVII.—Mother Baystate and Her Children,	277
XXVIII.—The Stone-Cutter's,	287
XXIX.—A Country of Joy,	295
XXX.—Another Country,	303
XXXI.—Indigenous Vexation,	314
XXXII.—Set Free,	323
XXXIII.—Why an Apple Falls,	334
XXXIV.—Grey Clouds at Sundown,	344
XXXV.—Mr. Penn's Pocket,	352
XXXVI.—Two Men in the Rain,	360
XXXVII.—The Bar-place,	367
XXXVIII.—Over the Bar,	375
XXXIX.—In Port,	381

MY BROTHER'S KEEPER:

CHAPTER I.

*When I fell sick, an' very sick,
An' very sick, just like to dee,
A gentleman o' good account,
He cam' on purpose to visit me.—Old Ballad.*

It was a blustering December day,—no snow to lay the dust or to allay the cold with its bright reflections; and Winter himself seemed shivering, despoiled of his ermine cloak.

In that very spirit in which some people seek out the worst side of human nature, the wind careered about,— picked up all the dust and straws it could find, and showered them upon the heads of innocent and well dressed people. Not exclusively, to be sure,—the wind was impartial in its bestowings; but if mischief may be measured by the trouble it gives and the effects it leaves behind it, then did "the upper ten" get more than their share that day. It mattered little to the chimney-sweeps that their caps were stuck with dry leaves, and their brown blankets flung about in every fantastical way—à la Don and à la Boreas,—the carters had no veils to blow off; and if now and then a rowdy's hat flew into the middle of the street, nobody pitied him and the hat was none the worse. But the ladies who fought the wind at every corner, and came upon an ambush of full grown zephyrs in most unexpected places, found the enemy's reinforcements to be far beyond their own; while hair was frizzed after every fashion not approved; the colour of dark hats became doubtful; and if white ones ever looked white again, it was only because in town one takes a medium standard of purity.

In the midst of it all the sky was sometimes quite clear, and in the sunshine the driver of some incoming stage loomed out from his high station, and hackney-coachmen became visible. Then with the next gust the clouds rushed on, as white and almost as light as snowflakes,—drifting, meeting, covering the blue, and causing an instant fall in the thermometer.

Through the throng of men and things a gig made its way, unmolested but not unheeded. Everybody looks at a doctor's gig, though everybody has seen one every day of his life,—everybody looks and wonders with a strange sort of interest. And there is always the same thing to be seen. On the one seat a remarkably comfortable-looking gentleman, in his multitude of greatcoats and wrappers (no doctor ever looked anything *but* comfortable); while the other seat contains with great ease a comparatively thin individual, hardly a sketch of the doctor, and usually habited in a cap, mittens, and a red worsted comforter. He enjoys moreover a share of the boot.

And it is no wonder that everybody looks; for there is a strange meeting of life and death in the air of that gig—its errand and itself so widely different!

The house towards which this one went had been already visited by the wind many times in the course of the day; and there it had demanded admittance as noisily as at any other house in the whole street. But of late the wind had grown respectful; and though just at the time when the doctor drove up Broadway it made one desperate dash at the third story windows, piling dry leaves and dust on every sash,—something it saw there seemed to calm its mood;— the wind not only went down sighing, but took the dry leaves with it.

CHAPTER II.

'I feel it not.'—'Then take it every hour.'
'It makes me worse.'—'Why then it shows its power.'—CRABBE.

'THE doctor's come, Miss Rosalie,' said a woman, opening the door of that very third story room. 'Been spry, aint he? I shouldn't wonder if his horse was somethin' more than common. But he's come, anyway. What's to be done with him?'

'Show him up here, Martha.'

And as the door closed the young lady's eyes came back to the bed by which she sat.

A child lay there, in that drowsiness which is of fever, not of sleep; to which the hot cheek and uneasy posture alike bore witness. She was not undressed, for the arm that lay above her head displayed a short merino sleeve at the shoulder; and at a very small distance down the bed one little shoe of childish cut moved restlessly from under the shawl fringe that half covered it. With what quick and fluttering action the fringe about her throat was stirred, the watcher noticed painfully; and softly drew it away, and was rewarded by the half unclosed eyes, and the lips that met to thank her.

'You have been asleep,' Rosalie said, resting her own upon them.

'I don't know,' said the child dreamily. 'Who's that coming up-stairs?'

'Doctor Buffem.' And even as she spoke, a long-continued and portentous creaking of boots came to a sudden stop at the door,—Doctor Buffem having paused for breath and admittance. The last was the easiest obtained.

'What the mischief! Miss Rosalie,' he said with some impatience. 'Why don't you emigrate to the stars at once? Venus would suit you well enough, or you might get a situation in Mars, you're of such a warlike disposition. You haven't got sense enough for Pallas, or you'd never be caught in the third story of a house while there were two below it.'

'I thought it would be quieter up here,' Rosalie said, with a face that was grave only because she had no heart to smile.

'Nonsense!' said the doctor, 'I should like to hear anybody make a noise in this house for once. Quieter! At this scale of elevation "the music of the spheres" is overpowering.' And putting his hands behind him the doctor marched off to the window, and with a very panting enunciation gave,—

'Yon tall anchoring bark
Diminish'd to a cock,—her cock a buoy.
The fishermen that walk the beach
Appear as mice.'

Very particularly comfortable he looked, with his gold spectacles and gold-beaded cane; and a head of his own which if not all of the same precious metal, had at least 'golden opinions.'—A singular contrast to the figure standing by the bedside, and wishing very intently that his gesticulations might have an end.

'Well, what's the matter with the child?' he said, wheeling suddenly round as if her existence had but just occurred to him. 'Out of breath with running up stairs, eh?'

And throwing down the shawl Dr. Buffem took the little hand in his, and scientifically applied his three fingers to the wrist.

'All dressed,—ready to go to Albany,' he remarked. 'Let's see your tongue. S, c, a, r,' said the doctor, looking round at Rosalie.

She gave no answer—that he could see, and none for him to hear. One quick bound of the heart—a bright spot that came and as quickly left her cheek, and she stood there as before, the hands perhaps holding each other in a somewhat firmer clasp.

The doctor replaced the shawl, straightened himself up, and began to talk.

'Here's a fine case,' he said; 'but I guess you and I can manage it. What sort of a nurse will you be, hey?'

'The best that I can, sir.'

'Hum—ah'—said the doctor, with a recollective glance at Rosalie's black dress which sent a thrill to her finger-ends,—the wound would not bear even that slight touch. 'Yes, I guess you'll do. Got a thermometer about the house?'

She bowed assentingly.

'Have it up here, then,—hang it anywhere except over the fire and outside the window, and keep it just at 70°,—no hotter, no colder. And don't let in more than half the sunlight at once,—keep the rest till afternoon,' said Doctor Buffem, walking off to the windows and closing the shutters. 'You're so close to the sun up here, Miss Rosalie, that he'll put out the eyes of well people if you give him a chance. There—I'll leave you one crack to put your face straight by,—important duty that in a sick-room. I'll come in again by-and-by, and bring you some powders,—came off without 'em this morning. And get her undressed and put to bed,' he added, with a nod at the sick child. 'She won't want to take much exercise to-day nor to-morrow. Ever had it yourself?'

'No sir.'

'Well—no, it's not well; but it can't be helped. Take care of you famously if you do get it.'

'What is the matter with me?' said the little patient, now speaking for the first time.

'Only scarlet fever,' said the doctor,—'that's not much. Worst thing is, it makes one look like a lobster.'

'Shall I be sick a great while?' said the child again.

'Hum—' said the doctor,—'depends entirely. Not if you make haste and get well. I'll cure you up in no time.'

The words seemed satisfactory enough, but they failed to give satisfaction. Hulda looked away from him to her sister, finding comfort in her look and smile, grave as they both were.

The doctor fidgetted about the room, kicked the fire, came back to ask questions, then stamped off to the door.

'Hark you, Miss Rosalie,' he said, 'don't forget why I left that crack in the window-shutter. Good-bye—I'll see you again this evening. And keep your spirits up,—there's nothing in life to put 'em down.'

But Rosalie thought that there was many a thing in life to do that office for her spirits had they needed it. In life! —With that thought came one of life's great antagonist, and sitting down once more by the bed she took her little sister on her lap, and began very tenderly that work of undressing which the doctor had recommended. Was there anything in death to depress her?

There had been,—the tokens of his power were not less plain upon her face than in her dress; and now—human nature lived still! Before those two sisters could be separated many a band must give way that passed about them, unseen in this world, but forming to the eyes of angels a golden tissue of love and confidence. Rosalie felt as if some hand were trying its strength even now. There was something in these quiet preparations for suffering that tried her extremely; and to brace her mind for possibilities, without that sudden strength which an emergency gives, was very hard. And more than once was her hand passed across her face with that feeling of which Rutherford wrote,—' O how sweet it is for a sinner to put his weakness in Christ's strengthening hand!—Weakness can speak and cry, when we have not a tongue.'

' Do you think I shall get well, Alie?' said little Hulda, looking up at her.

' I trust so, my darling.'

Steady and sweet the voice was as ever.

' Then what makes you look sorrowful?'

' Because you look sick. Is not that enough to make me sorrowful?'

' No,—not if I'm going to get well soon.' And as if but half satisfied with her sister's face, Hulda repeated,— ' Isn't he a good doctor? Won't he cure me?'"

' I believe he is a very good doctor; but dear Hulda I trust you in better hands than his.'

The child smiled with a perfect understanding of her words,—a look so quick and bright, that Rosalie was silent until her little charge was laid in the bed. Then Hulda spoke.

' Say that to me again.'

' I have done as the people did when Jesus was in the world,' Rosalie answered,—' when they brought their sick and laid them down at Jesus' feet, and besought him that he would heal them.'

'I wish you would ask him again,' said the child wearily closing her eyes, 'for my head aches very much.'

And kneeling down with the little hand fast in hers, Rosalie spoke once more the words of submission and entreaty,—that strange mingling of feeling which none but a Christian can either know or rest in. When she arose Hulda was asleep.

Carefully drawing the drapery around the bed corner, so as to shield the child's eyes yet more from the light, Rosalie began to busy herself in arranging the room for its new use. Unnecessary articles were put out, and the needful brought in; and the closet was so filled and arranged that the rest of the house should be but little called upon. At first Rosalie had half determined that none of the servants should be allowed to enter the sick-room; but Martha Jumps, light of heart as of foot, having declared that nothing short of a dismissal from the house should keep her from going where she pleased in it, she was made an exception,—and forthwith moved about with a great access of dignity.

'There aint the least bit of squeak leather in *my* shoes, I can tell you,' said Martha in a whisper, which low as it was penetrated to the remotest corner of the room. 'I could walk over hatching eggs and not scare the chickens. Tom Skiddy says—What next, Miss Rosalie?'

'That little thermometer that hangs in the front room down-stairs, Martha—and my desk, and the trivet.'

'Theometers, hey,' said Martha,—'that aint just the sort of doctor's stuff I took when I was a child, and yet I growed up as fast as most folks, too. What's the good of theometers?'

But she brought it.

'Has Mr. Thornton come home?' was Rosalie's last question.

'Not he!' said Martha emphatically. 'The idea! And what use, after all?'

'Ask him to come up here as soon as he does, Martha.' And then she sat down quietly to wait—that hardest of all things to do.

The sun was not long in finding his way to the horizon, and the darkness which had lain hid until his departure came forth,—at first slowly and tarrying in corners, then marching with swift steps over the whole city. The crowd gave way before her; foosteps were few and distinct; the hum and the roar were past; and every carriage now had credit for just its own noise and no other. The doctor had come on his promised visit, and had left medicine 'to be taken when she wakes up;' and still Rosalie sat there alone in the dim light from the fire, and the far off and shielded candle. The winds were whispering at the corners of the house, and anon sighing around it,—now raising and now depressing their voices, but never entirely silent. Footsteps now had a character and meaning, coming out as they did from the deep stillness and passing into other stillness as deep; and as an oyster-man went slowly through the street with his cart, his deep monotonous cry of 'Oys—ters!' chimed wildly and yet soothingly with the universal tone of all things else.

And so passed the evening until a loud ring sounded through the house, and the new comer had sprung up stairs and entered the sick-room, almost before the startled bell clapper had regained its equanimity.

'Hush!' was Rosalie's first greeting.

'I thought you wanted to see me,' said the young man, with a but half-checked step.

'Yes, but softly—you will wake Hulda.'

'No disparagement to your eyes, my dear—which are

as fine as can be no doubt—but I also must lay claim to some powers of vision. Hulda has been watching me ever since I came into the room. Now what is your pleasure? Martha having screamed 'scarlet fever!' after me as I came up-stairs, I am prepared for any disclosures. Is that really the state of the case?'

'So Dr. Buffem says.'

'Well I suppose he is at least on a par with his brethren in sagacity,' said Thornton, sitting down on the edge of the bed. 'How do you feel, young one? Hey-day!—don't you want to be kissed?'

'No,' said Hulda, who had turned her face very decidedly away. 'You've been smoking.'

'What a little goose you are!' said her brother, laughing and standing up again. 'And I suppose I may not even shake hands with you, my Lady Squeamish?'

But the lips that were hastily offered him showed no fear of his, and the hand that rested on his shoulder had no touch but of sisterly affection—unless a little want of comfort mingled therewith. Thornton returned the embrace very heartily.

'You are a dear girl,' he said, 'with all your prejudices. Now don't trouble yourself about this child—I daresay she will do well enough. Would it be any comfort to you if I sat up with her to-night?'

'No,' said Rosalie, with a smile which she could not repress at the very idea; 'for then I should have two people to take care of instead of one.'

'What are you going to give her?'

'Something I have here—I don't know what;—at twelve o'clock, Dr. Buffem said.'

'Well I will come in then and see how you get on, and give her the medicine.'

A very needless offer, but it was not refused; and when little Hulda awoke at midnight from uneasy dreams to the dazzling candle, it was to see the medicine spoon in the hands of Thornton, and that plan of arrangements sanctioned by her sister's quiet presence and smile. But it was Rosalie's arm that raised her up, and it was on Rosalie's bosom that her head lay; and if Hulda dreamed of angels that night, they all wore Rosalie's face.

CHAPTER III.

*Out of the day and night,
A joy has taken flight.*—SHELLEY.

For several days the doctor's visits were short and frequent; and his conversation was made up of little abrupt questions and ejaculations, assurances to Hulda that if he killed her he would have her buried, and earnest requests to Rosalie that she would furnish him with another patient. His first step was always towards the window; and having admitted a few of the proscribed sunbeams, he came back to the bed and made his observations, and once more closed the shutter. Counsel and warning about antimony and apple-water took up what further time the doctor saw fit to bestow in this quarter of his round; and then the room was left to the unquiet motions of the sick child, and the gentle and tender ministering of her nurse. Sometimes when Hulda was more than usually at ease, her eyes followed Rosalie about the room—watching with a dreamy pleasure the perfect doing of the one person whom she thought perfect,—noticing the noiseless placing of a stick of wood on the fire, and the laughing answer which the flames gave thereto; and sometimes her thoughts were held fast for a while, as the white ashes came over the red coals, and then dropped off, or the sap went singing out at the end of the stick, or the stick itself broke and fell down over the andirons. But her eyes got tired with the light and went after Rosalie, who was perhaps arranging the cups and napkin on the little stand; and if she went into the closet Hulda knew she had gone for an apple, and watched with some interest while the apple was made fast to a string, and that again to the mantelpiece. Then she noticed the desperate twists of the apple when it found itself at liberty to twist; and turning her head a little she listened to hear the first spurt of the apple-juice, and watched the bright drops as they came back from their tangent and fell into the little silver plate that awaited them; while the apple having waltzed to its heart's content, presented a steady front to the fire and rebelled against being roasted all round. Often Hulda fell asleep here, and then awoke in time to see the refractory apple, all brown and shrivelled, cut loose from the string and shut up in a silver pitcher with plenty of boiling water. At this point she always felt thirsty, and was quite ready for the tumbler by the time it came to her bedside; but though Rosalie held her up, and managed glass and spoon to admiration—tasted the apple-water too, lest it might be not sweet or not cool enough—Hulda could take but a few spoonfuls, and was glad to lie down again.

Thornton's visits were a little variety, but of no other use; though he always wore a look as if he knew he ought to do something, and hadn't the remotest idea what,—a look which his sister understood perfectly, and read with sometimes a smile and sometimes a sigh. The visits were always short. Hulda could bear very little talking or reading, and her greatest comfort was to have Rosalie's face on the pillow with her own, and to hear from her lips a verse of a hymn or from the Bible, or some little story or incident, or a few of her own sweet and quiet words. No one else entered the room, except to bring wood and water and Rosalie's meals; and on these occasions Martha Jumps restrained as much as possible her own love of talk, and said not many words more than were needful. The sounds from the street became to little Hulda's ear almost what they were to her sister's; and in the still, late evening she lay and listened to the oyster-man, with a strange feeling of dreariness and pleasure. And as in health, so in sickness, the morning never rose and the evening never fell, that Rosalie did not kneel by her little sister, and pray with her and for her in just such words as she could understand. Martha Jumps stayed her foot if perchance she entered the room at those times; and Thornton more than once found himself there, and wished himself away, and did not go.

'I wonder what Dr. Buffem would say to such proceedings!' he remarked one evening, when he had come softly in during the prayer and had stood watching and listening —too proud even to bend his head. 'In my opinion he would call them feverish. What would you say, Rosalie, if I should report— and if the doctor should issue contrary orders?'

'I should hear them,' she answered with a smile that told very plainly what more she would do.

'And by what token, my sage sister, do you prove yourself wiser than your physician?'

'O—by not 'thinking of men above what is written.''

"A most complete lady in the opinion of some three beside herself!'' said Thornton. 'Nevertheless I stand to the feverishness.'

'But it couldn't make me feverish,' said Hulda, putting in her word with a voice as pale and thin as her face. 'I like it—always.'

'Like it, you pickaninny! You don't know what you like.'

'It would be strange,' said Rosalie with a very gentle look at Hulda, and then turning one no less gentle but of somewhat different expression upon Thornton. 'It would be strange if a child brought up as she has been, to look upon God as her best friend, should be disturbed or wearied by all mention of his name.'

'You are looking marvellously pretty to-night,' was Thornton's cool reply, while he surveyed his sister as if he had not the remotest idea what she was talking about. 'I only hope you will keep on these wrappers when you come down stairs again. I am as tired of seeing you in that black dress as a man can be of seeing you at all, I suppose. Here—don't turn off with that face;—look up and kiss me before I go. What are you so grave about?'

She gave the required kiss but not the required answer; and moving away to the fire-place began to pile together the fallen brands—arranging and altering, as if in no haste to have the task finished.

'Well—what?' said Thornton following her. 'What have I said that was so dreadful? Did you never hear that

'A saint in crape is twice a saint in lawn?''

'You speak as if you did not know why I wear that black dress,' she said without looking at him.

'I don't know why the wearing is in the present tense, I'm sure. Give me the tongs—you know as much about fires as about some other things. I say it is a fashion I cannot abide; and if one must follow popular superstition for a time, the less time the better. Such a fire!—put together as if the world went by suggestion!'

'The world does not go by pounding,' said Rosalie, —'and your fire is going up chimney in the shape of sparks. Hadn't you better suggest to it to blaze?'

'I never made suggestions,' said he throwing down the tongs. 'What I've got to say comes out head first. Now here you persist in shutting yourself up, and trying to be as nun-like as possible. I wonder you submit to be called Rosalie! Why not 'Sister Ursula,' or some such sweet appellation?'

'I should not like to undertake any more Sisterhoods than I belong to at present,' said Rosalie with a slight smile.

'Well, leave off that dress, will you?' said Thornton. 'I abominate hoods of all kinds! And let us have pleasant recollections instead of disagreeable.'

'Disagreeable!' She stood silent and still, while the flickering light of the fire played over her face, and mingled curiously with the feelings that flitted to and fro there.

'Oh Thornton!' she said; 'would you forget our mother?'

Her hands were laid upon his shoulders now, and her eyes looked clear and full into his. He would willingly have freed himself from that light touch of reproof and sorrow, yet he did not try; but his own eyes fell, and it was with a very changed and softened expression that he answered,

'I would sometimes forget if I could that she is not here.'

She might have filled that mother's place for the way in which she looked at him. And then laying her head on his shoulder, while her hands were clasped about his neck, Rosalie said,—

'If you could. But oh my dear brother! never forget where she is! I would I could keep that before you every minute of your life.'

If the wings of the recording angel had touched him,

and the book been laid open before his eyes, Thornton could not have felt more sure that a new prayer for him was registered in heaven. And yet he did not answer according to that assurance—and there was no more spoken; for when Rosalie raised her head it was to bid him once more 'Goodnight,' and he left her without a word.

Hardly had little Hulda eaten that small allowance of tea and biscuit which she called her breakfast, next morning, before the doctor made his appearance. But everything was ready for him, and the room not only wore a comfortable but a comforted aspect; for Rosalie's face was a shade less anxious, and Hulda's face several shades more bright. So in answer to the doctor's inquiries she told him that she was a great deal better; though indeed she had been 'better' every time he had come.

'I shouldn't wonder if you were to be quite a respectable looking child, after all,' said Dr. Buffem, bending down to impress his approbation upon Hulda's forehead. 'One of these days—if you keep on. Feel most like an oyster or a clam this morning?'

'I don't know how they feel, sir,' said Hulda laughing.

'Don't laugh,' said the doctor—'that will never do. Not sick yet, Miss Rosalie? I had strong hopes you would be by this time. *She* looks like an oyster, don't she, Miss Tom Thumb?'

'No indeed!' said Hulda, quite forgetting her own name in the one bestowed on her sister; 'not a bit!'

'You think not?' said the doctor. 'Well I could swear there had been pearls in the vicinity—'A sea of melting pearl, which some call tears.' Who's been eating honey?'

'O Rosalie had it for her breakfast,' said Hulda.

'Hum—' said the doctor—'what have you had for yours? Eaten a whole beefsteak, eh?'

A VISITER.

'May I have some beefsteak?' said Hulda.

'Why no,' said Doctor Buffem, 'I should think not. Wait a day or two, Miss Rosalie, and then give her beefsteak, and a little antimony, a soda biscuit, a cup of chicken-broth, a buckwheat cake, a little salts or magnesia or castor oil—whichever she likes best—an oyster, a clam, a cup of tea; keep the room at 70°, and the sunlight out of doors, and then read Cowper.'

As the doctor stamped out of the room, Rosalie sat down by Hulda, and putting her arms round her laid her own head on the pillow, with a feeling of thankfulness that was too weary to do aught but rest. And rest fell like the dew upon sun-touched flowers. But before six quiet minutes had ticked away, the door opened again to admit Martha Jumps.

'Here's a to-do!' she said. 'Here's been Mrs. Arnet secluding herself down-stairs, to spring upon the doctor as *he* come down, for to find out whether she could see you with safety, as she says. And the doctor gave it to her well. He said there wasn't no danger for nobody but you; and he didn't think as it *was* quite safe, lookn' at it in that light, but he guessed you could stand it, he said. So now the sooner the quicker, Miss Rosalie. She smells dreadful strong of pickles.'

With this forewarning Rosalie felt no surprise that her visiter's salutation kept at the safe distance of a somewhat warding-off bow of the head; and as she herself did not feel impelled to advance nearer, they took chairs at opposite sides of the fire.

'Do you consider Hulda to be out of danger?' began Mrs. Arnet—who looked very much like a butterfly deprived of its moral expression.

'The doctor so considers her,' said a sweet voice from the other side of the fire-place.

'Well, my dear, he is quite right in endeavouring to keep up your spirits, but at the same time I must tell you that amendments are precarious things. Mrs. Forsyth lost a child with scarlet fever only last week, and she had been supposed to be out of danger for several days. It is a shocking disease.' And Mrs. Arnet made free use of her aromatic vinegar, while Rosalie's heart sought better help.

'When is Marion coming home?' she inquired presently.

'Soon,' said Mrs. Arnet. 'I have considered it quite a providential thing that she should be away just now, for I am sure nothing on earth would have kept her from coming to see you.'

Rosalie felt sure of it, too.

'She is so very imprudent,' pursued Mrs. Arnet. 'I believe she would just as soon as not sit up nights with anybody that had any disease. And if I remonstrated, she would probably tell me that she was safer there than doing nothing at home. For my part, I think one owes something to one's family.'

'And nothing to the family of one's adopted brother,' thought Rosalie. But she checked the thought, and answered quietly that family duties could hardly be overrated.

'Which reminds me that I am keeping you from yours,' said the lady. 'How is Thornton? He never comes to see us now, but I cannot blame him. Give him my best love, my dear.' And Mrs. Arnet's eyes sought her handkerchief, and her handkerchief sought her eyes,—but that was probably the fault of the aromatic vinegar. And too affected for more words, the lady bent her head graciously and left the room, giving Rosalie a wide berth as she went. In another minute Rosalie was up-stairs. There sat Thornton, reading the newspaper by the side of the sleeping Hulda.

'It is an extraordinary thing to see me, isn't it?' said he in answer to Rosalie's first look of pleasant surprise.

'But I thought you had gone out.

'One must go out in order to come in,' said Thornton. 'If you will promise to come down to dinner to-day, and let me order it when I like, I will come home.'

There needed no answer but what the eyes gave him.

'You look sorrowful, Alie,' said her brother. 'What has that woman been saying to you?'

'She left her best love for you,' said Rosalie.

Thornton's lip curled with no attempt at disguisement.

'I hope she did not come on purpose to bring it,' he said. 'If her love were in the market, the report would be, 'Supply light, and the market dull.''

'She says,' continued Rosalie, 'that if Marion had been at home nothing could have kept her from coming here.'

Thornton's eye flashed, but he only said, 'Of course.'

His sister looked at him, and then at the fire, and then at him again.

'Oh Thornton! will you never give that one little promise? for her sake—for mine?'

He answered, 'Never!' and went.

CHAPTER IV.

I cannot like the Quakers (as Desdemona would say) "to live with them." I am all over sophisticated—with humours, fancies, craving hourly sympathy. I must have books, pictures, theatres, chit-chat, scandal, jokes, ambiguities, and a thousand whim-whams which their simpler taste can do without.—CHARLES LAMB.

THE doctor entered his gig and drove swiftly up Broadway, until the sound of its paving stones gave place to the regular beat of his horse's feet upon the frozen ground. Swiftly on—past houses and stores, the main body of the city, and then the miserable advanced posts of its outskirt buildings. For the most part the doctor took a vista-like view between the two brown ears of his horse; but now and then his wig made a half revolution towards the one adventurous row of houses that marked the south side of Walker Street, or when the shouts of the skaters on the great pond at the corner of Canal, suggested various ideas that were pleasant only in a professional point of view. But every boy there skimmed over the smooth ice in utter defiance of the doctor, his skill, and his wig; and his good horse Hippocrates, unconscious that the weight he carried behind him was in any part made up of learning, left pond and skaters in the far distance, and trotted nimbly on through the region of market gardens, orchards, and country seats.

As near as might be to one of these the doctor checked his horse,—or I should rather say, as near as he chose; for though the iron gate was too far from the dwelling to let even its closing clang be heard, the many tracks on the road beyond shewed that few vehicles stopped where the gig had done. But the doctor preferred walking. The long ride had made him well acquainted with the state of the atmosphere, and Hippocrates was merrier than he when they reached the gate. So leaving the boy in the red comforter to do the best he could under the circumstances, Dr. Buffem swung to the gate, and strode away through an avenue of tall trees to the house. In summer they would have screened him from both sun and wind, but now the leafless branches only mocked him with the slight shadows they cast; and the pitiless breath of winter swept whistling through, until every twig shook and shivered in its power. The fallen leaves stuck crisp and frozen to the ground; and if there were any at large they had retreated into corners, and there lay huddled together.

Dr. Buffem pursued his walk and the wind pursued him,—the doctor in extreme dissatisfaction at the pinched face of nature. His own was not suffering in the same way, for not even the wind could get hold of such cheeks; but still it was great presumption for the wind to try: and the curiosity which would fain have made itself acquainted with the lining of his coat was no less unwarrantable. And though the sunshine was by no means so inquisitive, the doctor made up his mind that too much reserve was just as bad as too little. So he tramped along, pounding the frozen ridges with his heavy boots, and shaking himself from time to time to make sure that the enemy had carried nothing but the outworks. Even the nicely swept porch, and the roses that were trimmed and trained beyond the wind's power, had not one approving look. Dr. Buffem made for the knocker; and after a succession of raps that might have answered for half the Peerage, he gave an echo to the same upon the porch floor, while his eyes sought Hippocrates in the distance.

The knocks were immediately successful, but the doctor's back took no note thereof.

'The door stands open, friend Buffem,' said a quiet voice. 'Does thee require aught? The wind is cold.'

'Require?' said the doctor wheeling round—

'"Rest and a guide, and food and fire."—

'The wind's as keen as nineteen honed razors,—no sort of a wind to kiss pretty faces. Where are the men?'

'James Hoxton as thou knowest is yet ill,' replied the damsel, 'and Caleb Williams hath gone in search of letters,—and moreover tendeth not the door at any time.'

'The wiser man he,' replied the doctor. 'But James Hoxton's as well as a fish out of water—wriggling his way back at full speed. What's the news up in these Northern regions?—how long since the mercury shook hands with zero?'

'Here is fire,' said the damsel, opening a side door into a small specimen of wax work, 'and here thou mayest leave thy clogs. When thou art warm I will conduct thee upstairs.'

'Clogs?'—said the doctor. 'Well—" every Quakeress is a lily,"—but even lilies come out of what may be called mud's raw material. How thee must love John Frost, friend Rachel. Now then—"Lead on!—I'll follow thee!"'

Along the wide hall and up the broad easy steps of the old staircase, went Rachel in her sad-coloured gown and white cap,—fit genius to preside over so spotless a domain; and after her the doctor, who with some difficulty made her tripping steps the measure of his own. Trip, trip—a soft stuff-rustle and a slight key-jingle their proper accompaniment; while the doctor's heavy tread came like some strange instrument, played out of time.

Rachel crossed the upper hall, and opening the door into a room that stretched along that end of the house, she stepped back and left the doctor to enter. The room looked like the head-quarters of the Fairy Order. Like snow-wreaths hung the curtains—like patches of snow lay napkin and toilet cover and bed-quilt. The furniture was made of self-adjusting materials,—the table-cloth probably shook itself. More polished than 'our best society' were the andirons, and at the same time more reflecting; while the ashes, too well instructed to fly about the room or fall on the hearth, followed the soot up chimney. Too dry to sing, the wood burned noiselessly; only the dancing flames shewed some vagaries, and declared themselves beyond the sphere of Quakerdom.

In a quiet tête-à-tête with the fire Dr. Buffem found his patient; or rather he found her first in one of the reflecting andirons, which shewed the face and figure that her high-backed chair concealed.

Her cap, her grey dress, the smooth kerchief that lay folded across a breast as unruffled, proclaimed her to be of Rachel's order; but the pure sweetness of her face, the gravity without a touch of moroseness, spoke a yet more honourable distinction;—a heart unspotted from the world; a faith that having laid hold on eternal life, took all in the life that now is with meek tranquillity. If there was one ruling expression in her face, it was of charity—" which suffereth long, and is kind; thinketh no evil; is not easily provoked; beareth all things, believeth all things, hopeth all things, endureth all things." And as at the advancing step she half arose, and turned to greet her visitor, Dr. Buffem thought he had rarely seen a finer face.

'Friend Raynor, how art thou?' he said, flourishing out both hands. '"Do you think me a swallow, an arrow, or a bullet? Have I, in my poor and cold motion, the expedition of thought? I speeded hither with the very extremest inch of possibility"—unless indeed I had run over Rachel.'

'Friend Buffem, thou art welcome,' said the quakeress with a smile. 'I trust thy haste hath not put thee to inconvenience. I scarce expected thee to-day,—perhaps, said I, he will be better pleased to come to-morrow.'

'No indeed,' said the doctor,—'though to-morrow had been June, while this is without doubt December.'

'The cold hath not then abated?'

'Not the first fraction of a degree,' said the doctor. 'It is the most confoundedly sharp day we've had this winter.'

'Thee must indeed feel it severely if thee indulges in such expressions,' said the quakeress gravely. 'I have always found, friend Buffem, that inward chafing doeth far less good than that which is without.'

'Ay, so you say,' replied the doctor, as he toasted his hands impartially over the fire, 'but I like a little of both. Men's hair won't stay brushed, do what you will, and it won't be the real thing if you try to make it. No, no—get your temper up to boiling point and then fizz round a little,—my word for it you'll get warm.'

'Warm after the manner which savoureth of cold heartedness.'

'Not a bit of it!' said the doctor, who was putting himself through all his paces; 'cold is flat, and never savoured of anything. You let the water run in upon the fire and it'll put it out—therefore heat up your fire and blow up the water. Nothing like letting off steam once in a while. Whizz!—Puff!—there you are, reduced to cold water again; and nobody killed, either.'

'Nor hurt?' said the quakeress smiling. 'And thee would get up steam for the very purpose of letting it off, to no end?'

'Well,' said the doctor, 'I should hope it would have an end, certainly. As to the rest, most people keep it on hand —blow it off too,—saves an immense number of boilers.'

'It maketh a most uncomfortable noise the while,' said the quakeress,—'and hath not much sympathy with the command, "Study to be quiet."'

'But reflect upon the terrors of an explosion!' said the doctor. 'You don't suppose the same lesson is set for everybody. It's not in all human nature to be as patient as you are, my dear lady.'

'Nay, it lieth not in nature at all,' she answered earnestly, 'and yet it may be attained. "Great peace have they that love thy law, and nothing shall offend them." But who requireth thy care at Thornton Clyde's? I hear thou hast been much there of late.'

'Ah!' said the doctor—'who told you so? "Now when I ope my lips let no dog bark."'

'Rachel must needs go into town yesterday,' answered the quakeress, 'and not only did the purse find work, but the tongue. Thee knows young girls will be gossipping. But what aileth them there? and who? not Rosalie?'

'No,' said the doctor,—'Hulda. Only scarlet fever.'

'Poor child! poor dear child!' said the quakeress anxiously. 'And is she very ill? does thee think, speaking after the manner of men, that there is much danger?'

'Not much'—said the doctor,—'speaking, as you say, after the manner of men. Speaking after the manner of women, she has been wonderfully sick. But she's better now.'

'It rejoiceth my heart to hear thee say that. Poor

child!—and her dear sister! Sorely tried she hath already been, and hath borne the trial like a true child of God.'

'Sterling stuff,' said the doctor. 'But the child is better, so you may put all thoughts of a visit out of your head. I see what you're meditating. You can't be let out of the house yet. I want to set you up before our travellers get home.'

A moment's smile was followed by a look of deep grief and anxiety.

'Alas this war!—when will they get home?' she said clasping her hands.

'See here,' said the doctor,—don't you get up any steam; it wouldn't suit your constitution. What's the war to do?—I never heard in my life that a declaration of war kept old Boreas in order. Let them set their sails,—he'll give chase. What's the date of their last letter?'

'Far, far back; and doubtless Henry hath written since, but the letter hath failed to come. He pineth to be at home now.'

'I'll warrant him!' said the doctor,—'and for a brush with the English, too.'

'Nay, he saith only that all should be in their own country at such a time,' answered the quakeress deprecatingly.

'Ay—that's it. Why didn't he come last summer, when the war broke out?—travelling is deucedly inconvenient now-a-days.'

'Thou speakest unadvisedly, friend. However he would have come then, doubtless, only Penn—that silly boy—being ill, it was but brotherly kindness not to leave him.'

'Got himself stabbed in some brawl with those German students, didn't he?' said the doctor. 'I recollect. But he ought to be cured by this time, if there's a respectable surgeon on the Continent.'

'Henry wrote that he was better,' said the quakeress; 'and if nought hindered they were to take passage in the War Hawk on the first day of this month.'

'Well she's not in yet,' said Dr. Buffem, 'but the United States is. I suppose you've read the papers this morning?'

'Nay,' she answered.

'Glorious victory!' said the doctor rubbing his hands. 'Decatur has taken the Macedonian, forty-nine guns, and but twelve men killed and wounded.'

'And in the other vessel?' said Mrs. Raynor.

'A hundred or so—and two hundred prisoners. Glorious, isn't it?'

The satisfaction on his face was so far from being reflected, that Doctor Buffem held up both hands, exclaiming,

'A traitor, as I am alive!'

'Truly friend,' replied the quakeress calmly, 'I trust thy life is much surer than thy assertion. But who can glory or who can joy in such bloody doings!—They seem not much in the spirit of "Love your enemies."'

'Mustn't love your enemies so well as to let 'em eat you up, Mrs. Raynor,' said the doctor—'no kindness in that,—and for the rest Decatur's as kind hearted a man as ever lived. Now here for instance—when Capt. Garden came on board the United States to give up his sword, Decatur told him he could not take the sword of a man who had defended his ship so well, but he would receive his hand. Isn't that a christian spirit?'

'It seemeth like it—though truly forgiveness should be easy to the conqueror. But the War Hawk claimeth not to be one of these fighting vessels?'

I guess she carries Letters of Marque,' said the doctor with a satisfied air.

'And may she then even capture other ships on her passage?'

'Capture them? of course she may—if they don't capture her,—that's the trade our captains are driving just now. Better come into port with a prize or two than be carried off by an H. M. cruiser.'

'Danger either way! I would I had forborne the joy of his presence and bade him stay there!'

She rested her head on her hands, but the heaving of her breast alone told of the struggle within.

'Come, come,' said Dr. Buffem, in some doubt how to treat a case so far beyond the range of his professional skill,—'he wouldn't have staid there if you had bade him. And what then?—many a pretty man has smelt powder without getting singed. The chances are twenty to one of his getting home in most inglorious safety.'

The quakeress looked up, and her face was very calm—not even her lip trembled.

'Nay, friend Buffem,' she said, 'not so! There is neither chance for nor chance against; but the will of God. And truly I know that he ruleth the winds and the waves; and holdeth the hearts of kings and doubtless the hearts of seamen too—howbeit the flesh is weak, and faith sometimes faileth. My all is in his hands,—I will not fear to leave it there.'

'That's right, that's right,' said the doctor, assenting to her means of comfort as probably the best that could be had for her under the circumstances; 'keep your spirits up always, and I'll look out for the War Hawk and bring you the first news of her. But I want you to get stronger before she comes—there'll be one pair of good keen eyes on board.'

The mother's own filled at his words, but she made no answer.

'I guess they'll be the best cure, after all,' the doctor added. 'Nevertheless I think I shall send you away for a month, not for your sake at all, you know—for his. What do you say?'

'I will go whither thou wilt send me for that cause. But he is so well, they say, and so joyful with the thought of returning.'

'Hasn't heard enough from home to content him, I doubt,' said the doctor.

'I have written even more than seemed needful,' she answered smiling, 'but he hath strangely missed of some of my letters.'

'Well then it's all settled,' said the doctor. 'You're to go South, and I'm to look out for the War Hawk, and she's to come just when she likes. Friend Raynor I wish thee good morning.'

CHAPTER V.

*The yule-clog sparkled keen with frost,
No wing of wind the region swept,
But over all things brooding slept
The quiet sense of something lost.*—TENNYSON.

THE setting sun shone fairly upon the last day of December; and as his disk sank lower and lower behind the city, chimneys and dormant windows and now and then a towering story, glowed in the clear red light with singular brightness. The sadder for that. So very fair, and yet the end!—the end of the day, the end of the year. The last time the sun might shine upon 1812!—Cold and still the night set in; and the quiet stars in whose watch the new year should begin its reign, looked down with bright eyes upon the subsiding city and its kindling lights.

Rosalie stood watching it all,—watching the people as they hurried home, the parlour windows lit up, the bright doorways that appeared and vanished, the happy groups gathering at tea. She could see them across the way,—those fair shadows, young and old, moving about in the bright glow. And in the next house—and the next,—up and down, as far as she could see;—it was one line of telegraphing. Nor did the few windows where only firelight shone, flickering like the joy of human life, look less cheerful. She remembered the long talks, the sweet counsel given in that dusky light,—the eyes that had looked down upon her like heaven's own stars; but now the room was not darker than her heart.

It was not the first time she had stood there watching for her brother,—she had looked till each frequenter of that street was perfectly well known. It was not the first time she had watched in sadness. But she remembered that there had been a time when she was never suffered to watch there long—when a gentle hand would be passed round her waist, and she be drawn away from the window, with,

'We may not overrule these things, daughter—we must not be children in whom is no faith. Come and let us talk of the time when God shall wipe away all tears from our eyes.'

Pressing her hand upon her heart, Rosalie turned hastily from the window.

The fire gleamed faintly upon Hulda's little face and figure, stretched upon the sofa in the perfect rest of childhood; and above that one bright spot in the room, hung a picture that gave depth to all the shadows. Rosalie ventured but one glance at it, and kneeling down at her mother's chair, she laid her face on the cushion with a bitter weariness of heart that found poor relief in tears. Yet they were a relief; and after a while her mind lay quiet upon those words, "God is our refuge and strength: a very present help in trouble."

A soft touch on her neck aroused her, and with an almost bewildered start Rosalie looked up; but it was 'neither angel nor spirit'—it was only little Hulda.

'Are you sick, Alie?' asked the child.

'No love. Are you awake?'

'O yes,' said Hulda, laughing and wrapping her arms

round Rosalie's neck,—' don't that feel awake? Aren't we going to have tea, Alie?'

'I shall wait for Thornton, but you shall have yours, dear;' and getting up with the child in her arms, Rosalie carried her into the tea-room, and fell back into her own quiet performance of duties.

Hulda was in quite high spirits for her, and eat her supper on Rosalie's lap with great relish,—a relish partly derived from returning health, and partly from this first coming down-stairs.

'I wonder if Thornton hasn't gone to buy me a present!' she said. 'You know it's Newyear's eve, Rosalie, and you must hang up my stocking.'

'There is no fear of my forgetting that,' said her sister.

'No, for you never forget anything. But I wonder what'll be in it! Well, we'll see.'

'Yes, we shall see. So put your arms round my neck, Hulda, and I will carry you up-stairs. It is pleasanter there than here to-night.'

But the musing fit was strong upon her; and later in the evening, when her little charge was asleep, Rosalie's mind could do nothing but wander in a wilderness of recollections. Not a wilderness in one sense,—how fresh, how dear, they were!—and yet too much like a sweet land breeze from the coast that one has left.

Rosalie took out the stocking as Hulda had desired, and put together on a chair at the head of the bed all the various trifles that were to fill it; but when she had placed herself on a low seat before them, the stocking hung unregarded from her hand, and her thoughts flew away. There seemed a long vista opened before her; and furthest of all its objects—yet clear, distinct, even more so than those near by—she saw herself as a little child; before her eye had learned to know the evil that is in the world, or her heart had grown up to feel it. What a stream of sunshine lay there!—

"The sunshine and the merriment,
"The unsought, evergreen content,
 "Of that never cold time,
"The joy, that, like a clear breeze, went
 "Through and through the old time!"

And even in later times, where the shadow of life had begun to fall, the picture seemed hardly less fair. For about both, the child and the half-grown girl, had been wrapped the same atmosphere of love and guidance,—through which sweet medium all the breaths of sorrow and pain came softened. Even when they came from bitter causes—her father's death, her brother's gradual estrangement from home—his voluntary withdrawing from the hand in hand intercourse in which they had grown up,—even then there was sunshine at her mother's side—sunshine for her,—she had never failed to find it. But it reached not to the dark foreground; where scorched flowers and blackened stumps showed that Time had claimed the land, and had cleared it.

But little more than one year ago, Rosalie was nerving herself for the bitter future. It had come, and she had met it,—had lived through those first few months of grief not to be told nor thought of. But though her heart was quieter now, there were times which seemed to surpass all she had ever known for intensity of sorrow,—when her very life seemed to die within her, and desire to live and power to do could not be found,—when her mind dwelt with intense longing on the words, "I shall go to her, but she shall not return to me." Yet even then God had not forgotten his child, and in the breaking light her mind rested submissively upon this other text—" All the days of my appointed time will I wait, till my change come." And as the last storm-clouds roll away, and are gilt with the western light, so upon all her sorrow fell this assurance,—" Blessed are the dead that die in the Lord—they rest from their labours and their works do follow them."

"I do set my bow in the cloud, and it shall be for a token of the covenant between me and the earth!".

Rosalie had dwelt long upon the words, till all thought for herself was lost in joy for her mother's safety and assured blessedness, far from the weariness that pressed upon her own heart; and though the remembrance brought back one or two tears, they were quickly wiped away, and her whole soul was poured out in the prayer that she might one day 'go to her,'—and not only she, but the two dear ones yet left to her on earth. The desire could not be spoken—it was the very uplifting of the heart,—for them, for herself: and that she might faithfully perform the work that was put into her hands.

With a look where sorrow and submission and earnest purpose and endeavour, were like the pencilling upon a flower of most delicate growth and substance, Rosalie raised her head, and saw Thornton before her: leaning against the bedpost with his arms folded, and eyeing her gravely and considerately.

'What are you thinking of me for, Rosalie?' he said. 'Cannot you do enough of that work in the daytime, that you must spend half the night upon it?'

'Are you sure that I have?'

'If I had not been sure of it I should have claimed your attention when I first came in.'

'And it would have been gladly given.'

'Yes, I dare say,' said Thornton, 'but one may as well take the benefit of all that good angels are amind to do for one. I am almost sorry I did not, though. What have you got there? stockings to darn?'

'Only Hulda's stocking to fill with presents—you know it is New-year's eve.'

'Give me credit for remembering something once in the course of my life. I did recollect that there was a stocking to fill, and have brought home my quota.'

'I am so very glad!' said his sister with a look of great pleasure. 'Hulda would have been disappointed if you had forgotten her.'

'She don't owe me many thanks,' said Thornton, as he watched the fingers that were busy disposing of the presents and the face that bent over them. 'I believe she might have escaped my memory if her sweet guardian could have gone with her. But Hulda's presents were to pass through your hands—No—don't kiss me,—I tell you I don't deserve it. When you looked up a little while ago, I felt as if you were up in the sky, and I—I don't quite know where,—so I'll wait till we both get back to terra-firma again.'

'Do you call me her guardian?' said Rosalie with one look at him.

'Yes, and mine too. Why didn't you have tea to-night? Well—you look,—Want to know how I found it out?—because the table was untouched. Why didn't you?'

'O—I thought I would wait for you,' said she brightly.

'But why did you, after all? Don't you know I'm not worth the trouble?'

'O Thornton!' she said.

'What?'

'I was not going to say anything.'

'Your saying nothing usually tells all one wants to know, and a little more. Come, finish your work,—I shall play guardian to-night, and make you go down and eat as many oysters as an angel can reasonably be supposed to want. So make haste, for it is time such particular little bodies as you were in bed.'

He had named her right—she was indeed his guardian angel.

In the midst of all his reckless absence and waste of time, in the gayest hours of pleasure among his so-called best friends, there was still in his inmost heart the pure image of *one* Christian, whose profession he *knew* was not a name,—whose walk he knew was consistent; whose life he knew was gladly submitted to a higher will than her own. And often did that image come up before him, rebuking the light irreverent talk of his companions, making false their assertions, and reproving him for even listening and looking on. His mother had indeed won his respect no less; but she was older—it seemed more natural, to his notion, that Christianity and years should come together. But his sister —young like himself—younger than he,—beautiful, admired, complimented; and yet maintaining that pure elevation of heart and mind—that uncorrupted, untainted simplicity of aim, which not all his most unbelieving desires could find in those who are living without God in the world:—it vexed him sometimes, and sometimes it roused his pride and sometimes his discontent,—yet on the whole it pleased him. There was a strange kind of fascination in seeing one who ought naturally to look up to him for counsel and strength, assume, almost unconsciously, so high a stand above him; and array herself not more gently than firmly against so much that he liked and followed. And though he often laughed at her, sometimes stopped her mouth with a kiss, and sometimes got excessively provoked,—if he could have thought her one whit more tolerant of the things which he tolerated, one jot more indulgent towards the company and the pursuits in which he wasted his life—Thornton would have felt that the best thing he had in the world was gone from him. He watched her—she little thought with what jealous eyes; and at every instance of her unwavering truth—not only in word, but in that uprightness of heart which pierces through error and fallacy like a sunbeam—he smiled to himself; or rather to the best part of his nature against the worst. And yet upon those very points he would argue and dispute with her till he was tired. But this consciousness of her secret influence made him the more shy of submitting to it openly. He was content to go on after the old fashion; thinking Rosalie a piece of perfection, and not much concerning himself whether she were a *happy* piece of perfection or no.

CHAPTER VI.

Here she was wont to go! and here! and here!—BEN JONSON.

LITTLE Hulda had slept away all the early part of the New-year's morning, and it was not till after the rest of the family had long ago breakfasted that she sat up in bed and looked about for her stocking. For the doctor gave leave that she should go down stairs in the afternoon, only upon the easy condition of her keeping perfectly quiet all the morning; and now, bundled up in dressing-gown and shawls, she sat leaning on Rosalie and supported by her arms, to examine into the mysteries that had hung all night at the head of her bed. She was weak and pale still, and the touch of helplessness which illness had given her voice and manner went to her sister's heart. When Hulda was well and playing about, recollections came less readily; but now the season of itself brought enough—the filling of that stocking had been bitter work,—and when from time to time Hulda's gentle and still weary-looking eyes were raised to her sister's face with a smile of pleasure, or her lips put up to receive a kiss; or her little thin hands were clasped round Rosalie's neck, while the childish voice spoke its thanks with such an earnest yet subdued tone,—Rosalie heard again that truth which she never could forget—they were both motherless. Not Hulda in effect—her whole love and dependence had been transferred; and she clung to her sister with a trust that perhaps was the strongest she had ever felt, for it was undivided. But Rosalie—she could love no one now as Hulda loved her,—she had no one to look up to —no one to fall back upon in those times of weakness and weariness that stir the strongest resolution. No one on earth; and though smile and word and kiss came at Hulda's bidding, her heart yearned for a more far-seeing sympathy, —her head longed to lay itself down and rest, even as Hulda's was resting then. Bitterly she remembered that she was alone, and for a few minutes her mind bent down as before a tempest. And then, drawn like Æolian music from the very breath that made the whirlwind, came the words,

"*My presence shall go with thee, and I will give thee rest.*"

"The rest that remaineth"—she thought with swimming eyes; "for surely our heaven lieth not here-away."

'Hulda dear,' she said presently, bending down to look at the languid eyelids that could hardly be kept open, 'you are very tired. You must lie down and sleep again, and then by and by you shall be dressed and go down stairs.'

'But *you* ought to be dressed,' said the child rousing herself a little,—'you won't be ready to see people.'

'I am not going to see any body, love.'

'You needn't mind about me,' said Hulda, 'I'm so well now. And Martha could stay here.'

'Martha could not,' said her sister as she laid her on the bed, 'for I mean to have that pleasure myself.'

'O that's very good,' said Hulda, closing her eyes with a satisfied air; 'only it's a pity the people should be disappointed.'

And so Hulda fell asleep and Rosalie stood watching her; and the Newyear's sun mounted higher and higher in the clear sky; but 'under the sun' there was nothing new.

Unless perhaps the hopes and resolutions,—and they were but the tying of an old cord many times broken. It was Newyear's day in name, but it was Old year in reality. The same bright points—the same dark corners,—the same strife of human passions and weariness of human hearts,—the same trembling of the scales of that never-poised balance of society. There was more leisure taken, and more pleasure undertaken, than on ordinary days; but among all the host of pleasure-seekers that now began to spot the streets, the beggar's hand was still held out; the doctor's gig went its rounds; and friends looked their last, that Newyear's morning, at the faces of those to whom the new year had not come.

"Is there anything whereof it may be said, See, this is new?"

"Behold I create new heavens and a new earth; *and the former shall not be remembered, nor come into mind.*"

'Even sorrow shall be forgotten then,' Rosalie thought, as she stood watching little Hulda.

'Happy Newyear and good morning!' cried a bright voice, while the door was pushed gently open. 'How dost thou, fair Rosalie?—fairest of all cousins whether real or adopted. Here am I just arrived in time to dress for visiters, and that being done, I forthwith turn visiter myself. My dear your cheeks are as soft as ever, and your eyes as grave; and your mouth—well I won't detail that combination.'

'How pleasant it is to see you!' said Rosalie; as the young lady after a variety of salutations held her back within gazing distance.

'How pleasant it is to see you,—which proves me of a disposition neither envious nor jealous. What have you done to yourself, child?—or have I been looking at the dark side of human nature till my eyes are contracted and cannot bear the light?'

'Nothing has contracted your eyes since I saw them last,' said Rosalie smiling. 'I am in some doubt as to your judgment. Did you come here bareheaded in this weather?'

'Had to, my dear, because of my hair—there wouldn't be time to dress it again when I get home, you know. O I rode of course,—rumbled through the streets to the envy —or admiration—of all the gentlemen on foot.'

'No doubt! But would their admiration keep you from taking cold?'

'O yes—perfectly,—giddy heads never take cold,—you might as well talk of champagne's freezing. Some one of my elderly friends is at this moment detailing to mamma— 'My dear madam, I saw Miss Arnet this morning in a most dangerous situation.'—Nevertheless here I am safe. This child is better I hear. And how are you, Alie?'

'Well.'

'Well? you don't look it. I saw Thornton in Broadway with his troop—where was he going?'

'To have a salute fired for the Macedonian, I believe,' said Rosalie. 'A message came for him in all haste to say that she was just coming in.'

'O that Macedonian!' cried the young lady,—'there never was anything like it! You know they had a great naval ball at Washington for Captain Stewart and the rest; and I was there of course, and everybody else. And the room was dressed out with all manner of sea things—I should rather say sea-faring things—and with the colours of the Alert and the Guerriere on the walls. The city was illuminated too, that evening, because of the victory: and everybody was in the best possible spirits. Well about nine o'clock their was a stir in the room—we could not tell what about at first,—only the gentlemen began to rush down in the most extraordinary manner, and the ladies stood still and looked. Then suddenly came the most tremendous cheering outside the house!—one stream of cheers, that seemed to have no end; and word came up that Lieutenant Hamilton had just arrived with the Macedonian's colours!—it excites me even now to think of it.' She drew a long breath and went on.

'They all came back in a body presently, bringing Mr. Hamilton with them; for all his family were there at the ball. And then Captain Stewart and Captain Hull and some others, brought in the flag,—with such shouts and hurrahs and waving of handkerchiefs—and 'Hail Columbia' from the band. And then at supper they toasted Commodore Decatur and his officers and crew, with ten times ten, it seemed to me—instead of three times three. My dear, you never heard people shout as we did.'

'You among the rest?' said Rosalie smiling.

'I don't know—I'm sure I cried. And vos beaux yeux are sparkling even at my poor account. There go the guns!'

They both started up and stood listening; and while all the bells of the city rang out their gladness, the guns at the Battery gave a response for the old Thirteen—a pledge that not one of them should be wanting in the contest.

'The bells will ring for an hour yet,' said Marion as the last report died away, 'so you may as well sit down and listen at your leisure. Poor Mary Laton! how can she bear all this. Her oldest son was killed in the engagement. Well, I must go. How lovely you look, child!—these guns have put colour in your cheeks,—try and keep it for your visitors—O no, you will not see them. Poor child! and dear child, and every kind of a child that ever was well beloved, goodbye.' And giving Rosalie a half dozen kisses Miss Arnet quitted the room.

When little Hulda next awoke she found Martha keeping watch at her bedside.

Not indeed keeping watch of her,—for Martha's eyes were intent upon four long shining knitting-needles that were kicking about at a great rate; while below them depended a short worsted cylinder of clouded blue yarn.

'What *are* you doing, Martha?' said Hulda.

'Massy! child, how you scar't me! and made me drop a stitch into the bargain. Why I'm a knittin'—didn't you never see nobody knit afore?'

'O yes, but not such a looking thing as that,' said Hulda disapprovingly. 'What is it?'

'It's a firstrate lookin' thing, I can tell you,' said Martha —'firstrate feelin' too. It's a mitten.'

'What's a mitten?' said Hulda, who being a young lady convalescent and at leisure was well disposed to ask questions.

'Don't you know?—them things people wears on their hands. It aint a glove, but it kivers a person's hand just as well—some folks thinks better.'

'O I know now,' said Hulda—'it's like a little bag with a thumb to it.'

'Well I s'pose it does look considerable like that,' said Martha knitting away with renewed energy.

'Only a bag is shut up at one end—'said Hulda doubtfully.

'A thing can't be finished till it's done,' said Martha sententiously.

Hulda looked on for a while in silence.

'Is that little hole for the thumb to come out of?'

'For nothing else,' said Martha.

'But who are they for?' said Hulda,—'that is too big for you.'

'La sakes, Hulda, you aint waked up, be you? I guess it 'll be some time afore I want mittens to sew in. These is for the militie.'

'The militia?' said Hulda. 'Why they don't want mittens.'

'Don't they though?—then you know more about it than Tom Skiddy, for he says his hands gets awful cold sometimes, mornings. And you see, Hulda, the paper says the ladies up to Newburgh and Hudson and all along shore there, has been knittin' their fingers off; and sent I do' know how many pairs of socks and mittens—six hundred I guess, more or less—up to the Governor for the militie; and there was printed thanks to 'em in the paper,—so I don't see why folks here mustn't do nothing.'

'O yes, Rosalie told me about that,' said Hulda. 'But she said those were for the soldiers away off—somewhere where it's very cold.'

''Taint cold here, I s'pose,' said Martha,—'we don't have to make fires in *these* parts.'

'But it isn't so cold as some other places.'

'La child, so long's fingers gets froze, it don't make much odds about the theometer. And fingers *can* get froze in this town o' York—Tom Skiddy says so.'

'You like Tom Skiddy very much, don't you?' said Hulda.

'He aint so bad he couldn't be worse,' replied Martha, when her head had taken two or three turns as if her mind were balancing as well.

'But isn't he very good to you?' pursued Hulda.

'Good to me!' said Martha with a gyration of more dignity,—'he aint got *quite* so far as that yet. Once in a while I'm good to him,—and he's pretty good to himself. That's about the state of the case. Only I may as well give the mittens to the first militie-man that comes handy; instead of sending 'em off to nobody knows who, nor whether they'd fit.'

Hulda looked on again thoughtfully.

'Thornton don't wear mittens,' she said.

'I can't see why poor folks should lose their fingers because the Capting buys yaller gloves,' said Martha. And inspired by the freezing fingers hers flew the faster.

'How very quick you knit!' said Hulda.

'Don't I, though!' said Martha—'as quick as most folks. I always was spry. And you see, Hulda, I'll put blue and white fringe to the top; and the way they'll keep Tom Skiddy's fingers warm, 'll be a caution.'

CHAPTER VII.

> The wind has swept from the wide atmosphere
> Each vapour that obscured the sunset's ray,
> And pallid evening twines its beamy hair
> In duskier braids around the eyes of day;
> Silence and twilight, unbeloved of men,
> Creep hand in hand from yon obscurest glen.—SHELLEY.

IT was Sunday afternoon; and unlike most perfect things, the daylight lingered; and a fair specimen of winter drew slowly to its close. The last sunbeams played persuasively about the hard-featured city, as if to draw and lead its attention towards the great light of the world; even as had the light of truth that day touched some hearts that slowly moved off beyond its reach.

Little Hulda sat in her sister's lap by the parlour fire; sometimes putting forth simple questions and remarks in a very unostentatious way, and sometimes silently following her sister's eyes, as they gazed upon the fire or looked out into the darkening light. At the window, half withdrawn within the curtains, sat Thornton. He had but just come in, and seemed not to have brought his mind in with him, for his attention was given undividedly to the street. At least it seemed to be; but from a certain moody aspect, from the gloomy air with which he now and then nodded to a passer-by, his sister judged that his thoughts were busy not only within doors but within himself. Neither pleasantly nor profitably she thought,—it was more like the clouds which cover up the day than the darkness which precedes it.

Afraid that he should think she was watching him, her eye came back to the fire and then down to the little face on her breast. Hulda was observing her very anxiously, but the anxiety broke away and a smile came.

'Are you tired, Alie?' said the child stroking her face.

'A little.'

'Were you out this afternoon?' said Thornton abruptly turning his head.

'No—I staid with Hulda.'

'You were not with Hulda when I came in?'

'No.'

'Where then?'

'O with some scholars who are older and know less,' said Rosalie.

'In other words, with your kitchen Bible-class,' said Thornton in a way which gave the adjective its full effect.

She bowed her head slightly but without looking at him, and answered, 'Even so.'

Her brother eyed her for a minute and then said more softly,

'What do you do so for, Alie?—it's too absurd, and wrong. Tiring youself out as if you were not possessed of common sense.'

'Why you declared yourself "tired out" yesterday,' said his sister smiling.

'But I had been amusing myself—taking my pleasure.'

'And I have been taking mine.'

'Nonsense! Do you expect me to believe that you like to hear bad English and worse Theology if it is only kept in countenance by the kitchen dresser?'

'Not Theology at all,' said his sister, 'only the Bible; and that is sweet English to my ear, always.' And if it were not— Thornton, you would have liked to bear a hand in the destruction of the Bastile?'

'There you are—' said Thornton,—'off on some unpursuable tangent. The most impossible person to argue with I ever saw!' and his head turned to the window again.

'I haven't said any hymn to-night, Alie,' said little Hulda.

'Well dear, it is not too late.'

'O no,' said Hulda, 'but I haven't learned any new one.'

'Then tell me one of the old.'

Hulda considered a while, and began very slowly and distinctly.

"Little travellers Zionward,
 Each one entering into rest,
 In the kingdom of your Lord,
 In the mansions of the blest;
 There, to welcome, Jesus waits—
 Gives the crowns his followers win—
 Lift your heads, ye golden gates!
 Let the little travellers in!

 Who are they whose little feet,
 Pacing life's dark journey through,
 Now have reached that heavenly seat
 They had ever kept in view?
 'I from Greenland's frozen land;'
 'I from India's sultry plain;'
 'I from Afric's barren land;'
 'I from islands of the main.'

 'All our earthly journey past,
 'Every tear and pain gone by,
 'Here together met at last,
 'At the portal of the sky!

'Each the welcome 'Come' awaits,
'Conquerors over death and sin!'
Lift your heads, ye golden gates!
Let the little travellers in!"

Rosalie had listened with her face bent down and resting upon the child's head; drinking in the words with double pleasure from those little lips, and blessing God in her heart for the life and immortality so clearly brought to light, so simply put forth within the reach of a child's faith. She glanced towards her brother, but the moodiness was greater than ever.

'What makes you sigh, Alie?' said Hulda looking up. 'Don't you think that's a pretty hymn?'

'I do indeed. But Hulda, who are these little travellers?'

'You told me—the children that follow Christ.'

'And what does that mean?'

'You told me,' said Hulda again, with her usual smile at ascribing anything to her sister. 'I remember you said it was going after him with our hearts more than any other way. You said that merely to keep some of God's commands without trying to love him, was like walking backwards.'

'Yes, the people who are seeking *first* the kingdom of God are not yet free from sin—they do slip and fall sometimes—but that is their grief. Their faces are toward heaven,—their desire is to do the will of God, because he has loved them and given himself for them.'

'I wish I could—' said Hulda who was looking gravely into the fire,—'I do try. I like that hymn so much, Alie. It's so pleasant to think that there will be all sorts of poor little children in heaven,—and there they'll be just as happy as anyone else.'

'Yes—' said her sister with a long breath,—' all will be happy in heaven—and there will be no difference there. Those gates are open to all who follow Christ, and the little black children are as free to go in as the white. It is not any particular nation, nor any particular church, but "*the redeemed of the Lord*," that shall "return and come to Zion with songs and everlasting joy upon their heads. They shall obtain joy and gladness, and sorrow and sighing shall flee away."'

'Aren't you ready to have candles?' said Thornton suddenly quitting his seat at the window. 'It's excessively stupid sitting here in the dark.'

Rosalie reached out her hand to the bell-cord, while Hulda exclaimed,

'Stupid! O that was because you were too far off to hear what Alie was talking about.'

'It was *not* because I was too far off.'

'But how could you feel stupid, then?' said Hulda. 'I'm sure it was beautiful.'

'It,—what?'

'Why, what she was repeating to me.'

'So let it remain then,' said Thornton. 'Bring some more wood, Tom—and last night's paper.'

'You must not expect to find everybody as fond of my talk as you are, Hulda,' said Rosalie, with an attempt to bring down the child's look of astonishment. 'I am not a very brilliant expositor.'

'What is an expositor?' said Hulda.

'A person who explains particular passages or books.'

'*I* think you are brilliant,' said Hulda, with a smile that certainly was.

'Why don't you ask me who I heard this afternoon?' said Thornton abruptly.

'Gentlemen sometimes prefer to give an unsolicited account of their movements,' said his sister, with a look and smile that might have stroked any fur into order.

'You shall have it then,' he answered. 'I heard Will Ackerman and Lieutenant Knolles.'

A flush of deep feeling came to her face and left it as quickly, but she said nothing; only her eyes which had been raised to his with interested expectation fell again, and her cheek once more rested upon Hulda.

'We had a very fine walk,' Thornton went on, 'and then a game of billiards, and so home with the church-goers.'

Still she said nothing, nor raised her head, although its support was suddenly withdrawn; for Hulda having with some trouble taken the meaning of such strange words, started up and exclaimed,

'But it's *very* wrong to play billiards on Sunday and not go to church! Don't you know that, Thornton?'

'I know that you concern yourself with what is not your business,' said the young man hastily, his hand giving more evident token of his displeasure. But it did not reach Hulda's cheek, only the shielding hand of her sister.

An indignant outburst was upon the child's lips, but the same hand was there too; and before Hulda had made up her mind whether she was too frightened or too angry to cry, Rosalie had taken her quietly out of the room. Her doubts were easily resolved then, and long before they had reached the top of the stairs she was sobbing her little heart out upon Rosalie's neck. And more for her sister's wrong than her own,—the shielding hand was kissed and cried over a great many times before Hulda's grief would let her speak, or Rosalie's silent agitation submit to control. She bent herself then to the task of calming Hulda,—checking her displeased and exited speeches about Thornton, drying her tears, and endeavouring to make her understand that it was not always best for little girls to reprove their grown-up brothers. A difficult task! without compromising either Thornton or the truth.

'I don't care!' was Hulda's satisfactory conclusion,— 'I shoudn't love him if he was fifty times my brother! And I don't want to.'

'I love him very much, Hulda.'

'I shouldn't think you would!' and a fresh shower of tears was bestowed upon Rosalie's hand.

'Why my hand was not hurt,' said her sister.

'I don't care!' said Hulda,—'it makes no difference.'

'O you are wrong, dear child,' said Rosalie,—'you must love him and try to please him. Come, look up—a little impatience is not worth so many tears.'

The child looked up—inquiringly,—as if she had detected tears in her sister's voice; but Rosalie's face was calm, though very, very grave.

'If you will jump down from my lap and ring the bell,' she said, 'Martha shall bring your tea up here, and then we will talk and you shall go to bed.'

So the bell was rung and Martha came and went according to directions; but when she came the second time with the tray, Miss Jumps stood still.

'You aint afraid of getting fat, Miss Rosalie, be you?' she said,—'cause you'll be in no danger this some time— that a brave man couldn't face, as Tom says. Now there's bread and butter down stairs no thicker than a thought, and beef, and preserves—and I'll fetch you up a cup of tea that shall smoke so you can't see it. What'll you have? Air's good enough in its way, but folks can't live on nothing else.'

'Thank you Martha,' said her mistress, 'but I am not ready for tea yet. Ask Mr. Thornton when you go down how soon he wishes to have it.'

A SISTER'S LOVE.

'I smell salt water,' said Martha Jumps as she went down to the kitchen,—'I say I do, sartain sure. One of my forbears must have been a sailor, and no mistake.

'Tom!—Tom Skiddy!—go up to the parlour straight, and ask Mr. Thornton if he wants his tea to-night or to-morrow morning. I guess he'd just as soon wait till morning,—and I'd as soon he would and a little sooner.'

'It's like enough you'll be gratified then,' said Tom, 'for I was up to the parlour a matter of five minutes ago to ask when he wanted tea; and all I got was, that when he did he'd let me know.'

The evening had worn away, and Thornton and the newspaper still sat vis-à-vis at the table, when the door was quietly opened and Rosalie came in. He heard her well enough, but the debating mood he had been in resolved itself for the moment into a committee of pride and false shame —therefore he did not speak nor look up. Neither when her hand was laid on his forehead—and its touch said a great deal to him, as the fingers stroked back and played for a moment with his hair—did he see fit to notice it.

'Thornton,' said she softly, 'I wish you would put up the paper and talk to me.'

'Because you do not wish me to read the paper, or because you do wish to talk—which?'

'A little of both.'

'Well—' and he sent the paper skimming across the table— 'there.—Now I am ready to hear what you've got to say. Let me have the lecture at once and be done with it.'

'I have no lecture to give,' she said gently. 'I am neither wise nor strong-hearted enough to-night.'

'I should think you were troubled with small doubts of your own wisdom,' said Thornton,—'why did you interfere between me and Hulda?'

'To save her from unmerited punishment.'

'Unmerited! she was excessively impertinent.'

'She did not mean to be—you forget what a child she is,—and that you are her brother.'

'And therefore she may say what she likes, I suppose,' said Thornton. 'It's a privilege to have sisters at that rate!'

He had not looked at her since she came in, but the pure image in his heart was never brighter than at that moment—he felt what a privilege it was.

'Yes,' Rosalie answered, as she knelt at his side with her hand on his shoulder. 'Yes—it is a privilege to have sisters—and brothers,—to have any near and dear friends in this wide world;—an unspeakable blessing.'

'Is that the blessing you have been crying over to-night?' said Thornton, glancing at her in spite of himself. 'It seems not to afford you much satisfaction. I wish you would speak out at once!' he added impetuously. 'Why don't you tell me that I have done all manner of bad things—shocked you, disgraced myself, and so forth? Say—why don't you?'

'Because you had said it all to yourself before you came home,' she answered steadily and without looking at him.

The words were spoken very gently but in a way not to be contradicted—if indeed he had been so inclined; but among all the qualities, good, bad, and indifferent, that went to make up Thornton's character, a few had never been tampered with. Foremost among these stood truth. The very feeling which had moved him to tell how he had spent the afternoon, was partly good and partly bad. The strong contrast of the quiet rest of Rosalie's hope with his own restless cravings, had wrought upon a mind dissatisfied with itself till for a moment he was willing to make her dissatisfied; but another feeling had wrought too in prompt ing the disclosure—the consciousness that she thought he had been more faithful to her wishes than was the truth.

Therefore when she told him that he was displeased with himself, no word of equivocation passed his lips; though he coloured deeply.

'You speak with sufficient boldness!' he said. 'And you do not call this lecturing one?'

'No,' she said in the same quiet way, and resting her cheek on his shoulder. 'Neither do you. But you try so hard not to understand your own thoughts sometimes, that I thought I would give you a little help.'

'I hope you will explain your own words next.'

'You remind me,' she said with a little smile which came and went instantly, 'of some one who said he would give to a certain charity if no one asked him to give. If any one did, he should probably knock the man down and give nothing.'

'And the key to this fable?'—said Thornton.

'It is hardly needed. You know the truth—you appreciate it—there is not one part of your character but sides, in its own secret persuasions, with right against wrong. And yet when I, or public opinion, or especially your own conscience, says, "*this is the way—walk ye in it,*"—that moment you say "*Nay, but after the desires of my own heart will I walk.*"'

She paused a few moments and then went on.

'Thornton, I came down to ask one thing of you.'

'You had better not,' he said, but more gently than before,—'according to your statement of the case I shall not grant it. But let me hear—perhaps I am not in a perverse mood at present.'

'You must not be displeased with me—I wanted to ask,

to entreat, that you will never again in such circumstances let Hulda know where you have been or what you have been doing. Let her keep all her love and respect for you —all that childish faith and veneration for the Lord's day and his commands, which you sometimes please to call superstition. O Thornton! do not try to ruin more than one of our mother's children!'

Her arms were about his neck and her face laid against his for a moment, and then she was gone; and Thornton sat alone with his own reflections until the bright wood fire had become but a heap of white ashes, and Trinity church had told off more than one of the small hours.

He roused himself then, and stood up,—that same sweet presence about him yet, his mother's picture before him, and still sounding in his ears the words he had heard repeated to Hulda in the afternoon. He felt their power, even as some persons can appreciate a fine melody while yet they know not one note of music. He took his light and went thoughtfully up stairs, but Rosalie's door arrested him,—he opened it softly and went in.

The moon shown in brilliantly but failed to awaken the quiet sleepers. Both in most quiet rest,—yet Thornton saw and felt a difference. Hulda, with her arm across her sister's neck, was in the very luxuriance of sleep,—there were none of night's own visions, there was no lingering one of the day, to disturb her with its influence,—her little train of thought was noiseless as a train could be, and apparently glided through fairy-land. Her sister's slumber was not so deep; and though undisturbed, though the lines of the face were more absolutely quiet than Hulda's,—the mouth had not relaxed its gravity, nor were the eyelashes dry.

Thornton went to bed strangely dissatisfied with himself.

CHAPTER VIII.

*Wouldst thou go forth to bless. be sure of thine own ground,
Fix well thy centre first, then draw thy circles round.*—TRENCH.

DESPITE the night's fair promise the morning rose upon bad weather; but in the moral atmosphere the change had been the other way, and everything looked brighter. Though indeed according to one fancy the changes were much alike, and

"——the sulphurous rifts of passion and woe
Lay deep 'neath a silence pure and smooth,
Like burnt-out craters healed with snow."

'I am so glad it snows!' exclaimed Hulda dancing into the breakfast room. 'You know you said you would give me a sleigh-ride, Thornton, as soon as I was well enough, and we had some more——'

She stopped short, the evening before suddenly in her thoughts.

'As soon as we had some more what?' said her brother looking off the paper. 'Rain?'

'I was going to say snow,' said Hulda in a low voice.

'That is a tremendous word, certainly,—it is not surprising that you were afraid to speak it. See here, Hulda— I don't want two guardians, and I think on the whole I prefer Rosalie to your little ladyship,—so do you never take it upon you to give me advice. I am not gifted with the Moon's patience, unfortunately.'

'The Moon's patience!' said Hulda. 'I never heard of that before.'

'Why you know,' said Thornton, 'when a little dog once undertook to bark at the Moon, the Moon kept on shining.'

'I don't think you are like the Moon,' said Hulda laughing, but eyeing him a little askance,—'not a bit.'

'Never mind—in future you must deliver your opinions of me and my conduct to Rosalie, and she may repeat what of them she likes. Where is she this morning?'

She was at his side, even as he spoke; with a face so fair, so shadowless except for a little anxious feeling when she first looked at him—a half glance of inquiry as it were—that Thornton was too touched to speak; and taking both her hands, he kissed her first on one cheek and then on the other, wishing from his heart that he had ever done more to fill the vacant place of which that black dress spoke. Such a purpose had often been formed, but when it came to the point there was always some hindrance. He had not learned yet how hard it is to obey the second great command while disregarding the first.

'Then do you think you will give me a sleigh-ride, Thornton?' said Hulda, emboldened by something in his face to press her request.

'Half a dozen, if there is snow enough.'

'O that is very good of you!' said Hulda, 'because Alie don't like to go alone. I guess there'll be snow enough—I mean I think there will,—I saw one baker's sleigh go by.'

'Which proves nothing concerning *my* runners,' said Thornton, as he seated himself at the breakfast table. 'Bakers have a facility of enjoyment which belongs to few other people.'

'Have they?' said Hulda. 'But here comes another sleigh—I hear the bells.'

'And a remarkably slow tinkle they make,' said Thornton,—'I'll wager something that's a coal man. It's a singular fact that everybody is out of fuel as soon as a storm comes.'

'Yes it is a charcoal man,' said Hulda—'all white and black. And here comes somebody else.'

'Somebody else had better come here,' said her sister, 'or more than breakfast will get cold.'

'I'll come—' said the child, getting down with some reluctance from the chair where she had been kneeling, and taking a last peep out of the window,—'but it looks so nice out,—and the people look so funny,—just let me see what this one sleigh is—O such a queer one! like a little old coach without any wheels. And it's stopping at our door! —O Alie, I do believe it's Miss Bettie Morsel!'

And the next act being like to come off within doors, Hulda came to her breakfast.

The queer sleigh, which was in truth but a coach-body on runners, drew up at the door as she had said. A most literal drawing-up!—the driver tugging at his horse till both were slanted back at no inconsiderable angle. Then the driver got down and clapped his hands once or twice, and the horse shook his head to make sure he was all right again,—a fact attested by a miserable little bell that hung about him—somewhere. And the coach-body door being at length opened, a little dark figure darted out through the white medium and up the steps. But her ring was by no means in accordance with so fierce a beginning. It was a kind of gentle intimation that if it was all the same to everybody, she would like to come in—a mere suggestion that perhaps there might be somebody outside in the snow,—a ring which a thorough-bred waiter of the present day would go to sleep over, and dream of visiters.

But Martha Jumps, who was on duty while Tom carried buckwheats into the breakfast room, and whose eyes, ears, and understanding were always wide awake,—dropped her duster, settled her cap, and went to the door. And having presently detailed her message to Tom, Tom entered the breakfast-room and said,

'Miss Morsel, sir.'

'What the deuce have I to do with Miss Morsel?' said Thornton. 'Why don't you tell your mistress?'

Tom coloured up to his eyes but replied,

'That's what Martha said sir—she said she wanted to see you.'

'Martha humbugs you Tom, about ten times a day. But shew Miss Morsel in here, and then she can suit herself.'

'And give me another cup and saucer,' said his mistress. 'Is the parlour fire burning?'

'Well—pretty smart,' said Tom doubtfully,—'not over and above.'

'Never mind, ask Miss Morsel to walk in here.' And meeting her visiter at the door, Rosalie explained to her how she thought the warmest room was the best that morning.

'So good of you!' said Miss Morsel, who was a benign, anxious-looking, somewhat care-worn little personage. 'Yes it *is* rather cold this morning—the wind blows quite keen.' And she shivered in her winter habiliments, which were none of the thickest.'

'It is particularly cold at this time in the morning,' said Rosalie, as she brought Miss Morsel round to the side of the table next the fire. 'You must sit down and take some breakfast with us.'

'O no my dear—thank you, I can't indeed.'

'Not a cup of coffee?'

'Well, a single cup—' said Miss Morsel, her face brightening up under bright influences—for it was a wonderfully pleasant thing to be so gently put into that comfortable chair by the fire. 'I believe I must take a single cup—and only one lump of sugar if you please. It don't matter much about the size of it, but not *more* than one lump. I came out this morning—queer, isn't it?—but I came out to see your brother. Captain Thornton, *is* it a true statement of facts that the city's bombarded?'

'Not unless the reports have deafened my ears,' said Thornton, fortifying himself with half a cup of coffee before he spoke. 'I have heard nothing of it.'

'Well I thought it couldn't be,' said Miss Morsel, looking very much relieved, 'for I've heard nothing of it either; only last night a boy was screaming about the streets. It's astonishing to me that boys are suffered to go at large as they are.'

'Instead of shutting them up like any other wild animals,' said Thornton.

'That's just what I said to ma,' said Miss Morsel, 'that it ought to be,—and she said it never used to be in her time, that boys never were wild then nor girls neither. It was ma that was so scared last night, for she always thinks something is going to happen to her, though I tell her she's just as liable to live as I am. No my dear—no more. It's really a shame to eat two breakfasts, though to be sure something depends upon how much a person took at the first.'

'O have another cup!' said Thornton, 'and you'll stand the bombardment better.'

'I don't know about that,' said Miss Morsel, but hand-ing her cup at the same time,—'it seems too bad to enjoy oneself now-a-days. It's a good thing we're none of us married people, for separations in families are dreadful; and gentlemen are the property of the government now, I suppose, to have and to hold, as the saying is.'

It was hard to tell which was most discomposed by this speech—Tom or his master.

'Are married people essential to your idea of a family?' said Rosalie smiling.

'Certainly,' said the little woman gravely. 'Now for instance—I can't call myself a family you know,—it would be absurd.'

'Most true,' said Thornton. 'But here Rosalie and I have a family Miss Morsel, and if either of us should get married it would break it up at once.'

'O dear!' said Miss Morsel. 'How could that be?'

'Why, not to go any further,' said Thornton, 'Rosalie is so fond of having the upper hand, that she never would endure to see my wife manage me.'

'But your wife would be a very nice person, of course, said Miss Morsel, 'and—dear me! that is a great pity. I always thought you would all live together so delightfully. I declare it has quite spoiled my breakfast—though to be sure I had eaten all I could.'

'It must have been the bombardment,' said Thornton laughing.

'Well maybe,' said Miss Morsel. 'But now Captain Thornton, what is the news, really?'

'Really Miss Morsel, there isn't much. Bonaparte has blown up the Kremlin and left Moscow, and Lord Wellington has left Madrid—that's the last news from Europe. Out west here the Indians have been defeated and Tecumseh taken prisoner; and nearer home still, one of our harbours is blockaded by a gun brig, a 74, and two frigates.'

'What is a gun brig?' said Miss Morsel,—'a brig loaded with guns?'

'Sounds enough like it,' said Thornton.

'What a dreadful thing it must be to be blockaded!' said Miss Morsel. 'Which harbour is it?'

'Our own here—of New York.'

'New York harbour blockaded!' exclaimed Miss Morsel. 'And has the bay and Staten Island and Fort Hamilton, and all those beautiful places come into possession of the British?'

'I wish they had,' said Thornton. 'Never mind Miss Morsel,—there are a good many guns between you and them yet. Tom bring some more cakes.'

'What will they do there?' said Miss Morsel curiously.

'Find out how little of our bread and butter comes that way, maybe,' said Thornton. 'Miss Morsel— you have not half fortified yourself for a siege.'

'O dear!' said poor Miss Morsel. 'If I thought I was ever to be besieged and taken, I shouldn't eat another ounce from now till then. You don't really think there's any danger?'

'Not a bit!' said Thornton laughing. 'I should like to see anybody attempt it! I'll let you know a week beforehand, Miss Morsel, and you can put up your defences.'

'Thank you—I'm sure you're very kind,' said Miss Morsel, 'but then you know we haven't got any. We never did have anything that could be called arms in our house. But I must go—it's so warm here and pleasant that I believe I forgot there was anybody out in the cold. Poor man!' said Miss Morsel looking out at her driver, 'I daresay he's been clapping his hands this whole time, and not for joy, either. It was very extravagant in me to ride, but I wanted to know so much about things,—and I can't always keep warm in the snow—and I'm afraid to take cold, you know, for ma's sake.'

ing her cup at the same time,—'it seems too bad to enjoy oneself now-a-days. It's a good thing we're none of us married people, for separations in families are dreadful; and gentlemen are the property of the government now, I suppose, to have and to hold, as the saying is.'

It was hard to tell which was most discomposed by this speech—Tom or his master.

'Are married people essential to your idea of a family?' said Rosalie smiling.

'Certainly,' said the little woman gravely. 'Now for instance—I can't call myself a family you know,—it would be absurd.'

'Most true,' said Thornton. 'But here Rosalie and I have a family Miss Morsel, and if either of us should get married it would break it up at once.'

'O dear!' said Miss Morsel. 'How could that be?'

'Why, not to go any further,' said Thornton, 'Rosalie is so fond of having the upper hand, that she never would endure to see my wife manage me.'

'But your wife would be a very nice person, of course, said Miss Morsel, 'and—dear me! that is a great pity. I always thought you would all live together so delightfully. I declare it has quite spoiled my breakfast—though to be sure I had eaten all I could.'

'It must have been the bombardment,' said Thornton laughing.

'Well maybe,' said Miss Morsel. 'But now Captain Thornton, what is the news, really?'

'Really Miss Morsel, there isn't much. Bonaparte has blown up the Kremlin and left Moscow, and Lord Wellington has left Madrid—that's the last news from Europe. Out west here the Indians have been defeated and Tecumseh taken prisoner; and nearer home still, one of our harbours is blockaded by a gun brig, a 74, and two frigates.'

'What is a gun brig?' said Miss Morsel,—'a brig loaded with guns?'

'Sounds enough like it,' said Thornton.

'What a dreadful thing it must be to be blockaded!' said Miss Morsel. 'Which harbour is it?'

'Our own here—of New York.'

'New York harbour blockaded!' exclaimed Miss Morsel. 'And has the bay and Staten Island and Fort Hamilton, and all those beautiful places come into possession of the British?'

'I wish they had,' said Thornton. 'Never mind Miss Morsel,—there are a good many guns between you and them yet. Tom bring some more cakes.'

'What will they do there?' said Miss Morsel curiously.

'Find out how little of our bread and butter comes that way, maybe,' said Thornton. 'Miss Morsel— you have not half fortified yourself for a siege.'

'O dear!' said poor Miss Morsel. 'If I thought I was ever to be besieged and taken, I shouldn't eat another ounce from now till then. You don't really think there's any danger?'

'Not a bit!' said Thornton laughing. 'I should like to see anybody attempt it! I'll let you know a week beforehand, Miss Morsel, and you can put up your defences.'

'Thank you—I'm sure you're very kind,' said Miss Morsel, 'but then you know we haven't got any. We never did have anything that could be called arms in our house. But I must go—it's so warm here and pleasant that I believe I forgot there was anybody out in the cold. Poor man!' said Miss Morsel looking out at her driver, 'I daresay he's been clapping his hands this whole time, and not for joy, either. It was very extravagant in me to ride, but I wanted to know so much about things,—and I can't always keep warm in the snow—and I'm afraid to take cold, you know, for ma's sake.'

'You have not learned much, after all,' said Thornton.

'O a great deal! You say Cumsetah's certainly taken?'

'Tecumseh?' said Rosalie with a kind smile. 'Yes, I saw the account myself.'

'Thank you my dear—and for telling me the man's real name again,—I'm so apt to forget. But youe'r so good—and I do like to get things straight, though you wouldn't think it. Tecumseh—I sha'n't forget—you spoke it so distinctly for me. Do you know I always do understand what you say? Some people confuse me so,—and then I get hold of the wrong ball of yarn and begin at the toe of my stocking. Tecumseh—but who took him?'

'One of Harrison's officers,' said Thornton. 'But mind you tell the story to-day, Miss Morsel, for he'll probably escape before to-morrow.'

'Dreadful creature!' said Miss Morsel,—'I hope not. I hope they'll take good care of him though. Thank you my dear very much—your coffee was excellent.'

'I will try to have it just as good whenever you will come and breakfast with us,' said Rosalie as she shook hands with her poor little guest. 'I wish you would come oftener.'

'I'm sure you do!' said Miss Morsel earnestly; 'and there isn't much else in the world I am sure of. But you're like nobody else,—such Christmas presents and all,—and I haven't said a word about them—because I couldn't. I don't know now—were they yours or your brother's?'

'Not mine,' said Thornton,—'Rosalie does everything good that is done in this house. But mine shall come, Miss Morsel,—I shall remember it now, as surely as you will Tecumseh.'

'Tecumseh—yes, I'll remember. But you are all so good—to let me come and talk, talk,—not a bit like rich people,—and it's such a comfort sometimes,—and smile at me just as sweetly when I come as when I go. O there'll be one blessing upon your heads if words can call it down!'

And she slid out of the room; while Thornton having found out that he did not want to go and put her in the old coach-body, went—and made her perfectly happy thereby.

'Not quite *all* the good that is done in this house,' said his sister, meeting him when he came back with a look that was worth the purchase.

'The Sun has as much to do with the Moon's light as with his own,' said Thornton rather sadly. 'I am dark enough when I am turned away from you, Alie. You never turn from me—like a blessed child as you are.'

CHAPTER IX.

*But, brother, let your reprehension
Run in an easy current, not o'er high,
Carried with rashness, or devouring choler;
But rather use the soft persuading way.*—BEN JONSON.

A FINE body of snow lay on the ground. White, white,—cheerful and cold,—the trees rearing through the still air their part of the earth's burden; the sky in dazzling contrast to the bright roofs on which the sun poured down his full complement of rays,—in vain;—the snow laughed at them. A very merry laugh if it was a cold one.

The side-walks were cleared and dry; for in those unsophisticated days laws were not only made but enforced; and foot-passengers went comfortably along in their sphere of action, while a host of sleighs swept by in theirs. Neither division of the public crowded into an undistinguishable throng as now,—both people and sleighs had a pretty setting of air and snow,—then was it easy to see and to be seen.

In this reign of fur and velvet, cloth boots and wadded cloaks, the merging is a less matter; but when the weaker sex protected themselves with white dresses and stockings to match, and shoes that matched anything but the season,—when high-coloured and fly-away little capes were the best defence that the Commander-in-chief of the feminine forces allowed during a winter campaign,—then elbow-room was a thing of some moment. It would have been intolerable to have one's own scarlet wings confounded with a neighbouring pair of blue, and so to present the general appearance of a two-headed butterfly somewhat diversified as to his pinions; or worse still, to have no room for them to fly at all. But no such misfortune befell the ladies of 1813,— the field was clear, and spotted with butterflies as a field should be—each in its turn 'the observed of all observers.'

Thornton's horses were shaking their heads and jingling their bells at his door; snorting, and pawing the snow, and putting their heads together with every symptom of readiness and impatience,—the white foam frozen in a thick crust upon mouth and bit, the sun glancing from every metallic spot on the bright harness. On the steps stood Mr Clyde himself, in much the same mood as his horses,—the minute-hand of his watch seeming to mark the hours. One butterfly after another sailed down the street—or fluttered, as the case might be; now beating about in the cool wind, and then bearing down wing-and-wing upon the enemy; and soon espying Mr. Clyde's position, gracefully inclined its pretty head that way, and glanced at the gay horses. And Mr. Clyde's arms being for the tenth time forced from their position to return such courtesies, enwrapped themselves thereafter more closely than ever; and when the closing of the hall door drew his attention, he turned sharply round.

No butterfly stood there—and yet it might have been a creature with wings; but not such as are ever spread on earth except to fly away withal.

'What wonder will come next?' she said smiling. 'Thornton and his horses both here five minutes before the time!'

white snow with a sort of dainty regularity and precision; while the large grave-coloured and most comfortable looking sleigh, followed on at a pleasant but not breathless rate. The smile of the good quakeress to Rosalie was refreshing to see—so very bright and heartfelt.

Thornton however thought differently, for after conveying to his horses a very imperative request that they would go faster, he saw fit to express his distaste in words.

'I wish I could ever go through Broadway without meeting that turn-out!' he said.

'What is a turn-out?' said Hulda whose eyes were already half shut.

'I don't care much about it when I am alone,' Thornton went on without noticing her, 'but when you are with me I always get provoked.'

'That is unfortunate,' said Rosalie smiling. 'If I am such a magnet for disagreeableness I had better stay at home. I hope you don't get provoked at me?'

'You always will look so pleased to see her,' he said gloomily.

'So I am—I like her very much.'

'But I don't—there's the thing. And she looks at you just as I saw you once when you were a little child look at a canary bird in the hands of a school boy. And I say it provokes me.'

'What an imagination you have!' said his sister laughing. 'I noticed the particular pleasantness of her look towards you.'

'She had no business to look at me,' said Thornton. 'I don't know her and I don't want to.'

'The next time you come out,' said Rosalie raising her bright eyes to his face, 'I'll write a placard for the front of your cap—' Ladies will please keep their eyes off.''

'You are a saucy girl,' said her brother, whose displeasure was however evaporating. 'Do you mean to say that Mrs. Raynor did not think to herself what a poor forlorn child you were, and how much better off you would be in her sleigh than in mine?'

'She has called me a poor child very often, but not from any such reason,' said Rosalie, as the thought of the true one fell like a shadow upon her face. 'And she knows very little of me, Thornton, if she thinks that I wish myself out of your sleigh, or that I have one thought in my heart about you I am unwilling you should know.'

'There are several I don't wish to know,' said Thornton, —'I doubt some of them might make me feel uncomfortable. But I wish you would pull that veil back again Alie, for I have somehow got an uneasy notion that *I* am the wind blowing in your face.'

'You are full of notions to-day; but the wind does not trouble me at all now that we have turned. How pleasant it has been! I have enjoyed it so much.'

'Really?'

'Really.'

Thornton looked pleased.

'I have enjoyed it too, very much—with one or two drawbacks.'

'How did you ever get such a dislike to so excellent a person as Mrs. Raynor?' said his sister, as she arranged the little sleeping Hulda in a more comfortable position. 'You do not know her—and surely you never heard anything but good of her.'

'Never—I wish I had. If any one else would speak of her with a qualification perhaps I should not. I hate these dreadfully precise people.'

'O she is not a bit precise!' cried his sister—'not a

bit! Of course a quaker must talk after the quaker fashion, but her heart is as free as a child's.'

'Well that is a good thing about a heart, certainly,' said Thornton with a meditative air. 'But however it may be, the sight of her always gives me an uncomfortable sensation. I believe she reminds me of her son, and him I *do* know.'

'And do not like?'

'No ——'

'Why not?'

'I could give a very straight answer on the subject,' said the young man with a glance at his sister's face, 'but perhaps it's as well not. In general, he don't like me and I don't like him—nor his pursuits.'

'Did you ever hear that they were anything but creditable?' said Rosalie turning a startled look upon him.

'What is it to you whether they are or not?'

'Making the profession he does, I should be exceedingly sorry to think that he had disgraced it. Did you ever see or hear anything to make you think so?'

'Never—' said Thornton briefly.

And no more words were spoken till they were at home again.

The sleigh with black horses was at the door in five minutes after their own arrival, and Rosalie was called down to see her friend 'for a single moment only,' before she had time to do more than throw off her wrappers. And when she came into the parlour, her hair a little brushed back by the wind, and the glow of exercise and fresh air yet in her cheeks, the good quakeress took her in her arms and kissed her more than once before she spoke.

'I was so glad to see thee out,' she said,—'it is so good for thee. And how dost thou now, dear child? better?

Art thou learning to cast all thy care upon the strong hand that will not let it press thy little weak heart too heavily?'

The trembling lips could hardly answer,

'Sometimes.'

'" *I have chosen thee in the furnace of affliction*"'—said her friend tenderly. 'Chosen thee, love—not cast thee out thither. Thee must remember that. And also that other verse which saith, " Rejoice in the Lord *alway*." Now tell me—how doth thy sister?'

'O quite well again.'

'And thy brother—I saw him with thee even now. He hath thine eyes, Rosalie, but more self-willed. I love him for thy sake—ye are so much alike.'

But Rosalie's smile was like nobody but herself.

'And you are well again, too?' she said, as she sat on a low seat by her friend, looking up at her with the intense pleasure of having even for a moment comfort and counsel from one older than herself.

'Yes my child—or at the least so well that I am going away,—that is wherefore thou seest me now, and but an instant have I to stay. A week or two I shall be with my sister, which shall pleasure and I trust profit us both; and then shall I return again to wait.'

What for, the quakeress did not say, but she rose and took Rosalie in her arms as she had done before.

'Fare thee well, dear child! and the best of all blessings be upon thee. " *There be many that say,* '*Who will shew us any good?*' *Lord lift thou up the light of thy countenance upon us!*"'

'O that it might be upon *us!*' Rosalie thought, as she came back from the front door and went slowly up stairs to dress. 'Will that day ever come?' And then she remembered,

"*I had fainted, unless I had believed to see the goodness of the Lord in the land of the living.*"

'And what had your dear friend to say to you?' inquired Thornton when he came to dinner.

'Not much—just to bid me goodbye. She is going away for a few days.'

'Charming! We will go sleigh-riding every day. I shall take this opportunity to give my canary bird plenty of fresh air and exercise.'

'Your canary bird is much obliged to you for being glad when she is sorry,' said his sister smiling.

'Truly you are sorry sometimes when I am glad,' said Thornton.

'When the question is of things that do you mischief.'

'I wonder how you are to judge of that?' said he laughing and patting her cheek. 'Methinks your censorship is getting a little rampant. Don't you suppose now, my fair monitor, that if you went out a little more I should go out a little less?—that if you sometimes gave me your company abroad I should oftener give you mine at home?'

'You know I have had enough to hinder my going out.'

'Have had—but now?'

There was enough, now; but after a moment's struggle with herself Rosalie looked up and answered cheerfully,

'I will go with you wherever you wish me to go.'

'Is that said with a little Catholic reservation to your own better judgment?'

'No, to yours. I would trust you pretty implicitly if you once took the responsibility upon yourself.'

'I should like to know where it rests now?' said Thornton, looking half amused and half vexed. 'If you were not the steadiest little mouse that ever went about from corner to cupboard, the responsibility would be pretty well thrown upon my shoulders, I fancy. I'll take it, at all events. Will you go with me to the theatre to-night?'

'O I am not obliged to answer any but serious propositions,' said she smiling. 'You do not wish me to go with you there—let this be one of the evenings bestowed upon me at home.'

'Why shouldn't I wish you to go? What harm will it do you any more than other people?'

'I never mean to try and find out. But I would not go if I knew it would do me none.'

'Because you think actors must necessarily be bad people?'

'Not necessarily perhaps. But Thornton, if there was a gulf over which but one in a hundred could leap, while all the rest were dashed to pieces, what would you think of the rich people who hired them to try?'

'I will let you know my opinion of that amusement when it is advertised,' said her brother. 'But I tell you Alie, it's of no use to compare our opinions—we never were meant to live together.'

She laid her hands upon his shoulders, and looked up at him with a face so loving, so beseeching, so full of all that she could not say, that its light was half reflected. Her whole heart was in that look; and Thornton felt as he had never felt before, how true, how pure a heart it was—how unspeakably reasonable in all its requests. But his own unhumbled nature, the blind pride which will serve sin rather than God, because he is the *rightful* ruler of the universe, rose up within him; and silently laying his hand upon his sister's lips, Thornton disengaged himself and walked away to the dinner table.

CHAPTER X.

Jaques. Let's meet as little as we can.
Orlando. I do desire we may be better strangers.—*As You Like It.*

EVENING found Rosalie alone in the parlour. She had listened to her brother's departing step until even her fancy could hear it no longer, and the approaching ones were dull now and void of interest. The sleigh-bells jingled yet, almost as merrily as ever, but with a somewhat different effect; for the sun had taken leave of the cold earth, and Jack Frost had sent out his myrmidons. The little beggar children began to retreat slowly and shivering to their dens of sin and sorrow; hopeless of anything from the goers-by, whose rapid pace they could hardly check; and *home*, of one sort or another, seemed to be in everybody's heart. Why was it not in Thornton's?

His sister would have been comforted to know that it *was* in his heart,—that even then, as he met a party of gay friends and joined their walk, he remembered the one being whom he had never wished to see less unspotted from the world;—*more* pure, to his fancy, she could not be. He thought of her, and of the bright pleasure he might give and take where she was. And yet he came not,—and the soft twilight fell gently upon her, and gay lights blazed down upon him. Fit emblems of the spirit of each heart.

The one a bright artificial glare,—in the other a mingling of darkness indeed, but what light there was, from heaven!

So deep was Rosalie in her own reflections—devising ways and means to make herself more agreeable and home more attractive—that a ring at the door was unnoticed; and it was not till Tom announced,

'A gentleman, ma'am,'

that she recollected how much rather she would be alone. But he was there, and there was no help for it.

A young man, whose character lay not all on the surface. His aspect was singularly grave and quiet—by some people called morose; but the eye from its calm depth sent back no shadow of misanthropy, and if the mouth spoke self control it spoke with sweetness. And when a smile came—which indeed was not very often—the person in the world who liked him least would have done something to prolong or to bring it back. There was also about him a singular air of power, without the least assumption of it. It was the sort of fortress-like strength, the sure position taken and held unshrinkingly within the walls of truth and moral courage; and withal, the perfect freedom and fearlessness of one who has *himself* well in hand. Able too he seemed, to wage offensive warfare—yet he rarely did. The eye might fire and the cheek glow, and that sense of power strike disagreeably upon the beholder; but when the word came, it came with the very spirit of love and gentleness—and was the more powerful. The effect was neither hurt feeling nor wounded pride,—the effort was not to destroy but to build up. Yet for this very thing, so unlike themselves, many of his own age disliked and shunned him. They could not endure to trust a man thoroughly because his face commanded that trust; nor to feel themselves rebuked by his presence when he had not uttered a word.

For a moment, in the darkness, Rosalie looked with some doubt at the stranger; but she had quickly met him half way, with a look of great pleasure and the exclamation,

'Mr. Raynor!'

His look was as bright and more demonstrative, till he saw hers change and every particle of light pass from it; and not guessing the associations which a friend so long unseen had called up, not knowing what had taken place during his absence.; Mr. Raynor said with more anxious haste than caution,

'You are all well? your brother is not ordered away?'

'No, he is here and quite well,' she said, but turning a little from him.

'And your mother?'

It was too much. The heart's cry of sorrow was suppressed, but it was with almost passionate bitterness that Rosalie threw herself down on a seat, exclaiming,

'Well? O yes!—it is well with her! But for that my heart would have broken long ago!'

He understood it all then,—his eye took note of her dress—he knew what some lost letters would have told him; but shocked, grieved, as he was, a few minutes passed before he knew what to say or how to speak it. The words were spoken then with that quiet steadiness which insensibly gives strength.

'Yes, it is well!—Well with you too, my dear Miss Clyde—For "it cannot be ill with him whose God is"!'

O what a long breath answered him!—of weakness and weariness and faith, and again weakness! She did not move nor raise her head.

'Alie,' said little Hulda opening the door, 'may Tom get some New-year cookies for tea, or would you rather have only dough-nuts?'

Mr. Raynor turned quickly, and taking a chair at some distance from Rosalie he intercepted the little intruder, very much to her dissatisfaction.

'Let me go, sir, if you please,' she said; struggling, though very politely, to get away from the arm that was round her. 'Please sir let me go!'

'Not quite yet,' he said, gently placing her upon his lap and kissing her. 'Have you quite forgotten me, Hulda?'

'No sir, because I never saw you before.'

'That is being forgotten, with a witness. Did you never hear of a little girl who once took her doll out to ride, and then dropped that unfortunate young lady from the carriage window into the mud?'

'O yes!' said Hulda, 'indeed I have! And are you the nice gentleman that picked her up for me, sir?'

'I had the pleasure of picking her up for you. Whether I am nice or not you seem to be a little doubtful.'

'O I remember all about it!' said the child, sitting up now with a pleased and interested look. 'I haven't thought of it in a *great* while. I was so glad dolly's face was n't clear down in the mud—and oh the mud was so thick! And her dress was all black in front—do you remember?'

'No, I remember nothing about her dress.'

'Don't you?' said Hulda, 'well I remember perfectly well. And don't you remember sir how the other gentleman laughed because I loved my doll so much?'

'Nay I think that was not the reason he laughed.'

'O yes it must have been,' said Hulda, 'because you know there was nothing else to laugh at. But mayn't I go now, sir? I want to speak to Alie.'

'I don't think she wants you half so much as I do. How many new dolls have you had since then, Hulda?'

'O I haven't had any,' said she smiling. 'I've got the same one yet.'

'You must be a careful little body,' said her friend.

'Yes I suppose I am,' said Hulda folding her hands with a grave air, as if she had been about fifty; 'but then I don't play with dolls now much—I haven't much time.'

'Does Miss Rosalie keep you so busy? I should hardly have thought that.'

'O no, sir, *that* isn't the reason—she'd let me play a great deal. But then,' said Hulda, looking off with a contemplative face, 'I'd rather talk to her. Thornton always goes out, you know, and so she'd be all alone if it wasn't for me.'

A shade of very deep displeasure crossed the gentleman's face while she spoke; but happily absorbed in swinging her little feet and watching the shadows that flickered up and down the wall, Hulda saw it not. Neither did Rosalie, whose eyes were yet shielded by her hand. But old knowledge of the face and character supplied the want of sight,—her hand was taken down and she turned and spoke.

'What did you want of me, Hulda?'

'O—only about the cake for tea,' said Hulda twisting herself round. 'Tom didn't know whether you wanted him to get some New-year cookies.'

'Send for what you like, dear, and let us have tea at once.'

And Hulda went,—wondering very much at the kiss with which Mr. Raynor had released her; it was such a strange kiss—she could not tell what to make of it. Only it seemed to Hulda as if for some reason or other the strange gentleman liked her; and she began to like him in return very much.

He came and stood before the fire as she left the room, with a look that said his uppermost thoughts were not such as could be spoken nor yet easily put aside.

'You were expected earlier in the winter, Mr. Raynor,' said Rosalie, as if she had a mind they should at least not be dwelt upon.

'Yes, much earlier,' he said sitting down by her. 'But I am not accustomed to hear 'Mr. Raynor' from your lips, Miss Rosalie,—before I went away it was 'Mr. Henry.''

'O that was to distinguish you from Mr. Penn,' she said with a little flush that came somewhat unwittingly.

'And you do not mean to distinguish me any more?'

She did not look to see what he meant—the colour that came over her face seemed to say she would rather not know; it was more of distress than embarrassment; and she went on somewhat hastily, as if her object were but to talk —not to say any particular thing.

'My help is hardly needed to distinguish people that have lived so long abroad,—that is enough in this age of the world. But how grieved Mrs. Raynor will be that she has lost the first minutes of your arrival! She is quite well —I can tell you that. I saw her only this morning, and she left town at four o'clock.'

'So I found out when I reached the house; and my next move was to seek some way of following her to-night, but it was too late.'

'She has wished for you so earnestly! I think it was as much as even she could do to be patient.'

'I am sure it was more than I could do,' said the young man, who was apparently carrying on some under current of scrutiny or cogitation, and waiting for another look, which he could not get. 'My passage home was made in four different ships, and I left all my patience in the first.'

'Four different ships! Then you really did see some of the fighting that she feared so much?'

'I really did see and hear a good deal of it—felt a little

too. When we were two days out from Bordeaux,' he continued with no reply to her inquiring look, 'a British letter-of-marque fell in with us and took possession after we had run as hard as we could for eleven hours. Part of the men were left on board and the ship ordered for England; while I had the honor of being cared for—or I should say *not* cared for—in the brig. Then came up the Paul Jones, one of our privateers, took the brig and burnt her, and brought me home.'

'Unhurt through it all?'

'Except a very trifling wound from a splinter.'

She looked up then—one quick, earnest look,—and Mr. Raynor's smile said that he had got just what he wanted.

'I must go now,' he said quietly. 'Some business matters need attention, and there will be scant time to do anything in the morning. May I tell my mother that you are well? I hardly dare venture upon that unauthorized assertion.'

'O yes—I am quite well,—and give her my love, Mr Raynor.'

'If I can make up my mind to part with it.'

'Good evening,' said a third party who had entered the room. 'Have I the pleasure of seeing Mr. Raynor?'

'I am not sure sir,' was the somewhat grave reply, though accompanied with a not uncordial shake of the hand. 'But good evening Mr. Clyde—or I should rather say, how do you do, after so long a break in our intercourse.'

How well Thornton felt that whatever cordiality there might be in the salutation was for Rosalie's brother—not for him. Certainly his own greeting had been cold enough.

'Tea's ready,' said Hulda, suddenly adding her little person to the group,—' won't you come? O Thornton!—have *you* come home to tea?—how pleasant that will be!—there'll be four of us!'

Poor little Hulda! she might have said anything else her brother thought, with better effect. His cheek flushed with displeasure and mortification, and there was a minute of awkward silence. Then Rosalie came to his side, and linking her arm in his—caressingly, as he felt—she said,

'Thornton, cannot you persuade Mr. Raynor to drink tea with us instead of going home to take it alone?.'

Thornton felt that she stood by him, whoever else did not; and with a blessing in his heart that his lips did not speak, he gave the invitation—as he would have done anything else that she had asked at that moment.

Mr. Raynor looked at the brother and sister as they stood there, and though something of the shade which Hulda had before called forth came back, yet his face unbent, and in his answer there was no disturbing element unless a touch of quiet amusement.

'I cannot refuse to stay at your request Mr. Clyde, for I know you came because you thought I was here.'

And Thornton wondered whether his guest had lately studied witchcraft. It was odd too, but he would have given anything if Mr. Raynor had made himself less absolutely pleasant and agreeable for the next hour. In a half vexed half soothed state Thornton remained during tea; but when Mr. Raynor had gone and both his sisters were up-stairs, vexation soon got the upper hand.

'Where is Hulda?' he said when Rosalie came down.

'In bed.'

'Well that is a comfort. I do wish you would teach her to hold her tongue. Her way of saying things is perfectly spiteful.'

'If it is spiteful to be glad to have you at home,' said his sister as she took a low seat by him, 'you must bestow that epithet on me too.'

'Nonsense—glad indeed! What do you suppose she cares? As if it was not enough to find disagreeable company at home, without having all one's actions submitted to their approval.'

'But,' said Rosalie with a little hesitation, 'it does not matter what is done with the actions that oneself approves,—and the others can rarely be kept secret.'

'I presume not—so long as one has two sharp-eyed sisters,' said Thornton as he rose up and quitted the room. And the house-door's clang immediately followed.

Had she done wrong to say that? had she gone too far? She did not know—she could not resolve. Between the fear of displeasing him, of weakening her influence, and the earnest desire to speak a word for the truth whenever it might be spoken, Rosalie was often at a loss; and the eyes whose keenness he condemned had wept many tears before Thornton had gone far in his anger. On the whole the evening had been a sorrowful one. She had in a measure got accustomed to the old grievous things, but she felt now as if more were coming upon her,—a sort of undefined perception that her own trials were getting entwined with those of other people. But one thing seemed clear, and that was her duty. She thought long and earnestly of those words of Rutherford, "It is possible your success answer not your desire in this worthy cause: what then? Duties are ours, events are the Lord's." And striving to let her will as her hope, rest there, sleep had passed its quieting hand over her face long before her brother returned and came softly in to look at her. He had taken a great habit of doing this, of late.

CHAPTER XI.

*She doeth little kindnesses,
Which most leave undone, or despise;
For nought that sets one heart at ease,
And giveth happiness or peace,
Is low-esteemed in her eyes.*—LOWELL.

FULLY determined that if her brother had any cause of complaint against her it should not go unatoned for, Rosalie's first desire the next morning was to see him.

If he only knew!—she thought.

But he did not know—he could not guess that of all the cares upon her heart his welfare was the chiefest,—that for his sake she would have gone through any possible difficulty or danger. Sometimes she half thought he did know it,— that her love was appreciated if not quite returned; and sometimes she did not know what to think.

In this mood she got up as early as the tardy daylight would permit, and dressing herself softly that she might not wake Hulda, stood leaning against the door-post with clasped hands and a very grave, quiet face, waiting to hear him go down. She was not sure but this was one of his mornings for an early drill. The step came at last, and no sooner had it fairly past her door than her light foot followed. Down the stairs and into the breakfast-room—but he was not there. Had she mistaken another step for his? He came behind her at the moment, and with his lips upon her forehead inquired, 'What in the world she was after, at that time in the morning?'

'O, I was after you—' she said, looking up at him and then as quick down again; for something in his eyes had brought her very heart welling up to her own.

'To ask me to beg your pardon for last night's offences?' said Thornton, as he drew her to a seat by him on the sofa.

'No indeed!'

'It is done unasked then, Alie. I should hate myself for a month if I thought my words had grieved you half as much as they did me. I suppose I need not ask whether I am forgiven?'

He had no answer at all events.

'Hush—you are a foolish child,' Thornton said. 'Why Alie, what was it you took so much to heart?'

'Nothing—not that. But oh, Thornton,—I wish you knew me a little better!'

'So do not I—I know you quite well enough now for my own comfort. If I knew you any better I should probably absent myself permanently, and leave the field clear to some one who would take better care of you. As it is, Alie, I choose to persuade myself that we can live on together.'

What a look she turned on him.

'Well now let us hear what you have to say, pretty one,' said her brother admiringly. 'What has your little head been at work upon?'

'I was thinking—I was afraid that perhaps I had said too much last night,—more than I ought—to you. If you knew my feeling you would not blame me, but the words might seem unkind; and I was very sorry. I will try not to fail in that way again.'

'My dear little sister,' said Thornton laughing, 'you really are too absurd! To hear *you* make promises of amendment is very like hearing you say that for the future you intend to look pretty, or any such work of supererogation. You—who never thought said, or did anything but goodness in your whole life.'

'Which proves how little you know me.'

'We will agree to have different opinions on that point. At present you are my standard of perfection.'

'Ah but, you have no right to take any such standard, dear Thornton. Think what perfection is, and what the Bible standard, before you apply either word to me.'

'I must be allowed to have my own ideas on the subject, nevertheless,' said Thornton. 'But Alie, you fairly frightened me by getting up so early this morning. I didn't know but you were going to pay your friend Mrs. Raynor a visit.'

The implication raised so very slight a colour, that Thornton's spirits improved at once.

'Alie!' called out Hulda's little voice from over the balusters, 'won't you *please* come? because Martha isn't here, and I want to get up so much.'

'Run!' said Thornton laughing. 'It is hard to take care of two people, isn't it? Here you have been bestowing your attentions upon me, leaving that child to get out of bed alone at the risk of breaking her neck. I wonder, by the way, what 'getting up' is supposed to mean, in infant parlance.'

'And I wonder who gave you leave to come out and stand on the cold oil-cloth, little one?' said Rosalie as she ran up stairs and stooped down by the little night-gowned and night-capped figure. Hulda's arms were quickly about her sister's neck, and her little bare feet curled up in her lap; and then she was lifted up and carried back into the room.

'Who was that you were talking to?' said Hulda.

'Thornton.'

'Does he feel good natured this morning?'

'I did not ask him,' said Rosalie smiling. 'Do you?'

'O yes,' said Hulda, 'but then I didn't feel cross last night. I think it's very disagreeable to have people cross.'

'Then you and I will try to be always pleasant. If Thornton does not want the horses this morning, we will go and see Miss Morsel.'

The horses were not wanted, and after breakfast they set forth;—all but Hiram well pleased with the prospect. He thought it was hardly worth while to risk an overturn in a narrow street, for anything that street could contain. Not that he had the least intention of being overturned, by the by.

The street was narrow and the sleighing therein most disagreeable. Irregular heaps of snow that had been thrown from the side-walks stood up and shook hands across the narrow track which the sleighs of the milkman, the woodman, and the baker, had marked out for themselves. Nothing wider than those humble vehicles had been that way, and it was hard for anything wider to go,—the sleigh was obliged to content itself with having one runner at a time on smooth ground and the other on a snow-bank. Which state of things did not at all content Hiram. Ugly the snow-banks were, as well as inconvenient; for when gutters were choked up the unfortunate snow did duty instead, and no rigid enforcement of law prevailed in this district. Also the pigs had been dilatory in seeking their breakfast; and that which had been very white as it fell, was now agreeably diversified with cinders, cabbage leaves, lemon peels, potato parings, buckwheat cakes, oyster shells, and the like; according as dinner, breakfast, or supper, had been the last prominent meal in the different houses.

The house where Hiram at length paused, was distinguished by less of a snow bank and what there was, cleaner. No decorations lay there but dry Christmas greens—a wreath and a festoon, all falling to pieces and sinking into the snow: the hemlock leaves scattering about, and the cedar shrinking and shrivelling up within itself.

'O Miss Morsel has thrown away her wreath!' said Hulda.

'I don't know as you can get out, ma'am,' said Hiram, while he lent careful aid to the undertaking. 'The snow's right deep. It's an astonishing promotion to a street when the families keeps their carriage!'

But she got out nicely—as she did everything—and went lightly up the steps and opened the unlocked door; its want of fastening a sure sign that there was no family bond within. The house was but what a botanist would call 'an involucre.' That might be guessed from the sickly smell spread through the hall and passages,—one of those compounds which will not bear resolving.

Two flights of stairs and a short entry brought the visitors to Miss Morsel's door; where they had no sooner knocked than it was opened. Miss Morsel indeed, having watched the whole preliminaries from the first jingle of the sleigh bells, and having got very warm with anxiety lest the snow bank should prove insurmountable, was now equally cold with standing at her own door; and she would certainly have saved Rosalie the trouble of knocking had not elegant propriety, to her mind, forbidden it. So she stood as close to the door as she could get, and waited for her visitors to demand entrance. It was given them with every demonstration of joy.

The room looked comfortable, though with that strict, severe sort of comfort where everything is fastened up and fastened down, and must remain *just so* or it will *not* look comfortable. A doll's dress, sewed to the doll and not meant to be taken off.

Of the chintz curtains, Lydia Sharpe might have said that they had "no folds in nature—nor drapery,"—and yet they were curtains; and when they hung as they were bid, you did not at first see how old they were. The rug did not match the carpet but was a rug nevertheless; and of the fire appendages it could not be said in the words of the song,

> "The shovel and tongs
> To each other belongs"—

they belonged only to Miss Morsel.

The bed was not visible. Whether Miss Morsel kept it in the closet, and underwent severe bodily exercise to get it out every night—or whether she gave it her company in the closet, doth not appear. The chairs were rush-bottomed, and *begun* to be cushioned; and a little pine box by the fire held a supply of fuel—Rosalie was glad that she did not know for how long.

A few things in the room however, bore token of more outlay,—towards Miss Morsel's old mother her purse strings were evidently lenient. *Her* chair was most carefully cushioned—back, arms, and all; and the cover was of some red stuff, and her footstool clad with the same. By the window stood two or three geraniums in dark ruffled earthen pots; while a little work table, placed with evident care and tenderness, looked as if it and the books upon it were of no Miss Morsel's choice.

'I don't suppose there's anybody else in the world could have come here this morning!' said poor little Miss Morsel, taking hold of both Rosalie's hands and looking up into her face. 'Because I have felt rather down-hearted you see; and most people don't happen in when you feel so.'

'Then I have just come at the right time. How is your mother to-day?'

'O pretty well,' said Miss Morsel,—'though it does seem queer to call a person pretty that's got so little pretence to it. I'll tell her you're here.' And the fact was announced in no very measured voice.

'What's *she* come for?' was the old lady's first and most distinct question.

'Why to see you, ma—to see you and me.'

'O no,' said Mrs. Morsel, 'that's not it,—that couldn't be it. No person comes to see you and me now.'

'What do you suppose she did come for, then?' said Miss Morsel, who from policy or respect never argued with her mother.

'Well—perhaps she did—' said the old woman doubtfully. 'Miss Clyde, hey. Ask her to sit down, Bettie.'

But Miss Clyde was in no haste to sit down. She went to the window and looked at the plants; examined the state of the chair cushions, and recommended that two or three of them should be covered with some particularly bright chintz which she had at home.

'I will send Tom down with it,' she said. 'I think it will please your mother.'

'There's a scarcity of the people that ever think of that, now-a-days,' said Miss Morsel with a little sorrowful shake of her head. 'It's queer too, for if ever anybody wanted pleasing she does. But haven't you got everything in the world, at home! And after all, as I tell ma, there's no store closet like one's own heart.'

'What's she going to send down?' said old Mrs. Morsel.

5

'Bettie, tell her she needn't send no more o' them fine shirts—we don't take in sewing now.'

'She knew that before you did, ma,' replied her daughter.

'My eyes aint strong to do fine work now,' continued Mrs. Morsel, drawing herself up, 'and I like other work better. So does Bettie. We don't do it no longer. Tell her so.'

'It does really seem sometimes,' said the daughter in a kind of aside, 'as if ma'd forgot all the little English she ever did know! You would really suppose that she'd never been to school or studied grammar; and yet I daresay she used to know the noun of multitude and all those rules quite respectably for her age of society.'

'So that's what she come for?' said old Mrs. Morsel. 'I told you she wanted something. She must go to some poor person,—we don't take in sewing.'

'How much patience do you suppose Job had?' said Miss Morsel in the same undertone to Rosalie. 'Because sometimes I think he must have had so much more than me, that it's hardly worth while to try. Never mind her, dear,—just you sit down and tell me about the battles.'

'There's very little use in battles,' said the old woman. 'Folks said the Revolutionary War did the country a power of good, but *we* didn't get none of it. I've heerd tell of a great deal more than I ever was knowing to. *We've* been good for nothing since.'

'It's a singular fact,' said Miss Morsel softly, 'that if pa hadn't been killed in the Revolutionary War, we shouldn't have anything to live on now. Queer, isn't it?'

It was so queer, altogether, that Rosalie was somewhat divided between the desire to laugh and the desire to cry.

'But now do tell me,' continued Miss Morsel, 'you never *did* tell me—how did you get the pension money? who did the business?'

'O I spoke to a friend of mine about it,' said Rosalie.

'No wonder it got done, then,' said Miss Morsel, with a loving look up at her guest. 'I should think everybody would do any thing, and glad. Ah it's a great help in the world to be young, my dear,—and pretty—and rich! However, we all have what is best for us.'

'*I* don't think bread and cheese is a healthy dinner,' said Mrs. Morsel sourly. 'Bettie will have it sometimes. And she says it's best, and I say it aint.'

'Just think of her saying that!' said the daughter; evidently distressed that her guest should hear it, but only from the most generous and disinterested feeling. 'To be sure we do have it sometimes, but it's very good. I daresay those poor men that are out fighting Tecumseh don't get a bit better. But you said he was taken prisoner.'

'I thought,' said Rosalie softly, 'I thought you were taking better care of yourself,—you promised that you would.'

'Take good enough care, my dear—oh yes, so I do; but you see the thing is, ma's liable to be sick, of course—any body is; and if she is to be sick I should like her to have just what she's a mind to call for,—and the things wouldn't be few nor far between, neither. And it's so easy to take money out of the trunk when you've got it there ready.'

'But let her have it now—she shall never miss it, nor you either.'

'Yes, but I sha'n't let you do that,' said Miss Morsel, dashing off the tears which those glistening eyes had called up; 'so don't talk about it or you'll upset me at once. Everybody ought to live on his income,—and my income comes in regularly, and when it don't I'll let you know There's Hulda gone to sleep this minute.'

'No I haven't,' said Hulda, looking up with a weary little face. 'What made you throw away your greens, Miss Morsel?'

'Why they got dry and fell over the world, and made such a muss as I couldn't stand—so I thought they might come down. I reasoned in this way—if Christmas greens put me out of patience they won't do me much good,—and down they came. But I kept the laurel, because that isn't crumbly; and it helps one to think that there are woods in existence somewhere.'

'Why didn't you come before?' said the old woman suddenly turning towards her visiter. 'It's better than six months since you were here.'

'O no, it is not so many weeks,' said Rosalie smiling.

'It isn't more than half so many,' said Miss Morsel. 'You forget, ma.'

'Old folks always does forget,' said Mrs. Morsel with a somewhat piqued air. 'Only if they do, it's a wonder to my mind how young folks comes to know anything. They *don't* know much. I say it's six months.'

'You won't mind her, dear,' said Miss Morsel in a low voice,—'because she's had a good many sticks in her way, and somehow she likes to take 'em all. It's only a little cup of crossness she's got to pour out, and then she'll be done for a while. She used to have just what she wanted once, you know, and somehow it makes one good natured to be comfortable. But we are comfortable now, very,—if you have everything, you can't wish. I've nothing to complain of. I never wanted to complain since what you told me once —do you remember? how "when the children of Israel murmured, it displeased the Lord." I've thought of it a great many times.'

'It would be easy not to murmur if we thought more of

the promised land and less of the wilderness,' said Rosalie with a half-checked sigh.

'Yes dear. And I'm glad for my part to recollect that this isn't the promised land;—so in that point of view, you see, bread and cheese is quite wholesome.'

'Can you leave your mother for a while?' said Rosalie, 'I want you to go and take a sleigh ride. I came on purpose.'

'Did you really?' said Miss Morsel,—'then I'll go; though I don't think I could if you hadn't come on purpose. Just like you! I wonder who else would want to parade me up and down Broadway! and not in a close carriage, either. O yes—I can leave her,—Seraphina Wells 'll come in and sit here—ma likes Seraphina,—don't you ma? don't you like Seraphina Wells?'

'Not much—' said the old lady. 'She aint much but a giddy-go-round. No, I don't like her.'

'Just hear that, now!' said Miss Morsel. 'But she does like her, for all. Well I'll get ready dear, as soon as I can. But I don't know whether I ought to go—I felt so down this morning.'

'That's the very reason why you should go,' said Rosalie smiling. 'It will cheer you up.'

'O the snow is beautiful!' said Hulda.

'Snows aint much now-a-days,' said old Mrs. Morsel rubbing her hand back and forth over her knee. 'They aint like the snows in my time. They wouldn't hardly ha' been called a *flurry* of snow in my time.'

'Did you ever!' said Miss Morsel, pausing on her way to the closet. 'I shouldn't wonder if she'd say the people were worse then too.'

'How do you feel to-day, Mrs. Morsel?' said Rosalie, coming close to her chair.

'How should I feel?' said the old woman pettishly, but with more energy than she had before spoken. 'How would you feel if you was shut up in this chair with nobody to speak to, and no home nor nothing? The folks that has the world thinks it's easy to do without it. I tell you it isn't,— it's hard. It's a bad world, but I want it.'

'There is a better world,' said Rosalie gently,—'do you want that?'

'Suppose I want both?' said Mrs. Morsel in the same tone. 'What then?'

'Then make sure of the best first. "They that seek the Lord shall not want any good thing."'

'Ay—that's what you say,' replied Mrs. Morsel, rubbing her hand back and forth. 'That's what you say. I should like to see you try it once! Easy work to learn Bible verses and say 'em!'

'Yes, it is much easier than to follow them,' said Rosalie, —'I know that. But then you believe the Bible words, whether I obey them or not; and isn't it pleasant to think of heaven when we have a poor home on earth? and to remember that if not one friend ever comes to see us, yet that the angels of God are ever about his children, and that the Lord Jesus has promised to be always with those that serve him?'

The old woman's hand moved yet, but it was with a nervous, unsteady action, and her face in vain tried to maintain its cold dissatisfied look. Rosalie had stooped down and laid her hand upon the arm of the chair while she was speaking; and now one of the old shrivelled hands was laid tremblingly upon hers.

'That's true—that about the angels,' she said in a shaking voice, 'but I'm not one of them they should come to. What did you come here for?'

'Yes I'll go—' said Miss Morsel, coming back with her bonnet on. 'It *is* queer, isn't it? but I never can hear sleigh bells without wanting to run after 'em. I often think there must be a little perverseness tucked away in some corner of my existence.'

'Things always is tucked away in corners,' said old Mrs. Morsel, sinking back into her chair and her old manner at once. 'Corners aint no other use in a house.'

'That aint much use, to my mind,' said Miss Morsel. 'However, I'm going ma, so goodbye.'

She went—and to use her own expression "was cheered up higher than ever."

Leaving poor friends and poor circumstances behind, the sleigh now glided on to the other extreme of the city, as of life; and before a large house in State Street Hiram once more drew up. The door was quickly opened, and merely inquiring if Miss Arnet was at home, Rosalie sought the young lady up-stairs. There she sat in her dressing-room, ensconced in wrapper and cushions,—a book in her hand, her hair in the hands of her maid. Book and maid were at once dismissed; and seating Rosalie among the cushions, Miss Arnet stood before her to talk and arrange her hair at the same time.

'Where have you been? and what has made you do so unwonted a thing as to come here?'

'Truly, the simple desire to see you,' said Rosalie.

'The pleasantest reason in the world—and the rarest. What *did* that woman do with my comb! Poor little Hulda, you look tired to death. Where have you been whisked to this morning?'

'O we've been sleigh riding with Miss Morsel,' said Hulda with a look that bore out Miss Arnet's words.

Marion lifted up eyes and hands, which were by this time disengaged.

'You poor child! there wouldn't be the least atom of me left after such an experience. Here,' she continued, picking up Hulda and depositing her upon the sofa, 'won't that make you forget Miss Morsel? Don't pull down my hair, pet, in the intensity of your gratitude. Are my sofa cushions nice?'

'Very nice!' said Hulda smiling.

'Then lie still there and go to sleep—I sha'n't let Rosalie go for one good hour.'

'But why don't you come to see us as you used to?' said Hulda, when she had at last taken her arms from Miss Arnet's neck. 'I asked Thornton the other day, and he said—'

'What did he say?' inquired Marion.

'I don't believe I know,' said Hulda, 'it was so many queer words. He said he couldn't undertake—to account for young ladies' freaks.—Yes, that was it, because I said it over and over for fear I should forget it.'

Marion sprang up, and crossing the room to where Rosalie sat she said in a kind of indignant undertone,

'Is *that* the way I am understood? Is *that* what he thinks of me?'

'No—' was the quiet and sad reply.

Miss Arnet knelt down by her side, and leaning her elbows on the chair arm went on in the same vehement way,

'Then what does he mean by saying so? It is cruel to say what he does not think!—it is unjust!'

'He is neither to you, Marion. He is only cruel and unjust to himself.'

'Then what does this mean?' she repeated, but more quietly.

'It means only that he is not happy,' said his sister sorrowfully. 'You do not wonder at that?'

Marion's head drooped lower and rested upon her hands.

'What can I do?' she said at length. 'I will never subject myself to the miseries I have seen in my own uncle's family. Rosalie! he has ruined himself—he has ruined them,—in mind, character, and estate; and when he came here one night and said he had been playing with Thornton——'

For a minute the room was absolutely still, and the figures there might have been statues.

'I told Thornton at once,' said Miss Arnet raising her head, 'that unless he would promise me never to play for money again, I would have no more to do with him than with the rest of the world. And he would not give the promise—said he would not be dictated to by any woman—as if it was not more for his sake than my own, after all!

'Do you blame me?' she said, after another pause.

'No.'

But the word was spoken with such evident pain, that Miss Arnet put her arms about Rosalie and tried every word of soothing she could think of.

'I am very, very wrong to go this all over to you again!—you have enough of your own to bear. Only it is such a relief to speak out. Alie! what is the matter? you are not well—you are perfectly white.'

'Yes, quite well,' Rosalie said. But the bitterness of the thoughts and feelings that had been at work could no longer be kept in. Speak out Rosalie never did, now; but the sorrow that for a few moments held her in its strong grasp, told of heart sickness such as Marion could hardly comprehend. She was almost as much frightened as grieved.

'I don't know where my common sense went to this morning,' she said, when Rosalie had once looked up and given the assurance that there was nothing new the matter. 'It is a perfect shame for me to lean upon you—little frail thing that you are,—and younger than I am to begin with. I should think you would hate me Rosalie, for bringing this upon you.'

'My dear child, you have not brought it.'

'Well, but don't call me child,' said Miss Arnet, trying to take down her cousin's hands, 'because it's really absurd for me to look up to you,—I shall not do it any more, if I can help it. For the future, Alie, you may lean upon me. But indeed I have hard work sometimes. Mamma you know takes different ground—says I have behaved shockingly, and she has no patience with me. And it is not a light thing to see such a change in a friend one has always had.'

His sister knew that! But she sat up now, and pushing the hair back off her face with an expression of quiet patience, she said gently,

'I do not blame you, dear—I could not have advised you to do otherwise than you have done.'

'Perhaps it will all turn out well yet,' said Marion looking at her anxiously. 'Perhaps he will change his mind.'

'It may be that God will change it—' said his sister, though the calm words trembled a little,—and Miss Arnet knew then why she looked up to her. 'The grace of God which bringeth salvation hath done harder things than that.' And as her face once more rested on her hands, Rosalie added,

'" Let thy mercy, O Lord, be upon us, according as we hope in thee!"'

No more was said; and after a few moments Hulda was aroused and they went home.

CHAPTER XII.

I dare do all that may become a man ;
Who dares do more, is none.—Macbeth.

'WHAT a confoundedly stupid thing it is that people can't do as they choose!' said Thornton, throwing down the paper one morning.

'Do you think so?' said his sister. 'Now I think that much of the confusion of the world is because people *will* do as they choose.'

'What else should they do?'

'That depends— Choice is a poor reason if there be no reason in the choice.'

'Now here,' continued Thornton without heeding her, 'here has this precious court martial dismissed Capt. Lewis from the army, just because he chose to play cards.'

'Chose to gamble—' said Rosalie.

'Call it what you like—' said Thornton,—'I can't for the life of me see whose concern it was but his own. Why shouldn't he gamble—if it amuses him?'

'Why shouldn't he cut throats if it amuses him?'

'He may for what I care.'

'What are the reasons given for his dismissal?' said Rosalie,—'what is the verdict?'

'Here it is, in full.'

"HEAD QUARTERS, &c.

"At a general court martial, whereof Colonel Thomas Parker was president, was tried Captain Charles Lewis, of the 29th regiment, on the following charge and specifications:

"*Charge*—Conduct unbecoming an officer and a gentleman.

"Specification 1. Holding a faro-bank at his quarters near Buffalo, about the 6th Nov. 1812.

"Specif. 2. Gambling with his own waiter, and other soldiers, at faro, same time and place.

"Specif. 3. Winning and receiving money of soldiers, same time and place.

"Specif. 4. Boasting to his waiter, that he had won $60 with a pack of cards, about the same time and place.

"To which charge and specifications the prisoner pleaded not guilty of the charge—guilty of the first and third specifications, and not guilty of the fourth.

"The court, after mature deliberation, find the prisoner, Capt. Charles Lewis, *guilty* of the 1st, 2nd, 3rd, and 4th specifications; and *guilty* of the charge preferred against him; and *sentence* him to be *dismissed the service of the United States.*

"The General approves the sentence; and Capt. Charles Lewis is accordingly dismissed the service of the United States.

"(By order)
"JAMES BANKHEAD, brigade major."

'Pretty specimen of impertinent and unjust interference, isn't it?' said Thornton when he had finished.

'I know too little of military law to say whether it be unjust or no; but I should sooner call it humanity than impertinence—if it makes Capt. Lewis ashamed of what does not become the gentleman and ruins the man.'

'What nonsense you do talk!' said Thornton angrily, —'just because you know nothing about the matter—or think nothing.'

'Just because I know and think. O Thornton, you should not defend gambling!—it has lost us too much.'

'Lost! how do you know that I ever lost anything?'

'I know of one most precious thing,—I need not seek further.'

'It will be time enough to remind me of that when I have forgotten it,' said the young man with an uneasy change of posture.

She left her seat, and kneeling down by him leant her head on his shoulder.

'Is it possible that you can remember and disregard it? What would I not do—what would I not bear, to save you from these false friends—these degrading and ruining pursuits! To see you take the part of a man and a christian in the world. To see you live for something more than the day's laugh and the night's amusement. O Thornton, is it worthy of you? while this command stands unerased, "*I am the Almighty God. Walk before me and be thou perfect.*"'

He was looking down, somewhat sullenly; and neither by word nor look did he answer her words, nor the hand that drew back the hair from his forehead as caressingly as if he had been a child, nor the earnest eyes that he knew were studying his face. In his secret mind, Thornton felt very much as if he were Captain Lewis just hearing Major Bankhead dismiss him the service,—but if Rosalie's power was strong so also was his resistance.

'And you think,' he said, 'that people's hearts are always open to the view of their fellow creatures,—that secret good and evil do not exist.'

'I think anything else,' said his sister. 'But I must believe the words of Christ, and he says, "*Whosoever shall deny me before men, him will I also deny before my Father which is in heaven.*"'

How tenderly it was spoken! and yet how gravely too. Thornton thought he had got about enough. His next effort was in a different way.

'There is no doubt of your filling your place as a woman,' he said lightly. 'I will give my testimony to that effect whenever it is called for. But for the present, as you do not belong to my regiment suppose you let me repair to those that do. As to taking you for my commanding officer, I'll think about it,—it's not always safe to invest guardians with extraordinary powers. So let me go—here am I bound not neck and heels exactly, but neck and hand. You can rule enough of the lords of creation if you will only take the right way for it.'

She had not tried to interrupt his words, the drift of which she knew full well; and at last to get rid of the uneasy consciousness that her eye was upon him, Thornton turned suddenly and met it. The spark flew,—and the shock awoke all the old memories of his mother whose look he seemed to see again in those sweet eyes,—memories which were or tried to be ofttimes asleep. Putting his arm round Rosalie he drew her head down to his shoulder again.

'What has got into you to-day, pretty one?' he said. 'Cannot you be content to rule men in woman's own way, and leave them free in other respects?'

'You are not free—that is the very thing.'

'I won't fight you for that, seeing you are my sister,' said Thornton, 'but I must really demand an explanation.'

'"Whosoever committeth sin is the servant of sin,"'— said his sister sadly.

'You are cool in your remarks, at least,' said Thornton reddening. 'At the next one of that sort I shall take my departure. And I really had something to say to you.'

'What?' she said, looking up at him with a most disarming face as he now stood before her.

'Are you willing, Lady Paramount, that I should bring some of my friends here some evening?'

'I do not understand you Thornton—you have them whenever you please.'

'Of course! But I mean can I have you as well? will my canary bird please to be visible? Well?—what are you meditating? what sword thrust am I to have now?'

'Dear Thornton—I wish you would not talk so. I will see anybody you wish me to, of course—if—'

'Ay—there's a world-wide difference between your 'of course' and your 'if,'' said her brother dryly.

'You know there is nothing in the world I would not do for you unless I thought it wrong. I will see anybody you choose to bring here, and entertain them to the best of my power,—if the entertainment may be without cards or wine.'

Displeased as he was Thornton held his words in check. Hers had been spoken in so low a tone, at once so timid and so resolute, that it shamed him into gentleness. At last he spoke, but in a constrained voice.

'Why not say 'no' at once? it would be rather more frank, and save both time and trouble.'

'It would not have been what I meant. Is it quite impossible for gentlemen to spend a pleasant evening without those two things?'

'Quite impossible for me to offer it.'

'But why? One has surely a right to one's own opinions, and to the free expression of them.'

The word 'free' struck him disagreeably, and he was silent. Rosalie went on.

'I will do anything that I can to give you or your guests pleasure, Thornton,—I will lay myself out for their entertainment; but I will *not* countenance that which I disapprove.'

'You are not responsible for what I choose to give my guests—' said her brother.

She quietly repeated, 'I will not countenance it.'

'Why not?' said Thornton looking at her curiously. 'What voice has a canary bird in the matter? Can it make itself heard all alone?'

'It shall not go to swell the cry for evil.'

'My poor little canary bird!' said Thornton, but there was a touch of tenderness in the words that thrilled through her. 'My poor little canary bird,—I am afraid the cry will never join your sweet voice. And after all why should you care? You don't suppose I would permit anybody to drink too much in your presence?'

She smiled slightly and shook her head, but the eyes went down as gravely as before.

'Why not?' said Thornton, going back to the point. 'What concern is it of yours?'

The little smile came again, but the eyes were full that she raised to his face as she said,

'I know how I should feel if I were the sister of one of them at home.'

'You are a strange girl!' said Thornton. 'What are other people's brothers to you? I should think you might find your own enough to manage.'

'No, I would rather he should manage himself,' said his sister smiling.

'Which is a polite way of saying that he don't.'

'If you will go with me this afternoon, Thornton, I will shew you one good reason for what you call my whim.'

'My dear it might not be satisfactory to me,—or it might be too satisfactory—worse still. I will attend you where you like in the open air; but I don't wish to see any examples but yours, nor any cases of charity but myself—who am in desperate want of amusement just now. You may have my purse and welcome, though I suspect your own is the better filled; but as to the rest I should only discomfort myself without comforting anybody else. So goodbye, little guardian,—since you give me leave to go out by myself I will go.'

He went forth on his pleasure seeking, and Rosalie muffled herself up and set out on her expedition alone. It was a keen, wintry day,—the sky cold grey, the snow cold white; the wind sharpened upon snow crystals. The city vanes, like the Moorish astrologer's little horseman, pointed steadily to Baffin's Bay as the quarter whence the enemy might be expected; and a dismal appreciation of the fact seemed to have settled down upon the whole outer world. People looked blue and white and red and spotted,—men pocketed their hands and went along at an easy run; the unkempt portion of society hugged themselves in their rags and sought sheltered corners; and the few ladies who were abroad flitted along, the very sport of the wind. Rosalie would have been glad of her brother's arm, but it was not there and she passed on alone.

In one of the poor streets of the city lay the object of her walk,—a house as poor as the street, with tenants yet poorer. The house had two stories, the upper one reached by an out-of-doors staircase; at the head of which a door in two parts opened into the front room of that floor. Old furniture of various families and complexions, but neatly dusted and arranged, graced its walls; the bit of rag carpet was free from lint and wrinkles, and the cover of the little table without a spot on its white. A door stood half open into an adjoining room, where the darkened light and the low moans that now and then were heard, told their own story. An Irish woman opened the divided door in answer to Miss Clyde's knock, and softly closed it behind her.

'It's very kind of you to come, ma'am,' she said, 'and indeed it was too bold of us to ask—only they said Miss Clyde never refused any one. And indeed we didn't well know what to do.'

Another woman now entered from the back room, and courtesied to Rosalie but seemed as if she could not speak.

'Is he any better?' said the young lady softly.

'No Miss! not a bit! just the same! Out of his head always, and crying and moaning as you hear. Never a better son than himself!' she said, covering her face with her apron, 'till he took to drink.'

'But how did this happen?' said Rosalie as she sat down in the chair placed for her. 'I did not quite understand what was the matter.'

'Ye see Miss, he drives—that is, not now, poor soul, but he used,—he has a coach, and never a steadier nor a better man when himself. And a week ago come Thursday there was a party, they say, and he went—not to the party, at all at all, but with some that was going. And it's bitter could it was—and ye know yerself, ma'am, the could is a hard thing to bear, to them not dressed for it. Not but his coat was good, but it wouldn't stand that. And when he went for the gentleman it's like he took something warm just to help the coat as it were, and because of the waiting; but he never got to the place at all. The horses went on and throwed him off, and next morning they found him lying in the snow half dead and buried, and he the only hope of his mother! And he hasn't lift his head since they brought him home.'

The mother walked back into the other room to conceal or give way to her grief, for her sobs came mingled with the groans of the sick man.

'Has he been in the habit of drinking?' Rosalie inquired of the other woman.

'No Miss—he usen't—but he's took to it more in the could weather. And it's no good talking: for 'See mother,' he says, 'sure the gentlemen I drive don't know so much as meself on the box sometimes, and sure *they* can tell what's right,—why shouldn't Mike take a drop of comfort as well as the quality?' he says. 'Is drink worse out o'doors in the could nor it is in by the fire?' But he'll niver say that again, maybe!'

There was nothing to be done except in the way of money or sympathy. What words of comfort she could Rosalie spoke, and after promising to send a good physician she asked further concerning their wants. But these seemed at present to be few.

'The neighbors is very kind,' said the mother, who had returned to the front room. 'The tinman's wife below sent a fresh egg from her own hens, and the little china woman at the corner she just stewed oysters for him twice. But bless ye! it's himself couldn't touch neither of 'em! And what good 'll anything do him more! Yes Miss—I know the Lord is good—'a strong hold in the day o' trouble'—I learnt that long ago. But it's hard to trust—sometimes.— If it wasn't all I had in the world! And to die so too— without a thought on his mind at the last!'

Rosalie left the poor little abode, and remembered neither wind nor cold till a long walk through both had brought her to a very different establishment.

'Is Dr. Buffem at home?' she said to the servant who opened the door.

He was, by chance; and came bustling into the parlour in a great fit of amazement.

'Who gave you leave to come here in business hours?' he said. 'What's the matter? That chicken of yours can't be sick, or you'd never be here.'

Rosalie briefly preferred her request.

'You see sir,' she added, 'my trust among physicians is even less extensive than my acquaintance,—so I was forced to come to you.'

The doctor took snuff and shook his head.

'I'll tell you what *I* think,' he said—'*I* think you want a strait jacket. What business is it of yours if coachmen get run over every night?'

'It is every one's business to see that they do not die therefrom without help,' said Rosalie smiling.

'No it isn't—' said the doctor. 'Not yours.—Nonsense!'

'I am putting the business into your hands now, sir.'

'But if I go,' said the doctor, 'you know I should despatch him, the first thing. Immense saving of trouble!'

'I will trust you sir, with many thanks.'

'I haven't promised to go yet,' said Dr. Buffem. 'I've got two ladies and three gentlemen to attend to. Real ladies—who don't know that hackney coachmen have souls, —and gentlemen who don't know much about their own. Think of that!'

'I don't like to think of it sir—nor of them. And now I will not break up business hours any further. Dr. Buffem—'

'Yours to command!' said the doctor bowing.

But the cheek flushed a little and she stood hesitating.

'Out with it!' said the doctor. 'I know you are going to say something very impertinent.'

'These people are very poor,' she said, colouring more and more, 'and—'

'Hackney coachmen that drink always are,' said the doctor sententiously.

'And—if—Will you please send your bill to me, sir?'

'That you may break the amount to them by degrees?' said the doctor, looking at her across the finger and thumb which held a prepared pinch of snuff.

'Yes, if you choose to think so,' she said laughing. 'Only send it to me.'

'I'll be—no matter what—if I do!' said Dr. Buffem. 'Take yourself off, Miss Rosalie, and don't come here fooling old doctors. Here have you and your hackney coachman cost me more snuff than you'll ever bring me in. I've a great mind to make you pay interest in advance.'

But Rosalie negatived that and moved towards the door.

'It always puts me out of patience to be cheated!' said the doctor following her. 'See here—what's become of that boy who used to be always tied to your apron string? Have you seen him since he came home?'

'Only once sir.'

So ho!—'only once.' How did you know what boy I meant?—recognise the description, don't you? I'll send you some fever powders when you get home. Ah I thought I'd have my revenge. Talk to me of hackney coachmen, indeed! It'll be a large bill!—tremendous!'

The hour was late and dinner waiting when Rosalie reached home. Hulda was waiting too.

'O Alie why didn't you come before? Here has been that nice gentleman again. And there are two notes in the parlour.'

'Well let me take off my bonnet and then I will see to the notes.'

They were two, as Hulda had said. One to herself, the other to Thornton. The style and address of the one were peculiar, and Rosalie thought she remembered having seen it before,—thought she recollected that a similar invitation (as this looked to be) had kept her brother out much later than usual one night, and had been followed by days of peculiar distaste for home and her society. She would have given anything to put the note in that bright blaze before her, ere Thornton came in. For a moment the temptation was so strong that she thought she would do it,—thought she would risk anything to keep him even for once out of bad company. But she remembered that underhand dealings became not her, and could not benefit him in the long run,—she must let things have their way, and patiently wait and hope. With a half sigh she heard her brother come in and felt the note taken from her hand.

'What are you doing with my despatches?' he said.

'Holding them safe—and wanting very much to put them in the fire.'

'I should like to see you do that,' said Thornton as he refolded the note and put it in his pocket. 'What is the other?'

'Not much—a request from Mrs. Raynor that I will spend to-morrow with her.'

'And you will?'

'No.'

'Why not?'

'I do not wish to go.'

'I wonder if your foot ever trembles on the narrow bridge of truth?' said her brother, raising her face and surveying it intently.

'Not in this case. But don't you wish to go to dinner?'

'Well I certainly might be hungry,' said Thornton as

he followed her, 'for I have been parading and walking in the most exemplary and orthodox manner—quite à-la-bon fils. Where have you been?'

'Where I wish you had.'

'O—I remember, and cannot echo the wish. And you have been working yourself up to some untenable point of perfection, I suppose—à-la-vraie femme.'

'Only untenable to the people who never occupy it.'

'By the way,' said Thornton, 'just for the fun of the thing, I think I will have a party upon the proposed plan. Only I shall not fail to proclaim to the company whose 'hospitable thought 'contrived it all.'

'*I* had company this morning,' said Hulda, who thought she had been long enough unnoticed.

'Indeed!'. said her brother. 'Was it a wasp or a yellow-jacket?'

'He didn't wear a yellow jacket at all,' said Hulda,— 'it was a black one.'

Thornton burst out laughing.

'If I am to have *two* sisters to look after,' he said, 'I may as well build a castle at once. I really did not know you were grown up, Hulda.'

Not understanding Greek, Hulda was not in the least discomposed.

'You see Alie, I ran on before Martha to open the door, for I thought maybe it was you; and it was Mr. Raynor.'

'Mr. Raynor!' said Thornton, every particle of the laugh vanishing. 'What the deuce brought him here?'

'I don't think the deuce brought him here at all,' said Hulda, in a very dignified manner. 'I'm sure he was very pleasant, and a great deal more good natured than'—

'Hush, Hulda!' said her sister.

A silent play of knives and forks followed.

'And what had Mr. Raynor to say for himself?' inquired Thornton, when he had swallowed the first effervescence produced by this information.

'O not much,' said Hulda. 'Nothing at all for himself. He only kissed me and asked for Rosalie.'

Thornton carried his fork to his mouth with more expression than is usually bestowed upon salad, but verbal remark he made none.

CHAPTER XIII.

Not for my peace will I go far,
As wanderers do, that still do roam;
But make my strengths, such as they are,
Here in my bosom, and at home.—BEN JONSON.

'Miss ARNET, ma'am,' said Tom, opening the sitting-room door next morning.

'O Marion!' cried little Hulda springing towards her, 'is that you? I thought you never were coming here again.'

'I began to think so myself, pet. Good morning, Alie. Good morning, Captain Thornton! I saw your troop out, and supposed you were with them.'

'Good morning, Miss Arnet. I am sorry you should be disappointed, but I can soon go, if that be all.'

'You are excessively stiff and disagreeable this morning!' said Marion colouring. 'Can't one give one's cousin his title without being immediately hailed as Miss Arnet?'

'It is in the nature of ice to freeze, nevertheless,' said Thornton.

'Alie,' said Marion turning to her, 'I came to borrow this child—will you let her go?'

'Ah please do!' said Hulda who was bestowing on Miss Arnet a small hundred of kisses. 'I always like to go with you, Marion. But why don't you come here as you used to? —when we all love you so much.'

'Are you sure you do?' said Marion. 'Alie, you haven't spoken to me yet, except with those violet eyes of yours. Will you let Hulda go?'

'Yes, and glad. She is too quiet here with me sometimes.'

'O no I'm not,' said Hulda. 'But I like to go, too.'

'Then run and get ready, pet—get your bonnet, I mean. Don't put on another frock—I'll lace-ruffle you if it is necessary.'

'Why do you plague yourself with that child?' said Thornton.

'I do *not* plague myself with that child. Of all the children I ever saw, she is the least of a plague.'

'Your experience differs widely from mine.'

'You have not studied the subject of counterpoise Captain Thornton. Things to love one in this world are not so plenty that one can afford to put out the fire of a child's affection, for fear it should now and then fill the room with smoke.'

'Very rhetorically expressed,' said Thornton; 'and quite in Rosalie's style. I should think she had been giving you lessons.'

'She gives me a great many that I do not take,' said Marion with a sudden change of expression—'I wish I had ever been more ready to learn! I wish all the world were like her! Alie, my dear, what do you do to me? When you are silent I feel reproved for speaking, and when you speak I feel reproved for the way I have spoken. Your power is like nothing but the old fashion of a lock of hair round a love-letter—very strong, because nobody would break it. One would have small compunction about filing a chain in two, but who could struggle against such a lock as this?—'

'You are riding off too fast on your simile,' said her cousin. 'The hair bound up only the lady's own thoughts—and was destined to be untied, after all.'

'By the proper person,' said Marion. 'O yes—and I expect to see your power in other hands than your own, by and by. Which is the thing of all things that Thornton least likes to hear. I would not for something be the man to encounter him in such circumstances.'

'Are there any circumstances under which you *would* like to encounter me, Miss Arnet?'

'Did either of you ever hear,' said Rosalie, 'of the man who was so anxious to bring down a bird that when other shot failed he fired all his treasures into the tree-top? And he never perceived the while that he was standing upon a cricket, whose overthrow could yield him neither glory nor satisfaction.'

Marion's eyes filled to overflowing.

'I have felt it in my heart sometimes,' she said. 'But I would rather the cricket should bite my foot than send out such a soft little chirp as that. Here comes Hulda at last.'

'At last?' said Hulda. 'Why Martha said I had been no time at all. Good bye, dear Alie—you won't be lonely?'

'I shall be as happy as possible, to think you are, love.'

'Well do,' said Hulda, with a somewhat doubtful breath. 'Good bye, Thornton.'

'Good bye,' said her brother. 'Though I cannot conceive what is the use of having a ruffle to one's shirt if it is to be mussed up in that style.'

'Come away, my dear,' said Miss Arnet. 'Thornton doesn't like smoke.'

'Doesn't he!' said Hulda. 'Why I thought he liked it so much!'

The morning passed rather moodily. Thornton seemed disposed for home comforts—or home meditations, and yielded very little return for his sister's kind and delicate attempts to please him. When at last he roused himself to go out, however, he did condescend to signify his appreciation of them.

'You are like nobody else, Alie—nobody else in the world,—Marion is right there. But whether her growing like you would benefit me much, may be questioned. You are a stiff enough little child yourself, and I don't believe would shake her resolution if you could.'

'I am sure I have tried hard to shake yours.'

'My resolution won't shake—or if it does will do no more. It is fast at both ends. And that child thinks she can twirl me round her thumb—and so she can I suppose, in heart, but not in purpose. Well—I thought I had got used to it.——'

'But why cannot you talk to each other peaceably, at least?' said his sister.

'Because having said the most provoking things we could to each other, the less provoking come natural, I presume,' said Thornton. 'I don't think Marion could speak to me as she speaks to other people. There is a kind of lemon-squeezer effect about all she says.'

'I am sure she never speaks of other people as she speaks of you.'

'Well—it may be,' said Thornton. 'Snows, doesn't it?—But I tell you, Alie, it's of no use for you to look sober about this—if you wear such a face people will think my canary bird has a hard jailer.'

It was no prisoner's look that she turned to him, and for that he kissed her more than once before he went.

An hour passed by, and Rosalie had gone up to her

room, and was beginning the business of the toilette in a very leisurely and reflective sort of way, when Martha Jumps came in.

'My stars alive!' she said—'Well if you ain't all undressed at this very identical minute!'

'Well?—' said her mistress.

'Well's easy to spell,' said Martha sententiously, 'but whether the gentleman down stairs is agoing over the letters to himself, is a question.'

'What gentleman? I told Tom to let nobody in.'

'Very good,' said Martha, 'but you didn't tell me; and when Tom Skiddy's to the baker's he ain't at the front door, commonly. But do make haste, Miss Rosalie, because——'

'Because what?'

'O I don't know,' said Martha—''because' never stays put in my head,—it's a kind of floating population. I don't know who he asked for first, neither, but I told him Captain Thornton wa'n't home. I guess it don't much matter——' said Martha in a satisfied tone, as if it did matter a great deal but all the right way.

'Are you sure I am wanted at all, Martha?

'Sure as he is—and there's no going beyond that, ma'am. Now you'll soon be ready. My! what white arms! It's a mystery to me what ever does come over some folks's skins. Miss Rosalie! you forgetfullest of all ladies (in this house),' said Martha parenthetically, 'here's one of your rings on the washhand stand. There—do go.'

'Lovely she is, and he too,' said Martha Jumps to herself as she looked over the balustrade after her mistress, —'and he was here yesterday—that's more. Now if I wasn't honourable, which I am, wouldn't I go down and second all the motions through the keyhole! There—shut fast. Such doors! I should think cur'osity 'd die an unnatural death in this house, for want of air. Well—I'll go look after Tom Skiddy!'

It was indeed a lovely vision that Mr. Raynor saw when the opening door drew his eye in that direction. She was dressed according to the fashion of the day; but her look was like no fashion that the world ever saw.

'I could not come sooner, Mr. Raynor,' she said,—' if that is any apology for keeping you waiting so long.'

'I have been conversing with an ideal presence,' he said with a slight smile, ' and too pleasantly to find the time long. I wish I could hope to go over the same interview with the reality.'

'You have brought your mother back with you,' said Rosalie.

'Certainly—or rather she has brought me. But she was a little fatigued with the journey, and has not been able to go out since; or you would have seen her.'

'So I understood—so she said in the note she was so kind as to write me.'

'The note whose request you were *not* so kind as to comply with,' said he smiling. 'Why was it, Miss Rosalie? Has the old friendship died out on your side?'

'O no—' she said earnestly.

'It died out on mine, long ago,' said Mr. Raynor,—' at least if transformation be death; and I should like to have your consent to the new order of things.'

'No, the old one was too good to be changed. But Mr. Raynor '——

'But Miss Rosalie, if you please, I am not ready to quit the subject. I went to Europe with one thing in my mind that I had been forbidden to speak out—though I begged hard for permission. But because we were both so young,

I was required to go without telling you in words who was the best loved of all the friends I left in America—which indeed I thought you must know without words.'

She sat silently listening to him, with a face grave and quiet, as if her mind was but half upon what he said,—as if she knew it already—as if some emergency which she had expected and tried to ward off had come, and she knew what her answer must be, and was trying to strengthen her woman's heart and woman's voice to give it. A look very different from the almost sensitive timidity which reigned there when no deep feeling was in exercise. An expression which Mr. Raynor had seen but once before—and that was on the night of his arrival, when he had watched so long to see it change to one he remembered and liked much better. He did not like it now at all—he would rather have seen *herself* more present to her mind—her colour deeper, and her self-control less.

'Well,' he said at last—and though the voice was gentle it was very grave—'what are you plotting against me? I see you knew all this long ago, and that it has been not quite forgotten in the mean time. I have told you my thoughts, dear Rosalie—tell me yours.'

'I wish they had never been told me—that they had been left to my own imaginings. I wish, oh how much, that if you had any such thoughts before you went abroad, Mr. Raynor, you had left them all there.'

'You might as well wish that I was not Mr. Raynor, at once. And as to not telling them—I'm afraid I should not soon have you really at the head of my house if I waited for your ' imaginings ' to place you there. It is high time that my persuasions came in aid.'

She passed her hands over her face for a moment, and then clasping them together and looking up at him that he might see it was no unsettled purpose, she said,

'I cannot leave my brother, Mr. Raynor.'

He looked at her steadily for a moment,—and then as her eyes fell again he sprang up and stood before her.

'But Rosalie! what sort of a reason is that?'

'A good one, if you will take the right point of view,' she said with the same steadiness, except that his look or his words had somewhat moved her lips from their composure.

'Then I take the wrong. It does *not* follow, dear Rosalie, that of two people who love you with all their hearts you should choose the one who has always had you— unless he has all your heart as well.'

'But it does follow that I should give myself to the one who wants me most.'

'I will throw down my gauntlet upon that!'

'Ah you do not take the right point of view. He needs me more than you can understand.'

'I know he would miss you—he could not help that. But—would you have said this to me two years ago?'

'He would not have been left alone then.'

'And you are left alone now. Forgive me, dear Rosalie —I do not say it in unkindness—but ought you not to take some care of yourself? Is it quite right to think only of another's whims and fancies?'

'He has nothing to do with it,' she said quickly—'at least not in the way you suppose. But Mr. Raynor——' She paused a moment and then went on.

'I must tell you all—it is but just. Mr. Raynor, I am the only friend he has in the world! Of all the people with whom he most associates there is not one, there is not one! whose influence for good is at best more than neutral. He does not go the lengths that some of them go—he has a little remembrance yet of what he was—a sense of honour and truth as strong as he ever had. But if he has any regard for my words, any love for me—and you know not how much!—could I be justified in leaving him to the unmitigated influence of worthless companions and unworthy pursuits?'

She had spoken very low at first, with evident grief and mortification; looking up then with her whole heart in her eyes, and yet with those same meekly folded hands, as if beseeching him neither to urge nor distrust her.

He met the look, and then turning abruptly away he began to walk up and down the room; but more in excitement than in thoughtfulness. Walking as if the disturbed spirit could not subside, and without once looking towards Rosalie.

'You are displeased, Mr. Raynor,' she said at length. 'You think I am trifling with you.'

He came to the end of the sofa where she sat, and took her hand in both of his.

'Nothing upon earth could make me think that! But I cannot bring my mind to look at things as you do,—neither is the feeling wholly selfish. If you could see yourself with the eyes of a third person, Rosalie, you would understand one of the reasons why I want you to be my wife, much better than you can now. Is it right, I must ask you again, to forget yourself entirely? to take no care for yourself?'

'No—perhaps not—' she said, but the voice was less clear and steady—'in one respect you may be right. But one needs to take a very wide view of things. I do not speak without consideration. I know too, that it is not in my hands—that I have no power that is not given me,—and I cannot tell how things will turn out. But God seldom makes the whole path clear before us—it is only the first few steps. Should I therefore refuse to take them? O Mr. Raynor! you have known what it was to live without God and without hope in the world—is anything too much to bring one out of that condition?'

She gathered breath and went on.

'I have thought—very much of late—of the day when "them that sleep in Jesus God shall bring with him"— when the book of life shall be opened. It is not enough to know that her name is written there—to hope that mine stands by it——'

'I know it is not in my hands—' she went on presently, —'and yet I cannot leave him!'

She said no more, and sat silent, except for those silently flowing tears.

'I dare not urge you—' Mr. Raynor said then. 'I dare not put my own earthly happiness, nor even yours, dear Rosalie, in competition with another's eternal welfare. The sick of the palsy was healed for the faith of them that brought him. Surely if ever endeavours were blessed, yours might be! But tell me one thing—was this the *only* reason?'

'If there had been another you should never have heard this,' she said.

'I might have answered that myself.'

He stood silent and grave, as if the struggle were in his mind yet, till she rose up and said,

'Good bye, Mr. Raynor—you must not stay here any longer—and for the future we must be only common friends.'

'I must not stay here any longer at present,' he said with some emphasis, 'but I do not give up my claim—it is only postponed. Nay, do not contradict me. And we must *not* be common friends—for I have a more than brother's right to be called upon, and shall perhaps assume that right to watch over you, whether I have it or not. And as for you, dear child,—" The Lord bless thee, and keep thee: the Lord make his face shine upon thee, and be gracious unto thee: the Lord lift up his countenance upon thee, and give thee peace!"'

He went—and as the door closed behind him Rosalie felt as if she had taken leave of the sunshine of life, and turned her face unto the shadows. Hulda thought her sister very tired that evening;—and when late at night Thornton came home and went to take a look at the sweet face whose pleadings he so often disregarded, he found its expression more hard to read than usual. He was sure there had been sorrowful thoughts at work—that the fountain of tears was hardly at rest now; but for whom had they come? Not for herself. He could not trace one murmur on the placid brow, and the mouth seemed to speak what had been her last waking thoughts—" And now, Lord, what wait I for? my hope is in thee."

But had they been for him? Thornton puzzled over it till he was tired, and went to bed to dream that he had forbidden Mr. Raynor the house.

CHAPTER XIV.

*With thy clear keen joyance
Languor cannot be;
Shadow of annoyance
Never came near thee.*—SHELLY.

It was one of those warm foretokens of summer which are sometimes sent by the hand of April. With sympathetic laziness people strolled along through the sunshine; the street sprinklers passed on with their carts, and birds and radish boys were clamorous. The leaves came out apace but stealthily, and the very air was breathless. And yet there floated in from the storehouses of fresh things, fresh influences. The silence spoke of sweet sounds in the wilderness of nature, to the wilderness of men; and flowers came not on 'the wings of the wind,' but their own breath; and over all there was a sky so purely blue—so free from turmoil and pollution,—that it seemed as if the last revolution of the earth had rolled New York away from its own proper atmosphere, and bestowed it beneath a new canopy. How far removed from the sights and sounds—the steps, the rattling wheels, the drums, the cries, that spread themselves through the city.

So thought Miss Clyde, as with little Hulda in her hand she went slowly home from a walk. How few, she thought, how very few there were that appreciated or even noticed that 'clear expanse,'—how few that would not mourn if the word were sent to them, 'Come up hither.' The very birds were longing to try their wings in such an element; and man chose the dust, and looked down and not up. A little pressure of her hand brought her eyes down. Hulda was studying her face as intently as she had watched the sky.

'Are you tired, love?'

'O no,' said Hulda, 'but I didn't know what you were thinking of. There's a carriage at our door.'

Somewhat wondering with herself what could have made Mrs. Raynor go in and wait for her, Rosalie mounted the steps, and her wonder was not lessened to find Thornton in the parlour.

The good quakeress spoke not a word till she had kissed her first upon one cheek and then on the other, even more tenderly than usual.

'I have made acquaintance with thy brother,' she said then—'I would know everybody that loves thee and whom thou dost love.'

'That is not a very safe rule to go by neither,' said Thornton. 'In this case, Mrs. Raynor, Rosalie loves somebody very different from herself.'

Mrs. Raynor looked as if she knew it full well—or at least as if she thought the people who resembled Rosalie were few.

'And thou, dear little Hulda,' she said, sitting down and taking the child on her lap—'wilt thou come home with me and see my flowers?'

Hulda looked doubtfully towards her sister and then up at the soft, quiet eyes that looked down upon her. She had to resort to the childish formula of hesitation,

'I don't know, ma'am.'

'Yes, thou wilt come,' said the quakeress decisively—

'thy sister will not say nay to thy going. Thou and I will have the carriage all to ourselves, and we will get home before dinner.'

'But how shall I get back again?' said Hulda smiling.

'We will see—mayhap thy friend Henry Raynor will bring thee.'

'Is that the same Mr. Raynor that came here once—no, two times?' said Hulda.

'Truly love I think there is but one Henry Raynor,' said his mother.

'O then I should like to go, very much.'

And jumping down to ask her sister's leave, Hulda ran away up stairs.

'He hath taken a strange fancy to thy little pet,' said the quakeress, looking however rather towards Thornton.

'To Rosalie's pet, Mrs. Raynor—I am fonder of grown-up humanity.'

'Thou hast never known what it was to lose such a little pure spirit from thy house,' said the quakeress with a sigh, 'or thee would better appreciate it. But thou hast a large share, friend Thornton, and when "the cup runneth over," the drops are less precious.'

'I have not a drop too many,' said Thornton, with an expression he was hardly conscious of. 'You know it takes more to make some people happy than others, Mrs. Raynor.'

'I know there is but one thing which of itself bringeth happiness,' she said—'perhaps without that thy remark may be just. But here cometh one whose happiness is of easy growth. And yet, Rosalie, she demurreth about leaving thee even for one day.'

There was certainly considerable doubt on Hulda's mind except when she looked at Mrs. Raynor; but there she found something so attractive that she was allured on, and soon found herself doing anything else but fill a place in the carriage. Stowed away like a small parcel on the spacious seat, her little shoes in plain sight, with one hand stretched over Mrs. Raynor's soft dress and there held fast, Hulda watched through the front window the substantial back of Caleb Williams, and thought how very funny it was for a coachman to wear a grey coat. The carriage rolled smoothly on in the most regular and matter-of-fact way possible,—as if Caleb and his horses had made an arrangement that they were not to get home before a certain time, and therefore it was as well to take it easy.

Hulda remembered how Thornton's horses went now very fast and now slow, and then started off again at a most eccentric pace; but at this rate she could have slept all the way to Mrs. Raynor's with no disturbance. Arrived at the house another wonder awaited Hulda, for there was a footman all in grey too; and when she had followed Mrs. Raynor up stairs, and Rachel came at her mistress's call habited after the same sober fashion, Hulda began to feel as if all the world were turning mouse colour, and looked down at her crimson merino with feelings of amazement.

'Thee sees I have brought home little Hulda Clyde, Rachel,' said Mrs. Raynor. 'Will thee take off the child's bonnet and cloak, and see if perchance her feet be cold?'

'Yea verily,' said Rachel, when she had brought her mistress another dress. 'Art thou cold, Hulda?'

'O no,' said Hulda, whose mind had got beyond the cold region and was in a great puzzle, for Rachel had not only Mrs. Raynor's stuff gown but also her cap! 'I'm not cold at all.'

'Doth thy dress keep thee warm?' said Rachel, with a grave irony which Hulda did not understand.

'Yes ma'am,' she said, in a new difficulty from the similarity of neckerchiefs—'I suppose so—my frock and my coat.'

Rachel almost smiled at the grave little face—so sincere and so wide awake.

'Did thee ever see a fire-fly, child?' she inquired.

'No,' said Hulda, 'but Rosalie told me about them. They're such bright and beautiful things that go flying all about in the evening.'

'Now thou art all ready,' said Mrs. Raynor approaching them, 'and likewise I, and we will go down stairs.'

'There waiteth a woman this long time,' said Rachel, 'and she will not tell her want save to thee. James Hoxton hath brought her to the kitchen.'

'I will straightway go and see her,' said Mrs. Raynor. 'And for thee, little Hulda, wilt thou sit by thyself in the library until I come? and Rachel shall bring thee the cat.'

It never would have occurred to Hulda that a tortoise-shell cat could come to keep her bright dress company; and therefore when a grave knight of Malta walked in, she felt that he was one of the family.

'Art thou afraid to stay here alone?' said Rachel, when she had watched the knight's reception.

'Why what should I be afraid of?' said Hulda.

'Truly little one, thee has reason,' said the handmaid as she departed.

Hulda had sat some time upon the rug in front of the fire, and Maltese was quite expanding beneath her caresses; when somebody came in and took a chair behind her, and she was lifted up, cat and all, upon Mr. Raynor's lap. *He* was not in grey—Hulda saw that at a glance—but in a blue uniform with red facings, very much like her dress. She felt quite comforted. But when she got a fair view of his face—for at first it was too close to her own—she saw that he had his share of the sober colour, only worn differently. But what made him look so at her? There was something in his face that troubled her, and almost tearfully her eyes sought his. He smiled then, and drawing her head down till it rested against him, he asked how she was, and then after her sister.

'O she's very well,' said Hulda stroking the cat. 'I suppose she's always well for she never says she's sick. Do you think she'll miss me to-day, Mr. Raynor?'

'I do not believe she is sorry you came, dear Hulda, and I am very glad.'

Hulda thought that was very strange.

'Henry Raynor,' said his mother as she came into the room, 'go I pray thee and take off those trappings at once, my child; I like them not—they become no man—much less thee.'

'Then you must get down, little Hulda, for a while, if I am to go and change my dress.'

It was a great pity, Hulda thought, with an uncomfortable vision of her friend arrayed in the prevailing colour.

But when he came down again the dress was black and not grey; and Hulda went to her former seat with great satisfaction.

'The dinner waiteth,' said James Hoxton opening the door.

'You don't think yourself too old to be carried, Hulda?' said her friend.

'O no,' said Hulda, 'Alie very often carries me up stairs when I'm tired or sick.'

'I should think thy weight better suited to thy brother's arms than to thy sister's,' said Mrs. Raynor, 'as having more strength.'

'O her arms are *very* strong!' said Hulda from her place of elevation. 'They *never* get tired. And Thornton's not at home you know generally when I want to be carried —but Rosalie always is. She says gentlemen can't always be at home so much as ladies. But she don't hold me quite as well as you do, Mr. Raynor.'

And with one arm passed most confidingly round his neck, they went forth together and proceeded to the dinner table; where Hulda was as well taken care of as possible. Taken care of in more ways than one, though she was too young and unskilled to notice the delicate tact with which whenever her childish talk ran too close upon home affairs she was led off to another subject; nor how carefully she was kept, as far as might be, from making disclosures which indeed she knew not were such. And if she had been older she would have wondered at herself for her perfect at home feeling among such grave people;—for the freedom with which she talked,—her little voice making music such as it never yields when the chords have been once overstrained or the wires unstrung—most like a mountain rill in its sweet erratic course. And the older ones looked and listened—Mrs. Raynor with often a smile and sometimes with glistening eyes; while to his face the smile came less often, and there was only the look of interest and affection which won Hulda's heart yet more. And whenever the rill went too far in any one direction, it was only necessary to hold out a painted leaf—some bright word or question or anecdote—and the rill was tempted, and went that way. On the whole Hulda thought as she was carried back into the library, it had been one of the most satisfactory dinners she ever remembered.

'Hulda Clyde,' said Mrs. Raynor, 'I go up-stairs to sleep, as is my wont. What wilt thou do, my child?'

'O I will stay here,' said Hulda.

'You can content yourself for a while with the cat and me, I am sure,' said Mr. Raynor.

'O yes—and without the cat,' said Hulda contentedly.

He smiled, and his mother came up behind him, and passing her arm round his neck as if he had been a child, raised up his face and kissed it, and went away.

'What do you think of my being made a baby of yet, Hulda?'

'Thornton says that's what mamma used to do with Rosalie,' said Hulda, whose little avenues of thought all ran down to the same stronghold of love and confidence. 'Did you ever see my mamma, Mr. Raynor?'

'Yes, dear, often; and loved her very much.'

'I don't remember her a great deal,' said Hulda—'I believe I get her confused with Rosalie.'

She sat quiet a few minutes and then started up.

'Don't *you* want to go to sleep, Mr. Raynor?'

'Don't you?'

'O no—not a bit.'

'Neither do I.'

'Well that'll be very fair, then,' said Hulda laughing. 'But I should think you'd get tired of holding me, Mr. Raynor—most people don't like to.'

'I once had such a little sister as you are, Hulda—whom I loved better than almost anything else in the world. You remind me of her very much, and that is one reason why I like to hold you and kiss you and carry you, and do anything else with you and for you.'

'I'm very glad!' said Hulda, her smile half checked by something in his look and tone. 'So that's one reason. What's the other?'

He smiled and told her she must be content with hearing

one; and then asked her what she had been doing and learning lately.

'I don't learn a great deal,' said Hulda—'only arithmetic and geography and little, little bits of French lessons. And then I write—and I have one hymn to learn a week, and a little verse every day.'

'Tell me one of your hymns.'

'Then I will tell you the last one,' said Hulda.

> '"Around the throne of God in heaven,
>   Thousands of children stand;
> Children whose sins are all forgiven,
>   A holy, happy band—
>   Singing glory, glory, glory.
>
> '"What brought them to that world above—
>   That heaven so bright and fair—
> Where all is peace and joy and love?—
>   How came those children there,
>   Singing glory, glory, glory?
>
> '"Because the Saviour shed his blood
>   To wash away their sin;
> Bathed in that pure and precious flood,
>   Behold them white and clean—
>   Singing glory, glory, glory.
>
> '"On earth they sought their Saviour's grace,
>   On earth they loved his name;
> So now they see his blessed face,
>   And stand before the Lamb—
>   Singing glory, glory, glory."'

'Don't you think it's pretty?' said Hulda, when she had waited what she thought a reasonable time for Mr. Raynor to speak, and he had only drawn his arm closer about her.

'I think it is much more than pretty. Do you understand it all?'

'I believe so—' said Hulda—'Rosalie told me a great deal about it.'

'What?'

'Why she said that even children needed to be forgiven before they went to heaven—that was one thing in the first verse,—and that people ought to try to make this world as much like heaven as they could, and that if all was peace and joy and love there it ought to be here. And then in the third verse, that we didn't only need to be forgiven, but made good and to love all good things, and that if God didn't make us love him and like to serve him, we never could be happy in heaven even if we could get there. And she said the blood of Christ was called a flood because it was enough to save everybody in the whole world—and to make them clean, if they would only trust in it. And she said the last verse taught us that we must love and serve him now, while we are here, and then when we die he would receive us to himself.'

'And what does that word 'white' mean in the third verse—' Behold them white and clean'?'

'Don't it mean something like clean?' said Hulda.

'Something like, yes. It shews how very pure, how very holy, will all God's children be when he has taken them to heaven. As the Bible says—"they are without spot before the throne of God"—"without fault before him" —think how very holy one must be in whom the pure eye of God sees neither spot nor fault. Such are all the children about his throne—and because thus holy they are happy.'

'Do you think there is *nobody* that is quite good?' said Hulda with a face of very grave reflection.

'The Bible says, "there is not a just man upon earth that doeth good and sinneth not."'

'I know it does,' said Hulda, who was apparently a little troubled with some reservation in her mind. 'But that only says men. I don't suppose there are a great many.'

Mrs. Raynor came down from her nap in due time, and then proposed that they should go into the greenhouse. Hulda was enchanted; and ran about and admired and asked questions to the delight of both her friends.

'Would thee like some flowers to take home with thee?' said the good quakeress, drawing Hulda's head close to her. And Mr. Raynor's knife hardly waited the reply before it began its work. Hulda's little hands had as many as they could hold.

'And now thee must have one flower for thy sister— yea, Henry, thou art always right,' she said, as her son began to examine the respective merits of the white camellias. 'They are not the fairer.'

'O Mr. Raynor! you are cutting the very prettiest one!' cried Hulda. 'O it was too bad to take that.'

'Is it too pretty for your sister?'

'O I don't think so, of course,' said Hulda,—'but then it was your little bush.'

Hulda wondered at the smile that passed over his face, and looked if she might see it come again, but it came not.

He tied up her flowers and put them in water for her, and walked with her about the greenhouse till the last sunbeams had left it, and the flowers grew indistinct.

'Friend Henry,' said James Hoxton appearing at this juncture, 'thy mother waiteth for thee at tea.'

'James Hoxton is a quaker,' said Mr. Raynor with a smile at Hulda's look.

'Does *that* make him speak to you so?' said Hulda. 'You are not a quaker, Mr. Raynor?'

'No. If I were a quaker, Hulda, I should call my mother 'friend Joan.''

'Should you! But that would be very disrespectful,' said Hulda.

'No—not if I were a quaker.'

'O—' said Hulda, a little and only a little enlightened. 'I'm *very* glad you're not a quaker—I don't like grey at all;' though when she got to the tea table, Hulda could not help liking everything about Mrs. Raynor—even her grey dress.

Mr. Raynor took her home in the carriage after tea. Not sitting by his side but on his lap, and wrapped up in his arms as if she were a precious little thing that he was afraid to lose sight of. But he would not come in, though Hulda begged and entreated him. He carried her and her flowers up the steps and into the hall where Tom stood holding the door, and then ran down again and in a moment was in the carriage and off.

CHAPTER XV.

So th' one for wrong, the other strives for right.—Faëry Queen.

'Well, what sort of a time did you have among the quakers yesterday?' said Thornton when he saw Hulda at breakfast next morning.

'O it was beautiful!' said Hulda with a pause of delight in the midst of buttering her roll.

'What was beautiful?'

'O everything! And they were so kind to me—and I like Mr. Raynor *so* much! And the flowers—O Thornton, did you see mine that I brought home? and the camellia? That is Rosalie's; and it was the very prettiest one they had; and I told Mr. Raynor so, and yet he would cut it.'

'Perhaps he did not agree with you.'

'O yes he did. I thought he was going to cut a white one at first and then he chose this.'

'Then he did not choose the prettiest, to my fancy,' said Thornton.

'Why you don't know anything about it!' cried Hulda. 'I never saw such a beauty, and I don't believe you ever did.' And away she ran to bring ocular proof of the camellia's perfectness. No further argument was necessary; for admirable kind and culture had produced one of those exquisite results that the eye is never satisfied with seeing. Thornton silently took it in his hand to examine.

The flower was hardly at its full opening, two or three of the inner petals being yet inclined towards each other with a budlike effect; but the rest lay folded back in clear glossy beauty, leaf beyond leaf—each one as spotless and perfect as the last. They were of a delicious rose colour —not very deep, but pure, perfect, as a tint could be; and the stem, which had been cut some inches below the flower, spread out for it an admirable foil in two or three deep green leaves.

'Isn't that beautiful?' said Hulda, who stood at her brother's side with her little hands folded and her little face in a rival glow.

'Exquisite!—I never saw such a one! Alie, I must get you a plant. I wonder what is its name, if it has any.'

'There was a little stick stuck in the flower pot,' said Hulda, 'but I don't know what was on it.'

'Do you know?' said Thornton looking towards his sister.

'I think, I believe it is called Lady Hume's blush.'

Thornton laughed.

'This is probably a variety called Miss Clyde's blush. It might be at all events. Methinks the quakers performed some conjuration over you, Hulda,—it seems that you have suddenly become a little conductor—a sort of electric machine, charged by one party with a shock for another.'

'Shock!' said Hulda. 'But I don't think I have shocked anybody.'

'That is the very thing.'

'But what do you mean by Miss Clyde's blush?' said Hulda, who was getting excessively mystified.

'Ask her what she means by it,' said Thornton. 'Alie just ring your bell, will you? Tom—did you get my sword-belt?'

'No sir—Jansen said he thought all the Captains was a conspirating against him; and if they were Generals instead he couldn't do no more than he could,' he said.

'And what did you say to that?'

'I told him he was a considerable piece off from doing more than he could, yet, and I guessed he'd better send the belt home to-night and no more about it.'

'I guess so too, or there will be more. I shall dine out of town to-day, Rosalie, so you need not wait for me.'

'You will come home to tea?' she said as she rose and followed him out of the room.

Her look half inclined him to come to dinner as well, but he only laughed and said,

'You had better not ask me, because if I come I may bring you your hands full.'

'Bring anything in the world that will make home pleasant to you,' she said.

'O it's pleasant enough now—and you are charming, but "variety's the spice of life," you know Alie.'

'A most unhappy quotation in this case,' she said with a slight smile. 'That life must miserably dwindle and deteriorate which is fed upon spice alone. Suppose you try brown bread for one night?'

'You shall try red pepper for one night, to pay you for that,' said Thornton. 'Why shouldn't you and I be like two birds of Paradise,—sitting up in a tree and eating pimento berries?'

'What a naturalist you would make!' said his sister smiling. 'You would condemn the birds of Paradise to as unwholesome diet as you give yourself.'

'Unwholesome according to you.—'

He stood by her, he hardly knew why; but perhaps half in curiosity to see what she would say; for the changing light on her face told of varied thoughts and feelings. But when she spoke her voice trembled a little.

'" The kingdom of heaven is as a man travelling into a far country, who called his own servants, and delivered unto them his goods. And unto one he gave five talents, to another two, and to another one; to every man according to his several ability; and straightway took his journey.——

'" After a long time the Lord of those servants cometh and reckoneth with them. And so he that had received five talents, came and brought other five talents, saying, Lord, thou deliveredst to me five talents; behold, I have gained besides them five talents more. His Lord said unto him, Well done, good and faithful servant; thou hast been faithful over a few things, I will make thee ruler over many things: enter thou into the joy of thy Lord."

'Thornton—shall we live that life together?—the life of heirs of heaven?'

'I wish you would let go of my hand,' said her brother, with a motion as if he would shake it off. 'What upon earth is there in that immense quotation to call forth such a sorrowful face?'

'Because,' said his sister with a gush of tears, as she took away the offending hand; 'because "*there was one servant who went and digged in the earth, and hid his lord's money;*" and to him it was said, "*Depart.*"'

The tears were quickly wiped away, and again she looked up at him.

'Do you think it is very kind to take the edge off my day's pleasure by such a prelude?' said he.

'Yes—very kind—to say what should do it.'

'By what rule of sisterly affection?'

'The rule in my own heart,' she said with a sigh. 'What is a day's pleasure that my love should balance it against eternal life? There is time now to obey—an inch of time, —and then " the angel shall lift up his hand to heaven, and swear by Him that liveth forever and ever, that there shall be time no longer!'"

'And how do *you* know that I need time for anything of the sort?' said Thornton, when his silence had taken to itself displeasure. 'What right have you to suppose, that because " after the most straitest sect of our religion I do not live a Pharisee," I am therefore excluded from all its benefits? You see I can quote Scripture too.'

She did not raise her eyes, though the sudden flush on her brow told that his words had struck deep. It passed away, and she said—betaking herself to Bible words as if she would not trust her own,

'"I speak as unto wise men,—judge ye what I say."— " *Every man that hath this hope in him, purifieth himself even as He is pure.*'"

And Thornton turned and left her.

How he despised himself for what he had said! for the implication his words had carried! And against her—upon whose sincerity he would have staked his life.

Christian in the Slough of Despond struggled to get out, but always on the side next the wicket gate; while Pliable, having no desire but to be at ease—even in the City of Destruction—was well pleased to set his face thitherward to be clear of the Slough.

Thornton soon got rid of his discomfort,—only the remembered touch of his sister's hand was harder to shake off than the hand itself. Perhaps on the whole he was not sorry for this. In pursuit of bird's nests he was swinging himself over a precipice, with but one visible stay—and that stay the hand of a frail girl. He knew he had hold of her, or rather that her love and prayers had hold of him; and with little thought of her life of watching and anxiety, he swung himself off—and rejoiced in his freedom.

He resolved, as he walked up Broadway, that he would go home to tea that night, but not alone,—anything was better than a tête-à-tête with his sister; and besides, as he remarked to himself, 'it will never do to let her suppose there are no men in the world but Henry Raynor.'

Rosalie sat alone in her room, half reading, half dreaming in the warm spring air of the afternoon,—now applying herself to her book and now parleying with some old remembrance or association; sometimes raising her eyes to take in most unworldly pleasure from nature's own messengers, and then trying to bring her mind back to more fixedness of thought. But a sunbeam that at length fell on her book wound about her its silken bands of spirit influence; and laying her folded hands in the warm light, Rosalie leaned her head back and let the sunbeam take her whither it would.

It went first athwart the room to little Hulda; who tired with the day's play had curled herself up on the bed in childish attitude and sleep. Her doll lay there too, not far off; and a little silk scarf with which she had been playing was still about her, and answered the purposes of adornment more perfectly than ever. On all the sunbeam laid its light hand tenderly; and then it darted to the table beyond, where stood the little sleeper's dish of flowers. The camellia was there too, and one look Rosalie gave it; and then turning her head towards the window and leaning it back as before, her eye again followed the sunbeam—but this time upward,—her face a little graver perhaps—a little more removed from earth's affairs, but no less quiet than it had been before. And proving the truth of George Herbert's words,

"Then by a sunbeam I will climb to thee"

it was not long ere her mind had laid fast hold of the promise, "*Unto you that believe, shall the Sun of Righteousness arise, with healing in his beams.*"

The ray had done its work and gone, and 'the lesser light' had held forth her sceptre, when Martha Jumps, whose head and shoulders had been enjoying the afternoon out of an upper window, suddenly rushed into the room.

'Here's a whole army of men coming!'

'Americans, I hope,' said her mistress.

'La sakes, ma'am! to be sure they aint British! and when I said army I only meant the short for multitude. But it's such an unaccountable start for the Captain to come home to tea and bring people with him!'

'He so seldom brings a multitude, Martha, that I wish you would go and tell Tom to make sure that we have bread and cake enough for tea.'

'Let Tom Skiddy alone for that,' said Martha,—'he has a pretty good notion of his own how much bread it takes for one man's supper, and if he hasn't I have; and I'll go tell him as you say; but you see if there aint a multitude. To be sure one hat does look like a dozen—viewed out of a three-story, but I wouldn't wonder a bit if there was five. And Miss Rosalie, you mayn't be conscious that your hair is walking down the back of your neck. There—they're knocking at the door this blessed minute!'

But in spite of this announcement, Rosalie's eyes and mind went out of the window again so soon as she was alone. For sorrow had put her out of society, and joy had not as yet offered his hand to lead her back; and the gentle spirit which had once amused itself with and among people, now found their gay words but as the music of 'him that singeth songs to a heavy heart.' Her mind found rest and comfort in but one thing; and these visitors—'they knew it not, neither did they regard it.' And she must not only go among them, but must go as a Christian—to take and maintain that stand alone. To do nothing unbecoming her profession,—to be neither ashamed of it nor too forward in making it known,—to be ready always to speak the truth with boldness and yet with judgment.

For a moment it tried her,—for a moment she shrank from the trial; and then throwing off care and weakness upon the strong hand that could provide for both, she got up and lit a candle and began to arrange her hair.

Thornton came up stairs and through the open door so quietly while she was thus employed, that the first notice of his presence was its reflection in the glass before her.

'Well little Sweetbrier,' he said,—' beautifying yourself as usual. Are your pricklers in good order?'

'As blunt as possible.'

'Defend me from wounds with a blunt instrument!' said Thornton.

'As dull as possible then, if you like that better.'

'I do not like it at all my dear, only that you never were and never will be dull. There is nothing dull about you,' said he passing his hand over her hair.

'Whom have you got down-stairs?'

'Nobody.'

'Nobody! O I am so glad. Then Martha was mistaken.'

'Martha is as often mistaken as most people; but when I said nobody, Alie, I did not speak very literally and not at all prospectively. I should have said nobody to signify, at present. A few entities to come and a few nonentities to pave the way. So the re-arrangement of your hair will not be thrown away.'

'O it would not have been thrown away upon you,' she

said. 'But where did you pick up such a peculiar name for me?'

'What, Sweetbrier?—out of the abundance and exuberance of my fancy, my dear. I never attempt to argue with you, that I do not scratch my own fingers and find out how particularly sweet you are,—and the sweeter the more provoked. So you see—Come!'

CHAPTER XVI.

My name is Mr. Stephen, sir, I am this gentleman's own cousin, sir, his father is mine uncle, sir: I am somewhat melancholy, but you shall command me, sir, in whatever is incident to a gentleman.—BEN JONSON.

'It is one of the singular properties of Sweetbrier, gentlemen,' said Mr. Clyde, as he presented his sister to the three or four young men who were variously disposed about the drawingroom; 'that while seeming to be one of the meekest and sweetest of the rose tribe, it is yet armed at all points and capable of making war with considerable fierceness.'

'" 'Tis excellent to have a giant's strength!"' said one of the guests, who was given to quoting Shakspeare.

'And it is safe enough, lodged in such delicate hands,' said another who came forward with the air of an old acquaintance. 'We all know that Miss Clyde is never tyrannical, except in the way which is every lady's prerogative.

"The tyranness doth joy to see
The huge massacres which her eyes do make."'

'What a pleasant image!' said Rosalie smiling. 'It reminds one, Mr. Clinton, of the Bill of Mortality in the Spectator; where you find "Will Simple, smitten at the Opera by the glance of an eye that was aimed at one who stood by him."'

'I think I need no further explanation of Sweetbrier, after that,' said the gentleman.

'Mr. Raynor—' said Tom, suddenly throwing open the door; and more than one of the party looked round with a little start, which subsided as quickly when they found themselves mistaken.

The new comer was a most flourishing combination of youth, good looks, imperturbable good nature, a gay dress, and a most jaunty manner. As if the air were buoyant under his feet, so did he come forward, and his face was radiant as if Miss Clyde had been the sunshine of his existence.

'My dear Miss Clyde!—it is ages!—two whole ages—and a half—since I had the pleasure of seeing you. And how in the world I didn't get here as soon as I came home, I can't imagine; but the first thing I knew I found myself at Washington.'

'The power of attraction, Mr. Penn,' said Rosalie. 'Did you suppose that you of all people could resist its power?'

'I never did think so before,' said Penn, 'but it really seems to me that I must have resisted it pretty strongly when I went to Washington. I feel remarkably drawn, to-night.'

'Drawn and quartered—in a pleasant sense,' said one of the gentlemen, as Mr. Penn threw himself down on the sofa by Rosalie.

'Mr. Talbot is apparently one of the people who think sense is everything,' said Mr. Clinton.

'Ah that's a mistake,' said Penn. 'But my dear Miss Clyde, is there anything remarkable about your appearance to-night?'

'I hope not,' said Rosalie, while the others laughed and Mr. Clinton remarked,

'You ought to be able to answer that yourself, Penn.'

'Couldn't trust myself, that's all,' replied Mr. Penn, 'for in the present state of my eyesight it really strikes me with astonishment how anybody could go to Europe. And do you know Miss Clyde, that do all I would I couldn't make Harry come with me to-night? Positively couldn't—and he went somewhere else.'

'Probably for the same reason that you went to Washington,' said Thornton.

'No, it couldn't have been that,' said Penn, 'because he has seen Miss Clyde since he came home, which I had not. But I never knew him resist the power of attraction before.'

'You seem to be fairly entangled, Penn,' said Mr. Clinton.

'Certainly,' said Penn,—'revolving. Miss Clyde, it confuses my ideas in an extraordinary manner to see you again. And it's only by the merest chance in the world that I am here to-night, myself.'

'What unhappy corner of the world has just missed the pleasure of your company?' said Mr. Clinton.

'You may well call it an unhappy corner,' said Penn, 'for if a man is bound to be wretched anywhere, I suppose it is in a prison ship in a hot climate. I escaped pretty well though.'

'From the wretchedness or the ship?' said Rosalie.

'Both, Miss Clyde, I assure you. I'll tell you about it.'

'What nonsense you do talk, Penn,' said Thornton. 'You came home only three months ago from Europe.'

'Certainly,' said Penn, 'but that's quite long enough to stay in some places. Have you any idea where I have been since then?'

'Not much,' said Thornton,—'at Washington and here I suppose.'

'Tout au contraire,' replied Mr. Penn. 'I have been at the West Indies and a prisoner.'

'Were *you* one of the men who ran away with the Bermuda?' said Rosalie.

'My dear Miss Clyde, with your usual acuteness you have stated the case precisely. In fact I may say I was *the* man, the rest being highly gifted with timidity. But I thought a little interlude of running away would be refreshing, even if we were taken again, and was by no means of the opinion that H.B.M.'s cruisers had a natural right to everything they laid hands on. Holla—who comes here?'

'"Enter a fairy at one door,"' said the Shakspearian.

And the door softly opened and Hulda came in. Just enough awake to get off the bed and brush her hair, she had found her way down stairs, and now stood by the door with her ideas in a most puzzled state.

'What do you want, Hulda?' said her brother.

'I want—Rosalie,' said the child abstractedly, and taking another survey of the room.

'The Queen, my dear,' said Penn Raynor walking up to her, 'is at present sitting in state upon the sofa. Shall I have the honour of conducting you to her? And by what title will you be made known? Is this the little prime minister?'

'What sir?' said Hulda raising her childish eyes to his face, while everybody laughed.

'You are the Flying Squirrel, my dear, and I am his majesty's sloop of war Wild Cat,' said Penn, as he gave her one jump to his shoulder; and then carrying her to the sofa permitted her to kneel in his lap. 'Now who have I got for a prisoner?'

'You have got me,' said Hulda.

'And it strikes me that I have heard of you before,' said Penn. 'Isn't my cousin a great friend of yours?'

'I don't know, sir,' said Hulda.

'Why yes you do,' said Penn giving her a little shake. 'You spent the day with him yesterday, and he was off with you somewhere when I got home.'

'But I was at Mr. Raynor's yesterday,' said Hulda, 'and he isn't your cousin.'

'He is my cousin.'

'Is he?' said Hulda, leaning back and taking a complete survey of the questioner. 'He don't look a bit like you. I love Mr. Raynor very much.'

'Well so do I,' said Penn, who was highly delighted with the unconscious emphasis Hulda had bestowed upon her friend's name.

'But I thought you were going to tell us of your great adventures,' said Thornton impatiently,—' and you sit there talking to that child!'

'I perceive that you are still subject to your old periodical fits of insanity, Mr. Clyde,' said Penn. 'When you have sojourned for a short lifetime among the Quakers, you will learn that impatience is one of the useless luxuries of life. Though indeed if you had been in our prison-ship—— But I was going to tell you about it. You see my dear Miss Clyde, when I got to Washington I fell in with some friends—not of the Society, you may be sure—that were bound to try their hand at privateering. Of course they invited me to go, and of course I went.'

'To benefit the country or yourself?' said Thornton.

'Whichever might be,' said Penn, 'and I think in the long run we came out about equal. However, when we first started from Baltimore the thing paid pretty well. We cruised about, took a variety of vessels smaller than ourselves, and had more prisoners than we knew what to do with: which was all very pleasant, except that the prisoners had as good appetites as our own.'

'Remarkably inconsiderate of them,' said Mr. Clinton.

'Yes, it was,' said Penn, 'when you take into the account that the Flying Squirrel's capacity for provisions was by no means unlimited. It came to this point at last—whether we should all starve together as human beings, or the upperhand live and the rest go overboard.'

'Difficult point to round, that,' said Thornton.

'It did look so in the distance,' said Mr. Penn; 'but after all it's astonishing how many points the tide of circumstance carries one round—as our Captain poetically expressed it. When we did reach the point there was a ship in the offing—an Englishman she looked to be and was.'

'And she carried you round the point?' said Rosalie.

'Precisely, Miss Clyde—round more than one. She was a sloop of war—or a frigate—I don't know which,—only I know that she carried four times as many guns as we did. The game was up, of course, but we chose to let the enemy cry checkmate, and so ran—but what could the Squirrel do so far from land? for the storms had driven us out so far that we were near coming up on the other side. I don't know to this day whether our guns were heard in England or America. But we ran as I said—skimmed over the water like the cannon ball the Wild Cat sent after us.'

'Did it strike?' said Rosalie.

'Yes, Miss Clyde—it struck us—that if she was going to spit fire at that rate we had better stop,—just to save her from spontaneous combustion. So we did stop, and gave her as good as she sent.'

'But not quite so suggestive.'

'Not quite,' said Penn,—' our arguments were not quite so weighty. And you see the Wild Cat had set her mouth for our poor Squirrel,—and what could four guns do against eighteen, after all?'

'So the long and short of it was, that you had to strike your colours,' said Thornton.

'Even so,' said Penn,—'I had that pleasure myself. Struck 'em so they fell overboard too——gave the Eagle my own choice,—death instead of dishonour. But we were all sent to Kingston and cooped up on board the Goree. Such a place!—such bread and such rats!'

'You wished for the Wild Cat again, didn't you Penn?' said Thornton laughing.

'I nearly turned one myself,' said Penn. 'For if the bread *was* uneatable, that didn't make it pleasant to have rats and cockroaches running over you all night to get at it. I tell you what, I came near hating my ancestors for having come from England.'

'If they had not come you would have been an Englishman yourself,' said Rosalie smiling.

'I don't know about that,' said Mr. Penn; 'but if I were a Turk I'd have respectable prison ships. Why even the Hindoos put nobody but beggars in the animal asylums— and pay them!'

'I think you were paid for privateering,' said Thornton.

'We did not view it in that light,' said Penn. 'In fact all the light we had was reflected into a focus upon our plan of escape. The States or the bottom of the sea,—we soon made up our minds to have one or t'other. It's a pretty enough place there, too,' said Mr. Penn, who was warming to his subject; 'and bread fruits and cocoanuts look very nice, waving about in the wind; but they don't make your sour brown bread any sweeter. I think to people broiling on the Goree's deck, or smothering under her hatches, it was rather tantalizing to think of green trees anywhere. But it strengthened our plans.'

'What did you have to do there?' said Thornton. 'Anything?'

'Not much,' said Penn,—'what we had was done, I do assure you. Wishing and grumbling was pretty much the whole of it—and then planning. Those of us that were given to swearing kept themselves in good practice; but as I had been brought up by the Quakers I hadn't even that resource. I remember one night I was too melancholy to sleep—or too hot—I forget which; and just as early as the prisoners were allowed to go on deck, up I went.'

'Didn't throw yourself overboard, did you?' said Thornton. 'That would have answered for either heat or melancholy.'

'Yes, but it wouldn't have answered for me, though,' said Penn, 'so I only leaned over the side of the ship and wished myself a fish; for the water was still enough to give one the fidgets. Presently the rest began to gather about me, and we exchanged a few looks and words as we got a chance, in a kind of desperate way that said we wouldn't wait much longer. Which sentiment we all endorsed by flinging our breakfast overboard. 'What's that for?' said the boatswain. But we gave him no reply; and after a few not very sweet words he ordered eleven of the prisoners into the launch to go for water.'

'And you refused to go?' said Thornton.

'No we didn't—we went, with only a look at each other; and the boatswain and two soldiers went along for company. The bay was quite spotted with vessels that morning, but all sleepy, apparently, with the warm day; there was nobody astir. The frigates shewed their teeth and that was all; and the smaller vessels had both crew and cargo stowed away out of sight. Only one, the Bermuda, had her deck lumbered with buoys which she was to take out and lay in the channel. But we rowed on past them all to the shore, and filled our six water casks in less time than they ever were filled before.'

'And upset them coming back,' said Mr. Clinton.

'You would have been a help if you had been there, said Penn. 'No—we upset nothing but the calculations of the boatswain; for the minute we were far enough from shore I gave the signal that we had always agreed upon. "Squirrel!" I said—and we pounced upon both soldiers and boatswain and disarmed them in a trice. Then we rowed quietly along to the Bermuda.

'Now you see, Miss Clyde, we had two forts on our right hand and the Bermuda on our left; and beyond the Bermuda lay the sloop of war Nimrod, and the frigates Chaser and Charlemagne, but all as I said asleep. So when we reached the Bermuda we boarded her at once, and put her five men under hatches; and in less time than you can think the cables were cut and we pushing out.'

'And after that the time seemed long.'

'Indeed yes,' said Penn. 'I never saw a thing creep so in my life as she did for a few minutes. When we had made a little headway we set the launch adrift, with the boatswain and soldiers and two of our party that didn't bring their courage along, and then overhauled the schooner to see what we had to work with. We knew nothing about the channel, and there was no chart on board; but we found a compass, forty gallons of water, and provisions enough to keep us alive for ten days.'

'How about the rats?' said Thornton.

'Never saw one, all the time we were in the Bermuda— they were sent to the prison ships. Well, it was eleven o'clock by the time we were fairly off—sails set and arrangements made; and we threw over all the buoys but one, keeping that till we knew the trim of the vessel. I can't tell you how pleasant it was. The wind was a true American, and favoured us all it could; and we sat on deck and eat some bread that had not been once eaten already, with great satisfaction. I know I looked at my watch, and it was just one o'clock; but as I was replacing it in a leisurely kind of way, that smacked of enjoyment, the wind came sweeping along the deck and brought us the booming of two or three alarm guns.'

'And how did you feel then?' said Rosalie as Mr. Penn paused.

'Every man was on his feet, this way,' said Penn, putting down Hulda and springing up; 'but nobody spoke. And so we stood for one hour till the Nimrod came in sight. We had nothing but a foresail, mainsail, and jib, but we made them work as hard as they could: still at sundown the vessel was nearer and seemed to be looming up every minute. As soon as it was dark we took a short tack and sailed off in a different direction, but by eight o'clock there were her lights again shining out as if to look after us; and when the moon was up in the early morning, the Nimrod or something else was after us as hard as ever. We stood and watched for a while as the day came on—and the Nimrod too, for that matter; and then a bright thought came into my head. 'Rutgers,' said I—(you know him Thornton, he's one of your cronies); 'we may just as well capsize ourselves here as to be carried back to Kingston. I vote we throw over this other buoy.' Which we did at once; and only think, Miss Clyde,' said Penn planting himself before her, 'it trimmed the schooner precisely; and by eight o'clock we had sunk the Nimrod, and she had her hunting ground all to herself!'

'That was brave,' said Rosalie. 'And what a pleasant breakfast you must have had.'

'Indeed we did,' said Penn. 'But that was not all. We were chased several times more coming home, and got away well enough till we neared Cape May; and there was a 74 in the channel, two other craft trying to cut us off from the shore, and a pilot boat full of armed Englishmen in chase.'

'Then you felt like giving up the ship again,' said Mr. Clinton.

'We did give it up—it was all we could do,' said Penn. 'We just steered for land, and by the time the boat was within pistol shot, we beached our vessel on the Cape and jumped ashore. Saved ourselves and lost the Bermuda,— which was a pity, after such a week's voyage in her.'

'Lost your prisoners too,' said Thornton.

'Yes, but that didn't matter. They were not worth much. *We* came pretty near being heroes, though,—I tell you what, they made fuss enough for us in Philadelphia. We should have been fêted and feasted till this time, if we could have stayed and nobody else had come along.'

'Will you come so far as the next room and take a cup of coffee, Mr. Penn?' said Rosalie when the little buzz of comment and remark had died away.

'You had better,' said Thornton, 'for you will get nothing stronger in this house to-night, I warn you.'

'What new freak have you taken up, Thornton?' said one of the guests with a laugh.

'No freak of mine,' he answered emphatically. 'What do you think was the last thing on which my Lady Sweetbrier laid her ban?'

'Freaks?' suggested Penn.

'No truly,' said Thornton, 'this being one. She has lately found out by great study and research, that wine was not meant to make glad the heart of man'——

'Nor oil to make his face to shine,' said Penn.

—'And therefore that men should not drink it,' said Thornton with a slight frown; 'and shall not, in her presence.'

'It is no *new* freak, at least,' said his sister in a rather low tone, while everybody else stood silent.

'No, that it is not,' said Penn Raynor; 'for I do assure you that when I went to Europe she would honour my departure with no better libation than the pump could furnish.'

'Threw cold water on the whole proceeding,' said Mr. Clinton.

'Yes she did,' replied Penn,—'just as if I shouldn't see enough on the way over.'

'Miss Clyde has probably studied those fine lines in Milton about singularity,' said one of the young men who had spoken but seldom. 'Familiar with them, are you not, Miss Clyde?'

'I hardly dare say I am familiar with all the fine lines in Milton,' she answered quietly, though something in the speaker's tone gave her cheeks a deep tinge. And Thornton's caught it.

'I remember them,' he said, 'if she does not—and she might have sat for the picture.

> "Against allurement, custom, and a world
> Offended; fearless of reproach and scorn,
> Or violence."

'That is my sister precisely, Mr. Talbot! Now Alie we are ready for your coffee—or for anything else you choose to give us.'

It was spoken with flashing eyes; and was heard by Rosalie with fluttering lip and heart, and in deep silence by the rest.

'Whatever Hebe pours out is bound to be nectar,' said Penn Raynor with a gay laugh. 'My dear Miss Clyde, if you will take my arm with half the pleasure with which I shall take your coffee, my share in the felicity of the evening will be filled up.'

Rosalie's coffee came as near being nectar that night as human coffee could; and so far as she was better worth looking at than the Queen of Spades—so far as her voice and words were truer and purer than any toast that would have been honoured with three times three—so far Thornton could not help being satisfied. And what with coffee and music, Mr. Penn's sallies and Rosalie's skill, the evening was lively enough to satisfy anybody.

CHAPTER XVII.

> The skipper he stood beside the helm,
> With his pipe in his mouth,
> And watched how the veering flaw did blow
> The smoke, now west, now south.—LONGFELLOW.

THE Fourth of July fell on Sunday, and of course all celebration thereof was deferred until the next day.

But when Monday morning had but faintly broken through the gloom of Sunday night, the still air was enlivened with a roar of guns from the Battery; and again from the Hook, and then from Staten Island, and then from every other point and place that was happy enough to have a gun. And the hills sent back a roar as their part of the celebration,—and if the younger members of society were not heard above all, it certainly was not their fault. And from every hotel and public building, from every fort, and from every mast that rose into the clear air about the harbour, there floated a host of flags, streamers, pendants and pennons, that for variety of colour outshone the very tints of the morning.

While the citizens were thus variously engaged with gunpowder and bunting—fire crackers or cannon, hoisting flags or pocket-handkerchiefs, according to their age and ability,—while independence was noisily declaring itself on shore, a British flotilla lay off the Hook, and New York harbour was blockaded.

As the morning came on, a little fishing smack lying in Mosquito Cove began to cast off her ropes and unfurl her sail, and then quietly stood out from the Cove into the open water. For figurehead, the little vessel carried an image which the skill of the carver had quite failed to render as clear as he meant it to be. A pipe was the most self-evident thing about it; but except that the figure was tall and gaunt instead of short and thick, it might as well have graced the Flying Dutchman as any other craft that sailed. The stern of the vessel, however, made all plain; for there was inscribed in jaunty black characters,

"The Yankee."

And if the craft was Yankee, so seemingly were her crew. Three men in buff caps and fishing dress were on her deck,—one attending strictly to the helm, though looking as if he attended to nothing; another lounging off on the bowsprit, by way of keeping a sharp look-out; and the third taking many an elaborate measurement of the deck, to the tune and time of first Washington's March and then a jig.

Midway on the deck of the little vessel were three remarkable passengers—a calf, a sheep, and a goose. The two quadrupeds were tied vis-à-vis, with however no check upon their feet or their vocal powers; while the goose, detained within a large and very open coop, thrust her head and neck through the bars and screamed and hissed incessantly,—most of all when the unoccupied one of the crew paused in his walk to enjoin silence.

'I say Mr. Percival!' said this man approaching the helmsman with an air of great disgust, 'what an unendurable noise those creatures make! If you could have got some sort of live stock now that don't feel obliged to say all they have on their minds at once—that had grown up in a Quaker barnyard, suppose—wouldn't it have served your turn just as well?'

'Quaker fetching up don't change *all* natures,' said the helmsman, with one of those quick looks which shewed him wide awake in the midst of his apparent sluggishness.

'No, that's a fact,' said the other man with a laugh. 'Though if you mean that all the unchanged ones are akin to these respectable animals, my opinion is about as far from yours as the Eagle down yonder is from the 74.'

The helmsman sent another quick glance down the bay, and then slowly moving the tiller so as to turn the vessel a little further off shore, he answered,

'We don't fly so far apart as that, Mr. Penn, not by two or three points. But you spoke of silence.'

'There's a delicate hint,' said the other, laughing again and pushing back his buff cap—to the disclosure of more ambrosially curled locks than fishermen are wont to wear. 'Never mind, Mr. Percival—the cackle of your live stock will either drown my voice or blend. When shall we be at the banks?'

'Late enough for a hot dinner first,' said Mr. Percival.

'Hot?' said Penn.

'Aye,' said the skipper.

'Curious what an amount of cold materials appear at such dinners,' said Mr. Penn. 'However—

"How sleep the brave who sink to rest"—

and I can swim like a cat too,—I have none of Falstaff's alacrity in sinking.' And he began his whistle and his walk again.

The sun was rising higher and higher, nor did the flood tide itself make swifter progress than the flood of sunlight.

Over the city with its tall spires and smoking chimneys,—over the green shores of Staten Island and New Jersey,—most of all upon the waters of the bay, did the sunlight come down and call forth beauty. The sails of the different vessels shone white and glistering, and the blue water sparkled and rippled and curled as if it were disporting itself. By means of a fresh north wind the little fishing smack went steadily on against the tide—courtesying along, and now and then dipping her bow that some fair wave might break over it. If the lookout had been a pilot he would but have said to the helmsman ' Thus ! '—so unerring a course did the Yankee's wooden pipe point out.

Sailing quietly along 'thus,' the little smack had come within full sight of a British sloop, the Eagle, then cruising about the hook in the capacity of tender to the Poictiers—a 74 gun ship and one of the blockading vessels. And as the Eagle's lookout did not belie her name, she was not long in discovering the little Yankee, and that her head was towards the fishing banks.

Swift sail made the Eagle ; but as her white canvass came flying towards the Yankee, that imperturbable craft neither fled nor fainted—neither ran in shore nor towards home, but went courtesying on as before, towards the banks.

' The fish bite well to-day,' remarked the skipper, when one of his keen looks had taken the latest news from the Eagle.

' Sizeable fish, too,' remarked Mr. Penn, who was now rocking lazily against the mast. ' Easy to catch and easy to land—hey, Mr. Percival ? '

' Thereafter as may be,' replied the skipper. ' But the race is not always to the swift. '

8

'On the wing, I declare she is,' said Mr. Penn after another pause. 'Swoops—don't she!'

Even as he spoke the Eagle rounded to and hailed, her brass howitzer glimmering in the sun.

'Smack Yankee, of New York,' returned the skipper.

'Live stock aboard?'

'Aye—' said the skipper, his words strongly borne out by Mr. Penn, who by a timely insinuation had greatly increased the wrath of the goose.

'What else?'

'Nothing.'

'All geese aboard?' was the next question, followed by a peal of laughter.

'Birds of a feather,' replied Mr. Percival with an unmoved face.

'Sail away then,' returned the man in the Eagle—'make a straight line for the Commodore, five miles down.'

'Aye, aye, sir,' said the skipper, putting up the helm as if to obey. This brought the smack alongside the Eagle, and not more than three yards off; but the next word came like a cannon-shot from the little vessel.

'Lawrence!'—shouted Mr. Percival; in a moment the Yankee's deck was covered with armed men. Pouring forth from the cabin and fore peak where they had been concealed, the little band, some thirty in number, saluted the Eagle with a fierce volley from their muskets, before which her startled crew sank back into the hold without even attempting to discharge their howitzer. The deck was clear.

'Cease firing!' called out Mr. Percival. And with that a man cautiously emerging from the hold came forth and struck the Eagle's colours. In another minute the stars and stripes stretched off upon the breeze, and Mr. Percival and Penn Raynor were on the deck.

It was no joyous thing to take possession of. The master's mate of the Poictiers lay there dead, and near him a midshipman mortally wounded; and of two marines that had fallen one was also dead. Nine other seamen and marines were in the hold. Briefly and gravely Mr. Percival made known his orders.

The Eagle changed her course again and stood for Sandy Hook. There the body of the mate was sent ashore and buried with military honours. The wounded men were carefully attended to; the prisoners secured: and the Eagle set sail for New York.

'I call this a decided improvement on the Yankee,' said Penn Raynor, as he stood by sailing-master Percival who had taken his old place at the helm. 'We shall make quicker time to New York too, by something.'

'At the Battery before sundown,' was the reply.

'But why the mischief, Mr. Percival, don't you use that howitzer for a speaking trumpet, and talk a little? The quiet of your vessel has been unheard of, all day. Talk of "darkness visible!"—Why don't you?'

The skipper's look for a moment betokened a stern reply, but he only said,

'Your cousin would not have asked that question, Mr. Penn.'

'Very likely,' said Penn; 'and the same might be said of all the questions I ever did ask, probably, but I like to have 'em answered nevertheless.'

'Go down in the cabin then,' said the sailing master briefly.

'What's in the cabin?' said Penn. '"Silence more profound?" I suppose if I went to the bottom of the sea it might be deeper yet.'

Again Mr. Percival looked at him, and then forward to

where the sloop's prow was cleaving the blue water; and half musingly half in answer, he said,

'I cannot fire rejoicings over my prisoners' heads, Mr. Penn, nor one gun to reach a vessel that is bound on her last voyage.'

'The prisoners' heads are intelligible,' said Penn, 'though I should think they might come on deck; but as for your poetical effusion, it might go on the shelf with all the Greek books I used at College. I say why not fire half a dozen shots?'

'And I tell you,' said the master, speaking with an emphasis that brought his voice down below its usual pitch, 'that there is one below who is nigh done with the world for ever,—do you want to roar into his ears that the world is all alive and kicking?'

'Is he so much hurt as that?' said Penn with a sobered face. 'You might have known that I didn't know what I was talking about, Mr. Percival.'

'I knew it,' said the skipper. Then in a quieter voice he added, 'I wish we had your cousin here, Mr. Penn.'

'Here!' said Penn—'Henry Raynor on a privateering expedition! Then will you see me chief confidant of the Great Mogul and adviser extraordinary to the Kham of Tartary.'

'He can fight,' said the skipper coolly. 'There was nót a better man of all that the Paul Jones took from that brig.'

'Fight—yes, with anybody,' said Penn, 'but what do you want of him now? There's no work for him now on board the Eagle, that I see.'

'You don't see far, Mr. Penn,' said the master. 'There is work for him—and not one of us is fit to do it—work below, to give that craft a chart and compass and set her off on the right tack. Think of that man dying there, and not a soul that can speak a word to him.'

'We shall be at the Battery by sundown, said' Penn, who preferred to choose his own thoughts.

'Aye,' said Mr. Percival, and the conversation ceased.

It blew lightly from the south now, and the Eagle skimmed along with a full sail and a motionless rudder. In the west the sun was rapidly nearing the Jersey hills, and light streaks and flakes of cloud bedecked the sky, and embroidered its blue with their own gold and rose colour. The bay caught the bright tints, and glowed and shone in competition; and on shore everything glittered that could, and those better things that could not, shone with a more refreshing light.

In a perfect bath of sunbeams the Eagle came up the bay; the American flag fluttering lightly out, and the English colours which hung too low for the breeze, drooping down and scarce stirring their folds. On and on—till she neared the Battery—and from the crowds assembled there went up a shout as from one voice.

Then every gun roared out its welcome, and the vessel was made fast and her captors sprang ashore; and quiet found but one resting-place—it was where the two wounded men were gently carried through the crowd, and their nine comrades came after as prisoners.

CHAPTER XVIII.

*Just so romances are, for what else
Is in them all but love and battles?
O' th' first of these we have no great matter
To treat of, but a world o' th' latter.*—HUDIBRAS.

'You don't mean to say, Tom Skiddy,' said Martha, as she stood leaning against the breakfast room door one morning with her hands behind her; 'you don't mean to tell me that he *never* comes in?'

'Never comes in—' replied Tom, who was assiduously dressing the line of knives and forks.

'Why I let him once myself—' said Martha with a very triumphant twist of her mouth. 'Now what do you say to that, Tom Skiddy?'

'I say he never comes in, Martha Jumps. I don't say he never *did* come in, in the course of his existence—I've let him in myself, maybe two or three times; but he never *does* come in,—not this whole summer.'

'And so many times as Hulda's been there, too,' said Martha parenthetically.

'Just brings her up the steps and sets her down in the hall,' said Tom, 'and then off he goes before you can say Jack Robinson.'

''Taint likely he'd stop if you did get it out, seeing it

aint his name,' observed Martha; 'so that's not much to the point.'

'Everything needn't be pointed in this world,' said Tom dryly.

'That's lucky,' said Martha,—''cause some things don't take one so well as some others.'

And Martha swayed herself and the door pleasantly back and forth, while Tom's motions grew dignified.

'Well that is queer, aint it?' said Miss Jumps at length. 'Now Tom, you're cute enough sometimes—what's the sense of it?'

'This is one of the other times,' said Tom, as he gave the salt-cellars a composing little shake and set them right and left in their places.

'O—that's it,' said Martha. 'But after all it aint worth while to keep one's sense for too uncommon occurrences; and I tell you I can't stay but a minute and a quarter, so say on, —what's the use of a man's keeping out when he's dying to come in?'

'He's mighty tenacitous of life then,' said Tom.

'Don't tell me!' said Martha impatiently. 'I know! so do you.'

'I know one thing,' said Tom,—'I wish Miss Rosalie 'd get sick.' And Tom shook his head and went into the pantry for mats.

'What are you up to, Tom Skiddy?' said Martha admiringly.

'I should be up to something—seeing where I come from,' said Tom.

'Where was that?' said Martha, 'Egypt?'

Tom signified that he was a chip of the true Charter Oak.

'Well, that's saying something for you, if it aint for

Connecticut,' observed Martha. 'Then it was some one else came out of the Phœnix's ash-pan. After all, Connecticut aint the biggest state in the United,—not by several.'

'And a pint of pippins aint so large as a bushel of lady apples,' said Tom shortly.

'Lady apples don't grow in Connecticut, then?' said Martha with a face of grave inquiry.

'Aint much need—' said Tom. 'The market's run down with 'em from other places.'

'The market 'll bear up under 'em this some time yet,' said Martha—'the good ones. But I say, Tom Skiddy— what would you do suppos'n Miss Rosalie should take sick?'

'Just tell him—I'd fetch him in quick enough.'

'Do you s'pose he'd come?' said Martha.

'I guess likely,' said Tom. 'He'd be took all of a sudden, you see, and wouldn't stop to think.'

'It's a nice thing to amuse yourself,' said Martha as she moved meditatively away, 'but it aint best to be *too* mischievous, Tom Skiddy.'

Tom was right.

Often as little Hulda spent the day at the 'Quakerage,' as Thornton called it; often as her friend brought her home; he never came further than the hall door. And though her little hand and voice made many an effort to bring him in, they won nothing beyond a smile and a kiss, or a kind-spoken 'Not to-day.'

Meanwhile the year went on, and the war with its varying fortune traversed sea and land. The English papers set forth that "the American navy must be annihilated," "the turbulent inhabitants must be tamed," and "the Americans beaten into submission;" and nevertheless the papers on this side the sea continued to chronicle such items as these:

"The privateer Paul Jones, of this port, was spoken on

the 16th April, having in her company the British ship Lord Sidmouth, her prize, with a valuable cargo, and $80,000 in specie."

"The privateer Comet, of Baltimore, fell in with an English ship, brig, and schooner, under convoy of a Portuguese brig of 16 guns, which she engaged, and captured all three in less than an hour."

And then came the less pleasant intelligence, "The Lord Sidmouth, prize to the privateer Paul Jones, was recaptured on Sunday afternoon within Gull light, near New London, by the British frigate Orpheus. On the same day the Orpheus captured two other American ships."

But as the papers said again,—

"The spirit of our transatlantic brethren, in conformity with the spirit of true republicanism, rises with every succeeding miscarriage and defeat."

Then came the battles of Lake Erie, and of the Thames; and the American papers found full employment for all their exclamation points.

One Saturday evening, late in October, the city was in an unusual state of murmur and commotion,—tea-time seemed to have no power to send people home; and night fell on even busier streets than the day had seen. Busy tongues and busy feet kept pace with each other, and the city seemed to have poured itself out into the chief thoroughfares. And as the great wave of people rolled steadily on and down, the upper part of the city became more and more deserted; and once off the pavements, the watchman and his sonorous cry of 'All's well!' were the most notable subjects of attention.

No city stir had reached the 'Quakerage,'—indeed a bustling crowd could hardly abide there, but would, like a swarm of bees, seek some rougher place whereon to cling

And if silence reigned without, and swayed her sceptre over tree and bush, her rule was no less complete within. There was talk enough in the kitchen, but the quiet 'thee' and 'thou,' 'nay' and 'yea, verily,' of Rachel and her companions, sent forth no more than a gentle murmur which had rather a lullaby effect. And up-stairs the wood snapped and crackled audibly enough to attest the stillness. Whatever Mr. Penn had done with himself, he was not there; and Mr. Henry sat writing, and his mother with her usual busy play of knitting-needles. The cat dozed before the fire, sending forth occasional long and sleepy purrs as if they scarce paid for the trouble; now and then getting up to take a dreamy survey of his master or mistress, and then curling down again, as by the sheer force of necessity.

Nor were those green eyes the only ones that took note of Mr. Henry. His mother looked at him often in the slight pauses of her work: when a needle was knit off, or the heel finished, or when the turn came in knitting the gore. He looked tired she thought, and so he did, and was; being one of those spirits so absolutely at rest within themselves that their energies work hard for other people,—and then need from still others, rest and refreshment.

'Henry,' said the quakeress at length, 'move thy head further to the right, that I may see thee.'

He smiled as he complied, and said,

'Well, mother?'

'I thought to see if the shadow on thine eyes came only from the lamp,' she answered.

'There is no undue shade upon them now, is there mother?'

'Nay,' said the quakeress, though her look was a little wistful,—'truly I think there is nothing undue about thee.' But she eyed him still; and he threw down his pen and came and took part of her ample footstool.

'If I interfere with your feet, mother, you can put them on my lap. Are you troubling yourself about me?'

'I would I could remove all trouble from thee, dear,' she said.

'That would not be well for me—since it is not done,' he answered gently. 'Why mother, have you forgot your favourite saying, "patience reacheth all"?'

The quakeress bent down, and stroking both hands across his forehead she kissed it two or three times.

'Go back to thy work, dear child,' she said, 'and surely the Lord is with thee in all that thou doest. Go back, Henry—I will not have thee sit here—thou art a strong reproof to me.'

He went as she bade him, but wrote less steadily than before; breaking off now and then to talk or ask some question, until his letters were done and ready for sealing. The taper was lit and the melted wax was just in a right state for the first letter, when there came a rush through the house——it might have been the wind, but it was only Mr. Penn.

Slam went the door, whirl went the table an inch or two from its place, and down went Mrs. Raynor's ball of yarn upon the cat, ere Mr. Penn had the floor to his satisfaction and could give utterance to his sentiments.

'"United States Brig Niagara,"' he began—'" off the Western Sister, head of Lake Erie, Sept. 10, 1813, 4 P. M.

'" Dear General—We have met the enemy—and they are ours. Two ships, two brigs, one schooner, and one sloop. Yours, with great respect and esteem, O. H. PERRY."'

His breath quite spent with the various exclamation points which were introduced to suit his fancy, Mr. Penn stood still to take the effect of his intrusion.

Mr. Henry looked up at him for a moment with some

gravity; and then looking down again with a smile which if not sympathetic was at least kindly, he threw aside the wrapper on which the melted wax had dropped in the wrong place, took another and went on sealing his letters. The quakeress felt herself more aggrieved.

'Whom dost thou respect and esteem?' she inquired with some severity.

'What ma'am?' said Penn. 'Harry!—just look at that!'

For the knight of Malta, being aroused by the summary descent of the ball upon his nose, immediately rolled over upon his back, and seizing the intruder in both paws inflicted a perfect battery of kicks with his hind feet; biting it from time to time and then kicking the harder. Nor did the rapid unwinding of the yarn and the partial entanglement to which the knight found himself subjected, at all mitigate his wrath.

'Thou art as unmannerly as the cat,' said Mrs. Raynor, while Penn testified his delight at the feline antics by several of his own. But Mr. Henry stooped down, and bringing his fingers into ticklish contact with the back of the cat's head, so distracted his attention that the ball was allowed to roll away.

'How much mischief thee does contrive to do in the course of the year, Penn,' said the quakeress.

'In a small way, ma'am,' said her nephew as he picked up the ball and presented it.

'But how would thee like to knit with thy yarn all wet?' said Mrs. Raynor, beginning to wind and finding her own in that condition.

'I think I should like it decidedly, if I'd been knitting dry yarn all my life,' replied Mr. Penn. 'But how *can* you be sitting here! Harry, have you seen the illuminations?'

'I have not been out of the house since sundown.'

'Then come now—ah do!' said his cousin. 'Let's go and take Miss Clyde to see them—will you?'

'No,' said Mr. Raynor.

'But why not? you are just hindering my pleasure.'

'I do not hinder your taking anybody you like, except myself, Penn.'

'I'm not sure that she'd go with me, though,' said Penn. 'However, I can try. And you had much better come too —I tell you they're worth seeing. So reconsider the matter and come.'

Penn went, and Mr. Raynor somewhat thoughtfully laid his letters together, then took them again and retouched the directions.

'Does thee think Rosalie will go with that boy?' said the quakeress.

'I do not know indeed, mother.'

'Art thou going out thyself?'

'So far as the post-office—perhaps nowhere else.'

'Thee does not care for these silly shows, Henry?' said the quakeress with a half doubtful look at her son.

He smiled as he answered,

'I care a good deal for the occasion, mother—not so much for the show.'

'Thee would have made a beautiful Friend!' said his mother, with another look that was a little regretful at the calm, dignified face before her. 'It is the only thing about thee that I cannot understand.'

He did not attempt to explain it, though for a moment the bright play of eye and mouth half saved him the trouble; but he said,

'I will be as good a friend as I can in this dress, mother —and for the rest, thee does not wish I should give thee any other name than that?'

She answered his smile—as anybody must—and he left the room.

Meanwhile Mr. Penn presented himself to the assembled gaze of Rosalie, Thornton, and Dr. Buffem; for if the old Doctor felt himself in want of tea when in Rosalie's neighbourhood, he often went to get it from her hand,—or as Thornton declared, for the express purpose of snubbing him if he was at home and finding it out if he was not. Therefore in the expectation of being snubbed, Mr. Clyde was rarely very gracious, and was really glad on the present occasion to have Penn come in and go shares with him.

'I hope you have not been out yet, Miss Clyde?' said Penn—'I mean to see the illuminations?'

No, Miss Clyde had not.

'Because in that case,' said Penn, 'I have come to offer my poor services. I tried to bring better ones and couldn't get them.'

'Where is your cousin to-night, Mr. Penn?' said the Doctor.

'Writing love-letters, I should think by the quantity,' said Penn. 'He didn't give me a chance to try the quality.'

'The wiser man he,' said the Doctor. 'And so you have not been out, Miss Rosalie? Must go, my dear——

> "Unmuffle, ye fair stars, and thou fair moon,
> That wont'st to love the traveller's benison"——

What would the illumination be without you?'

'The moon is not favourable to illuminations, sir,' said Rosalie.

'Depends upon what sort of a moon it is,' said the Doctor. 'I'd risk such a planet anywhere. And there are some transparencies about you, too. How many enemies do you suppose now you'll meet in the streets to-night?'

'Enemies to me as a moon?' said Rosalie smiling—'all the illuminators I suspect, and perhaps some other people.'

'Have a care!' said the Doctor with a threatening gesture of his finger. 'Don't you exasperate me. I mean enemies on Commodore Perry's principle——"We have met the enemy—and they are ours!" What do you think of that?'

The gentlemen laughed, but Rosalie did not put her thoughts into words.

'By the way!' said the Doctor—'I should think you'd have enemies in earnest! What's this I heard about you the other day?'

'I have not the least idea,' said Rosalie.

The Doctor finished his cup of tea, and then rising from the table and planting himself upon the hearth rug, he repeated with many a flourish:

> "Though we eat little flesh and drink no wine,
> Yet let's be merry: we'll have tea and toast;
> Custards for supper, and an endless host
> Of syllabubs and jellies and mince pies,
> And other such lady-like luxuries,—
> Feasting on which we will philosophize."

'Goodnight Miss Rosalie—you've been the death of two of my patients already, keeping me here so long. Mr. Penn—if anything happens to the moon to-night I'll be the death of you—or as I don't fight duels I'll turn you over to your cousin. Captain Thornton—your most obedient!'

'What a——' said Thornton, and put the rest in his teacup.

'Yes, how much we are losing,' said Penn.

'Get ready, do!' said Thornton impatiently, 'and we will all go together.' And upon that promise Rosalie went.

It was a pretty thing to walk through the rows of gleaming houses, and to observe the variety wrought by the taste the economy, or the patriotism of their owners. Some fronts were lighted from garret to cellar—the house looking out with all its eyes, and those bright ones, upon the thronged streets. And now and then might be seen a dwelling that was seemingly the abode of little beside a regard for the world's opinion; and a few groans once in a while, shewed that opinion to be unappeased. The public buildings displayed transparencies as well as lights.

'Look, Miss Clyde!' Penn Raynor exclaimed, as they came near the City Hall; 'do you see that window with Lake Erie and the fleets?—isn't it capital! And here in this other are Lawrence's last words, poor fellow!—" Don't give up the ship!"—Perry had that written on his flag before the battle. And Tammany Hall has got Perry himself, changing his ship in the very thick of it.'

The transparencies shone forth, and the spectators cheered, and the different national airs floated sweetly down from the City Hall on the night wind, as drummers and all the sons of Æolus did their best; as Rosalie with her two supporters moved slowly down to get a better view of the Park Theatre. It was brilliant with lights and transparencies,—the fight between the Hornet and Peacock, among others; and Commodore Perry's concise announcement,

"We have met the enemy—and they are ours."

'Miss Clyde,' said Penn Raynor, 'you must let go of me if you please—I can't stand that,—and I really shouldn't like to hurrah with a lady on my arm. But if they shout again I must.'

Rosalie laughed and released him, then and afterwards, whenever his feelings required; and would gladly have let him go altogether that she might be the more sure of Thornton. He spoke from time to time with some of his friends, but gave no signs of joining them until Penn had come back from a final cheer for Commodore Perry.

'Will that last you till you get home, Penn?' he inquired.

'Probably,' said Mr. Penn—'unless I meet Perry himself—or Harrison.'

'Then I shall leave my sister in your charge,' said Thornton. But as he felt her hand involuntarily take closer hold of his arm, Thornton added with a half apologetic tone,

'I shall be home soon, Alie—before you are asleep, I dare say.'

She could only let him go—but so sorrowful were the thoughts sent after him, that not for some minutes did she remember the poor protection in which she was left. It was first brought to mind, when as Mr. Penn's eyes were engaged with the transparencies, the crowd and she came in rather rough contact. She spoke at once,

'You see what you have brought upon yourself, Mr. Penn,—I must take you away from Commodore Perry, and you must take me home.'

'With the greatest pleasure!' said Penn, who never forgot his good nature,—'that is if I can—the crowd is so thick. Hadn't you better go down as far as the City Hotel?'

'No I think not.'

'What made me speak of it,' said Penn, as they turned and began to walk up Broadway, 'the people are all going down just now, and you'd find it easier. I'm afraid it will be hard work for you to get along this way.'

It was rather hard work, and once Rosalie was nearly borne back by the down tide of population; when her other hand was taken and put on somebody's arm, and a quiet 'good evening, Miss Rosalie,' announced Mr. Raynor. If Miss Rosalie felt relief, so did Mr. Penn.

'It is the most remarkable thing in the world, Harry, that you always come just when I want you.'

'It was not *because* you wanted me, in this case,' said his cousin.

'No, very likely not,' said Penn, 'but a bright idea has just come into my head; and I believe there'll be time for it yet, if Miss Clyde will only let me leave her with you—she has so little way to go now.'

'She will let you with pleasure,' said Mr. Raynor.

'I dare say she will—she was always so good,' said Penn; and darting off without more ado, he left Rosalie to wonder that one man's way through the world should be so different from another's,—the crowd touched her no more that night.

'Do you know, Miss Rosalie,' said Mr. Raynor, as he stood with his hand on the bell, 'that in this good city you need better protection on some nights than on others?'

'Yes,' she said quickly, 'but—' and then checking herself, she simply added, 'I know it.'

Mr. Raynor looked at her for a moment—for every pane of glass in the whole house gave forth light; but as if he guessed what she did not tell him he asked no further questions. The bell was rung and they parted.

When Mr. Raynor reached his own home, he found that Mr. Penn had employed his spare time in getting candles and putting them in every window that he dared appropriate.

His own rooms and Mr. Henry's and all that belonged to nobody in particular—the garret—even the dining room had Mr. Penn enlivened to the extent of his power; and the house looked like a hotel of patriotism and treason. But the candles burned as if there had been never a quaker nor a traitor in the whole world.

CHAPTER XIX.

The neighbourhood were at their wits end, to consider what would be the issue.—L'ESTRANGE.

'ARE the Clydes coming to-night, mamma?' said Miss Clinton, as she took a last elaborate back and front view of herself.

'Yes, my dear—I suppose so—I invited them of course.'

'But I mean are they *coming*—what *does* ail the neck of this dress?'

'Nothing at all.'

'Nothing at all! when it twists round and puckers—'

'When you twist round.'

'When I don't. And just see mamma—the waist is a great deal too long.'

'I don't perceive it, indeed.'

'Because you don't look, ma'am. Let me shew you—— where's a card—now what do you think of that?—two inches below the sleeve, mamma!'

'I think my dear, that your grandmother would have thought two inches below the sleeve was no waist at all.'

'Very likely ma'am, but the old lady didn't know everything. What makes you think the Clydes will come? They might have forgotten to send regrets.'

'I saw Mr. Clyde in the street to-day, and he said he should certainly come and bring his sister.'

'I should think he might, it will be such a small party. But it's a dreadful thing to be so long out of society! one grows so shockingly old. Why mamma, she must be more than twenty.'

'Well my dear, so must you, if you live long enough.'

'My dear ma'am what things you do always say to bring down one's spirits!—Just like Marion Arnet,—she told me the other day——By the by she's just as much off as ever with Thornton Clyde.'

'Is that what she told you?'

'La no, mamma—what an idea! But I mean there's not the least prospect of their ever making it up.' And Miss Clinton surveyed herself in the glass with much complacency.

'I can't conceive what concern it is of yours, my dear.'

'No ma'am—perhaps not,—but one likes to talk.'

'I think however that one should talk goodnaturedly, when one can,' said Mrs. Clinton, as she got up and peeped over her daughter's shoulder. 'Dear me—I look pale tonight! How should you like to have such remarks made about you, my dear?'

'Dear mamma!—as if I ever, ever could be such a fool! But Rosalie never does make disagreeable speeches, so I'm quite willing she should come; especially as she's so grave now and quiet. I suppose her engrossing power can hardly have survived these two years of seclusion.'

Miss Clinton wondered *how* it had survived, when she saw Rosalie enter the room and perceived that the engrossing power was in full force. It was only natural she tried to persuade herself, that people should crowd about one whom they had seen but seldom for a year or two; but a mere greeting did not seem to content them, and there were as many new as old friends in the circle that soon formed about Miss Clyde. Only over one person she seemed to have lost her power. Mr. Raynor went up and paid his respects, and came away again,—therefore, as Miss Clinton remarked to herself, ' there could have been nothing in *that*.' The power had not descended to her, however, for he attached himself perseveringly to two old ladies; and was deep in a discussion upon the state of the roads, the streets, and the atmosphere, and just having his juvenile inexperience enlightened on the subject of hailstorms, when his fair hostess claimed his attention.

' Mr. Raynor, doesn't it seem very dull to you here, after Paris ? '

' As the daylight after gas.'

' Well, that is pretty bad. Things look beautiful by gaslight, don't you think so ? '

' Beautiful ?—some things,' said the gentleman, whose eye had made a momentary excursion after his thoughts. ' But candlelight is in general thought more becoming Miss Clinton.'

' Do you think so? The other room is lighted with candles—let us go in there and see if the people look different.'

' By what rule of comparison will you judge of different people by different lights ? ' said Mr. Raynor, as he obediently gave the lady his arm.

' O we can compare each other,' said Miss Clinton laughing. ' But candles must be the most becoming, as you say, for all the oldest people have got in here to have the benefit of it.'

He looked grave and she changed the subject.

' How well Miss Clyde looks to-night—only rather pale.'

' What shade of colour puts a lady beyond the charge of paleness ? '

'O I don't know—but she keeps herself so shut up.'

'I have reason to believe that you are mistaken there, Miss Clinton. I have certainly received the impression that Miss Clyde walks a great deal.'

'What *is* mamma whispering about?' said Miss Clinton as they slowly paced back again. 'Wanting Miss Clyde to sing—and she won't, or don't—which is it? Miss Arnet will—no she don't choose, I know from her look.'

'Will you sing?' inquired Mr. Raynor, who really liked his companion better at the piano than anywhere else.

'O not for anything—there, some one else is going. And now Miss Clyde has got away to talk to Mrs. Delt. I would give the world for her coolness and self-possession—I never *could* cross a room alone.'

'Will you cross it with me, then?' said Penn Raynor presenting himself. 'Here am I Miss Clinton—at your service,—totally disengaged because nobody will take the trouble to engage me.'

'But I am not disengaged—' said Miss Clinton.

'Mrs. Clinton says,' pursued Penn, 'that she shall call upon Harry next,—so there's a decided opening.'

'Then we will walk over to the piano together,' said the lady, 'and secure a good place.'

'Aye, take my arm too,' said Penn. 'Just as well, you know Miss Clinton—only the old line about two strings to your bow, *renversé*—as we used to say in Paris.'

'As *we* used to say,' said his cousin smiling.

'O deuce take it Harry—you're so precise,—one word that you don't understand is as good as another. But I say how charming Miss Clyde looks—and everybody.'

'Mr. Penn is quite impartial in his admiration,' said Miss Clinton.

'Always was,' said Penn. 'I'm a sort of a bee—or a

BEES AND BUTTERFLIES.

butterfly—I declare I don't know which, but I guess it's the butterfly. I wonder why people call bees so industrious? Butterflies go round just as much, only they dress up for the occasion and go by the force of sunshine. Now the bees seem moved by the mere power of business—or buzziness.'

'You've been studying natural history, Mr. Penn,' said Miss Clinton laughing.

'O yes—in the Champs Elysées,—good place that to study butterflies. Especially with a bee along to keep you in order. Harry is a nice bee though—he never cries hum.'

'And never stings, I hope?' said Miss Clinton insinuatingly.

'Ah there's a question. But he don't plunge his sting so far in that you can't get it out,—and I suppose he'd tell you it was for your especial benefit, then.'

'You would think Penn spoke from experience,' said Mr. Raynor, 'but I assure you he is cased in armour of proof. Too nimble moreover, and too skilled in intricate passages. Like the bee-moth—only not so mischievous.'

'Too bad that, I declare,' said Penn. 'I shall not rest now till I have executed some desperate piece of mischief. Do you remember Harry how I carried off Miss Clyde's bouquet once?'

'Yes,' said his cousin rather gloomily.

'Carried it off? how?' said Miss Clinton. 'I shall hold mine very fast.'

Penn went into some laughing threats concerning the bouquet, and his cousin as if old recollections had taken off present restraint, looked over the heads about him with very little care whether he were watched or not.

It was a wearisome thing, he thought, to see her sitting there and not to be allowed to go and talk to her,—to have been so long in the same room and yet to have had only the greeting of a common acquaintance;—nor quite that, for it had been graver and more quickly ended; yet he would not have changed it for one of a class. In a very abstracted state of mind he obeyed Mrs. Clinton's call to the piano, and sang.

> 'I have seen what the world calls rich and rare,
>   Beyond the broad ocean's foam;
> But the brightest of all that met me there,
>   Was the vision of one at home.
> A flower! a flower!—how fair it bloomed!
>   I had never seen such before,—
> And my fancy the full belief assumed,
>   That the world could show no more.
>
> 'I dreamed a dream as I passed along—
>   A dream, sweet vision! of thee.
> Might so perfect a thing to me belong,
>   Then perfect my life would be.
> The flower, the flower—I saw it droop!—
>   For a bitter wind swept by.
> But it twined itself with a weaker group,
>   And no power to take had I.
>
> 'The dream is broken—the hope is flown,—
>   Or held by a faint 'perchance;'
> And the joy of that home is fainter grown
>   Which I thought she would enhance.
> The flower, the flower!—it bloometh yet,—
>   Grows sweeter—I know not how!
> But the beauty on which my love was set,
>   Hath my heart's deep reverence now.
>
> 'That wish of my life, it doth not fade—
>   My life and it are one.
> Yet well could I rest amid the shade,
>   Were my flower but in the sun.

> My flower! my flower! thy bended head
>   Is dearer than worlds to me.
> I would give up life and take death instead,
>   My flower's strong shield to be!'

The song was not much in itself, certainly; but there was a power in the fine voice and the deep feeling and expression with which every word was given, that held the listeners motionless; and from end to end of the still room was the song heard. It was not till the voice ceased, and the singer had played a few soft notes that might almost have been involuntary—so exactly did they carry out the spirit of the song; that the ladies recollected their pocket-handkerchiefs, and Penn Raynor exclaimed,

'Who upon earth's that, Harry?'

'Who upon earth is what?' said his cousin striking another chord.

'Yes, did you ever know her, Mr. Raynor?' said the lady of the house.

'Did I ever know whom, ma'am?' he said half turning about.

'Why this lady of the song. There's no description given of her, either—I don't know how it is—but it is all so life-like that I feel as if I must have seen her. Is there really such a flower in the world?'

It was with a singular smile that he heard her—a smile that to any keen eye would have said enough. But lightly touching the keys again, his answer was given with perfect gravity.

'If there be, Mrs. Clinton, you will find it in the genus woman, and in that species where Nature and Christianity have both done their best.'

'O I have no doubt Mr. Raynor knows the original,' said Miss Arnet. 'He always had a preoccupied air,—as if

9

he were saying to himself, "I have seen better faces in my time, than stand on any shoulders that I see before me at this instant."'

'True—at this instant,' said Mr. Raynor looking down at the keys. 'But what a character to give of me!'

'Deserved—' said Miss Arnet.

'By your favour, no,' said he rousing himself. 'In the first place, I am *not* always thinking of ladies' faces, heterodox as that may seem. And in the second—'

'No second to that, I beg.'

'But it's very provoking to be made to cry over a rival beauty,' said Miss Clinton.

'Rival beauties?' said Mr. Raynor. 'Did you ever hear of a belle that was rivalled by a wild flower?'.

'No—did you?'

'A belle thought to try the matter once, so she made a great effort and went to take a walk in the country.'

'What slander!' said two or three indignant voices.

'But do let him go on,' said Miss Arnet.

'Well—as story-tellers say—the lady went into the woods, with her hoop and her lace ruffles and her diamonds and her white gloves'—

'Don't you think diamonds and white gloves pretty?' interrupted Miss Clinton.

'Certainly—so did this lady. She went on, expecting to make a great impression upon her rivals; but the difficulty was to find them. First she perceived the Columbines. But she didn't feel as if they were rivals, though they were all red and yellow like herself'—

'You are atrocious!'

'As to her dress, of course—but they hung down their heads and she thought the world was wide enough for her and the Columbines too. Their hoops were so small, and they were such good little things that nodded to everybody.'

'I am not a good little thing, that's one comfort,' said Miss Arnet.

'The lady was puzzled to find a rival. The Dandelions were pretty, but common, and low bred; and the Anemones had 'no complexion,'—any man would be out of his senses to look at such a piece of wax-work.'

The ladies exchanged glances.

'But at length she came to the violet, and there she stood a long time. Was the violet a rival? She tried her by all the tests. She walked before her and threw her into the shade—the violet looked fairer than ever, and just as good-natured. That was not like a rival. But then some people who came by looked first at the violet—and that was. At last she inquired anxiously if the violet was invited to Mrs. Peony's ball of next week. But the violet said she had never been to a ball and did not even know Mrs. Peony by sight. That settled the matter, she could never be a belle. So our friend called her a sweet little creature, and reached home with but one source of dissatisfaction.'

'What was that?' eagerly exclaimed the circle, closing about Mr. Raynor as he sat on the music stool.

'She had forgotten to ask where the violet bought her perfume.'

'O you horrid man!' said Miss Clinton; and 'you are too bad!'—'you are perfectly scandalous!' echoed about.

'The ladies have been so much interested in the story,' said Thornton Clyde, 'that they have forgotten to find out why Mr. Raynor took them into the woods.'

'You are in no doubt on the subject, Mr. Clyde?' said the person spoken of, as he rose and passed through their circle.

'I am in no doubt on several subjects,' said Thornton dryly. 'Yet now I think of it, Mr. Raynor, why was not the rose your chosen subject of comparison?'

'Should a princess by the popular vote dare compare herself with a queen in her own right?' said Mr. Raynor.

'And does the queen never have the popular vote?' said Thornton.

'Sometimes—' Mr. Raynor said, with a glance at the court just then holden by Rosalie. But he himself turned and went into the next room, merely pausing to shake hands with Dr. Buffem, who now made his appearance.

'A pretty pass things have come to!' said the Doctor, walking straight up to the court. 'Mrs. Clinton—good evening! Miss Clinton—your humble servant! A pretty pass things have come to! A hedge-row of boys round a lady and never a gateway for a man to get through. I'll make a clearance!—Miss Rosalie—enchanting princess—"Queen of my soul! Light of my eyes!"—shall I rescue you from your enchanted ring?—shall I send them about their business?—though indeed my mind misgives me they have none. "To men addicted to delights, business is an interruption."'

'The doctor is personifying business to-night then,' said one of the gentlemen who had been set aside.

'What then?' said the doctor. 'I tell you I sha'n't quit the ring these twenty years.'

'You'll have a chance to carry everybody off in that time, doctor,' said Penn.

'Everybody?' said the doctor.

'"Fair Bessie Bell I lo'ed yestreen,
    And thought I ne'er could alter;
But Mary Gray's twa pawky een,
    They gar my fancy falter."

'Now my dear, take my arm, and let us have a comfortable little walk. Now how do you get on at home—and what rambles has the Sister of Charity been taking lately? Did you hear of the cat that fell out of a two story window yesterday?'

'No indeed,' said Rosalie smiling.

'Ah that was a great case!' said the doctor gravely—'a great case! Fell on her feet you know of course, and all that, but must have deranged the circulation. I said it must have interfered with the ordinary course of things very much, but some people thought not. But the cat has not spoken since.'

'Nor mewed?' said Rosalie.

'You hush!' said the doctor, 'and don't put yourself into a consultation. But what have you been about? and how are the pets at home? One of 'em I see looks flourishing.'

'Yes, they are both very well.'

'And their sister aint.—Don't tell me—I know—I read you like a book. Let me feel your pulse.—That's it—strong enough, but a little fluttering. I read you just like a dictionary, my dear—words and definitions. Now Miss Rosalie, I'm going to prescribe for you; and do you mind and follow orders. *A large dose of care for yourself, taken night and morning in a little less care for other people.*'

'That last is a hard medicine to get, sir.'

'Not a bit of it—ask anybody, and they'll give you as much as you want. And see here—look up at me—*don't you wash it down with anything.* Shake it down, if you like, to the tune of a hop or two—and season with "Quips, and pranks and wreathed smiles."'

'Not such a one as that!—I declare you are flying in

the face of my prescription and me together. I'll fix you!—wait till I find one of my assistants!—'

'Do you condescend to keep any, sir?' said Rosalie, as the doctor began to walk her about the room in a somewhat rummaging style.

'The secret society of medicine, my dear, has its officers. You wait—not long neither. Now,' said Dr. Buffem, pushing quietly through a narrow opening, and indicating with his thumb one particular velvet collar; 'now there is one that I always employ for Miss Clinton, but that won't do for you. I must find an engraving, or a book—or a bookworm!' he said, bringing Rosalie with a short turn into the library. 'Friend Henry, what art thou about?'

Mr. Raynor started and turned round from the table where he stood.

'Not studying that print?' said the doctor.

'Not at all.'

'No I thought not. Well here is one of my patients whom I want to leave in your hands—otherwise on your arm,—"for I must quit the busy haunts of men."—Fact, and no fib, Miss Rosalie—I declare your eye is as good as a policeman! Well Mr. Henry—are you going to do as I bid you? or must I find somebody else?'

'And how came Miss Clyde to be under your care, sir?' said Mr. Raynor, when the proposed transfer had been made.

'How came she to be under my care?—why because I took charge of her. Anything to say against it? What the deuce do you mean by asking such a question, sir?'

'Patients usually seek the doctor,' said Mr. Raynor with a slight smile.

'She never does,' said Dr. Buffem. 'Great peculiarity in her case! I've been prescribing for her to-night.

'And the prescription?'

'A trifle, a trifle—' said the doctor. 'A little good sense and insensibility.

> '"Sound sleep by night; study and ease
> Together mixed; sweet recreation,
> And innocence which most doth please
> With meditation."'

And with a profound flourish the doctor moved off.

Mr. Raynor began quietly to turn over the engravings and to comment upon them, until his companion looked up and answered; and then he said,

'That is a most admirable prescription—if it be made up like Bunyan's, with 'a promise or two.''

'They are all that I need to take.'

'No—not quite,' he said, establishing her hand upon his arm, and taking her away from the eyes and tongues of several people who seemed inclined to 'fall in' and make a circle.

'What then?' said Rosalie, trying to rouse herself and shake off the influence of two or three of the evening's events. 'Sound sleep I do take, enough of it, and study too; though sometimes to be sure of a rather juvenile sort—teaching Hulda and not myself. But I often make longer and deeper excursions and incursions alone. What more do I need?'

'I could easier shew you than tell you,' he said with a smile. 'My ideas on the subject can never be put in words—and you could never follow them. Such care as fresh air and sunshine take of the flowers,—as you of Hulda,—such care as I would take of the most precious thing in the world, if I had it. And after all that tells you nothing.'

She thought it told her a good deal too much, and though words fluttered to her lips they came not forth.

'Are you tired of walking about?' Mr. Raynor said in the same quiet way. 'I will find you a seat in the neighbourhood of what Dr. Buffem might call 'sweet recreation,'—here in the midst of geraniums and myrtles and your namesakes, the roses. What do you think of these pretty painted faces, and how would you characterise them?'

'The geraniums? As beautiful and showy, but I think not very loveable. Yet all the power they have is in exercise—there are no wasted advantages,—they have made the most of themselves.'

'Yes, and have advanced steadily to perfection. Then here is the myrtle,—of most rare beauty and purity and exquisiteness—if one may use the word. Exceeding sweet too, and elegant in a high degree. But its sweetness you must seek out for yourself,—the common course of things does not call it forth. For all but the eye's perception, the greenhouse were as sweet without its myrtle. And among flowers as among characters, the strongest power of attraction is that involuntary sweetness which some few breathe forth.

'I will not trust myself to speak of the roses,' he said presently, 'but you must remember that I watch with jealous eyes the care you bestow upon mine.'

'Deep in the flowers!' said Penn Raynor coming up to them. 'Miss Clyde, Harry's love for roses has lately become what *I* call a passion.'

'Eye deep or thought deep?' said Thornton who had followed.

'My thought and eye have kept sufficiently close company,' said Mr. Raynor.

Thornton looked at him and then at his sister.

'Rosalie, I thought you wanted to go home so early.'

'Is it late?' she said, rising quick and taking his arm.

'Late for you, little precision.'

'But she cannot go yet!' exclaimed Penn. 'You must take her into the supper room, first.'

'I will have that pleasure myself,' said Mr. Raynor.

And Thornton had no resource but to let him have it, and Rosalie too, for the time.

CHAPTER XX.

> Nay, an' I take the humour of a thing once,
> I am like your tailor's needle, I go through.—BEN JONSON.

WINTER and night reigned together; but while the night looked down with steady gaze upon the pranks of her colleague, winter ran on in his career, and caught nothing of her still influence. The wind as it whirled about the house drew whatever it could lay hands on into the same giddy dance; and tried every casement, and planted an ambuscade of puffs at every door. Then it roared in the chimney, and then sighed itself away as in penitence for its misdeeds; but in reality it was but waiting for breath and a fresh partner. The moon was making her way westward, bearing steadily on through the clouds which came up from some exhaustless storehouse in the northwest: looking dark at the horizon, but lighter and more flaky beneath the moon's inspection, and sometimes speeding away in such haste that she rode clear and unincumbered for a few minutes, till the next battalion came up.

In Mrs. Raynor's library the curtains were let fall and the fire blazing; and the table waited but the arrival of the teapot and Mr. Henry.

Mr. Penn was already there, reading the newspaper *all*

over, and in every dull paragraph indulging himself with very audible asides and interjections.

'What in the world has Harry done with himself?' he said at length, carefully bestowing the paper, blanket-wise, upon the knight of Malta; who crawled out, shook himself, and curled down again immediately by Mrs. Raynor who was counting stitches on a grey stocking.

'Very interesting news, Sir Brian,' said Penn, pursuing him with the paper.

'What did thee observe, Penn?' said Mrs. Raynor, when she had finished the stitches.

'Throwing words to the cat, ma'am.'

'Did thee say there was any news?'

'Not much,' said Penn,—'what there is smells mouldy. Dull as the editor's brains. Commodore Rogers is in,—not much in that quarter, neither—only thirty prisoners. It must have been a dreadfully moping cruise. But I say, where's Harry? aren't you frightened to death about him? Does he ever stay out so late without leaving word where he's gone?'

'How thee does run on!' said Mrs. Raynor, who had been hurried along the stream of Penn's wild and unquaker-like sentiments without chance to say a word.

'Where does thee think thy tongue will lead thee some day, Penn?'

'Into the house of some rich lady I hope, ma'am—I can't afford to marry a poor one,—and

> '"Whoso stands still,
> Go back he will."'

'Thy backward steps of speech will be few,' said the quakeress.

'But now just see the state of things,' said her nephew

'Down-stairs Rachel is endeavouring to stay the ebullition of wrath'—

'Penn! bethink thee!' said his aunt.

—'From the kettle ma'am—at being kept so long on the fire,—there never was a quaker teakettle yet, that I can find out. And Master Harry, presuming upon his importance'—

'Upon what dost thou presume?' said his cousin's voice behind him.

'Upon your absence,' said Penn jumping up. 'Now then—"Blow winds and crack your cheeks"—and Boil teakettle and put the fire out.'

'And sit down Penn, and be quiet—a more impossible thing than either.'

'But how long since you entered the genus felis, felicitous, and wore cushioned feet?' said Penn. 'Sir Brian might envy the softness of your steps.'

'One can do a good deal under cover,' said Mr. Henry.

'Well I suppose you don't mean to do anything more to-night,' said Penn. 'Your day's work's done, isn't it?'

'Yes—the day's work.'

'Thou art not going out again?' said the quakeress.

'Yes mother, for a while. I have promised to spend a part of the night with one who is sick.'

'Then the carriage must go for thee' said his mother; 'therefore give thine orders.'

'What do you plague yourself with these sick folks for, Harry?' said Penn.

'Somebody must—or rather somebody ought.'

'But there's no comfort in life if you have to spend your days in hunting up distressed people, and your nights in watching them,' said Penn, as he helped himself to a pleasant piece of toast.

The comfort of his life, or rather the joy of it, was a doubtful thing, Mr. Raynor thought; but he simply said,

'This occasion is not of my own seeking, Penn.'

'O then of course. But what a good thing it is that nobody ever wants me. Harry, what a fine night we had last night, didn't we?'

'How thee talks, silly child!' said Mrs. Raynor. 'It rained steadily.'

'Not at Mrs. Clinton's ma'am.—It didn't rain anything there but champagne and sweet words and things of that sort. And I wish you had heard Harry sing!—he surpassed himself, and made me open my eyes. Such a song! Do you know, aunt, *I* believe he's going to be married.'

'Not till I have been your groomsman,' said Mr. Raynor, while his mother turned one quick anxious look at the imperturbably grave face before her.

'Ah me! don't speak of that,' said Penn.

> '"A silver ladle to my dish
> Is all I want—is all I wish"—

but unless a man has the dish, how can he ever hope for the ladle?'

'Make the dish,' said his cousin.

'Don't know how, Harry—and take too long. Besides, one wants mettle to begin with—and I'd rather chase the lady than the dish.'

'Penn, Penn—thee is incorrigible!' said his aunt. 'Does thee never remember thy name?'

'O dear! what a name!' said Penn. 'Do I ever forget it? I am constantly expecting that somebody will give me the nom de plume of Goosequill—only I'm not a writer; and certainly the misfortunes and disappointments of life have not cut me up in the least. I do wish the war would break out here in New York, or else that they'd order me off to the frontiers. A real good fight with the British once a week, and an occasional interlude with the Indians, would keep up a man's spirits amazingly.'

'Hush Penn, you are wrong to talk so here,' said his cousin, while Mrs. Raynor laid down her knitting and sought for words. 'Thought may be free, but speech should be a little restrained sometimes.'

'Why does thee say *here?*' inquired the quakeress, but half pleased at the mildness of the reproof.

'My dear mother, Penn is not signing his name—he is only making flourishes.'

'Can't help it Harry—' said the young gentleman in question,—' you may write my epitaph beforehand—

'"With one sole Penn I wrote this book,
Made of a grey goose quill.
A Penn it was when I it took,
And a Penn I leave it still.'"

'Pens *may* be mended,' said his cousin.

'If you know how. And I can't help it, Harry—it's a—a—what the deuce is the quaker for confounded!—I mean,' said Penn, hurrying on, 'to have nothing to do is a—'

'A thing which no man should complain of,' said his cousin. 'I will give you something to do this very night.'

'No, pray don't,' said Penn most unaffectedly; 'because if you make me go with you I must go, and I would much rather be somewhere else. I think I will go and see how Miss Clyde is after the party—or Miss Clinton.'

'I hope thee will expend all thy adjectives in the street before thee goes to see ladies, Penn,' said the quakeress.

'They've got brothers—both of 'em,' said Penn in a half

undertone. 'But never fear me, ma'am,' he added aloud. '"I'll aggravate my voice so, that I'll roar you gently as a sucking dove—I'll roar you an 't'were any nightingale."'

'If thee will read play-books,' said the quakeress with some displeasure, 'thee must not repeat them here.'

'That's a study book,' said Penn—'the boy's first lessons in English and elocution.'

'Are you going out as soon as we have done tea, Penn?' said his cousin. 'Because in that case we will go together so far as our roads do.'

'Just as soon as I have satisfied the cravings of a youthful appetite,' replied Mr. Penn, who was regaling himself with plum sweetmeats.

'Do plums never make thee sick, Penn?' enquired his aunt.

'Never did, ma'am—except once when I cried for 'em,' replied Mr. Penn.

'And must thee really go out again, Henry?' said Mrs. Raynor as they left the table.

'O yes—' he answered cheerfully. 'It does not trouble you to have me go mother, if I can do anybody any good?'

'Dear child!' she said. 'I wish some one would try to do thee good. Methinketh thou art more grave, Henry, more silent than was thy wont.'

'Talked himself out to Miss Clyde last night,' suggested Penn, with a fresh attack upon the plums.

'Which did not befall thee,' said his cousin; and turning to his mother Mr. Raynor spoke a quieting word or two and left the room.

The night had worn away to its decline, and the spread of stars was wheeling westward, where the moon had long since gone down, when Mr. Henry gave up his place to another watcher and left the sick room, followed by the heart's blessing of its poor tenant. Body and mind had profited by his ministrations; and that night had shed heaven's own dew upon one soul, long shrivelled beneath the burden and heat of the day, contracted and deadened with the drought of all comfort, and covered with the world's dust.

With the strong feeling of the scene upon him, Mr. Raynor got into his carriage and passed rapidly along the silent streets; thinking of their busy inhabitants—hurrying even in sleep across the bridge of life, and one by one dropping through its many pitfalls, to be seen no more till the sea shall give up its dead. How dim and visionary earth seems from the banks of the Jordan; as the mists of that river of death which once hung like a thick curtain before the gate of the Celestial City, now roll off behind the pilgrim, and rest upon the kingdoms of this world and the glory of them! And what was any other work, to the one purpose and endeavour 'that by any means he might save some.'

His thoughts flew to another person who he knew thought and felt with him—yet to her practice it was hard to reconcile himself in all respects. Mr. Raynor threw himself into the other corner of the carriage, and watched for so much sight of her as the outside of her house could give.

A bright light met his gaze. Not the halo with which his fancy always invested her, but a red flickering glare that it was hard to locate precisely, in the uncertain black of the night, though it was in the direction of the Clyde house; and now he noticed that bells were ringing, and that the men hurrying along the streets stopped from time to time to pick up the fire-buckets which the startled sleepers left their beds to throw out.

Mr. Raynor left his carriage, and choosing some point beyond the scene of action where Caleb Williams might await his coming, he mingled with the crowd and went on afoot. Among the crowd but faster than they,—the mind giving winged spurs which carried him on beyond all that ran for profit or duty or fun; making his way spirit-like, without jostling or being jostled, and with unconscious care eschewing every possible hindrance or delay. One point he soon made sure—the fire was not in Thornton's house but opposite; and changing his course for the freer space of a cross street, Mr. Raynor made a slight circuit and admitted himself by a side door. It was open of course, for the firemen had free passage to every house in the neighbourhood, and after a word to the policeman on duty he entered the hall.

'Bless you, Mr. Raynor!' said Martha Jumps, who was taking care of any article she could find, not very careful what that might be; 'did you ever hear whether pillows go safe, packed in teacups?—I mean!—I'm at the end of my wits!—And there's the hearthrugs. How did you ever come to get here at this identical minute and everything in a blaze?—O she's in the back parlour and we're packing up.'

In that fiercely lighted room, the red glare dancing upon wall and ceiling like a thing possessed, the cries of the throng outside inspired by the firemen's trumpets, the dash of water upon window and door, the loud tramp of men through the hall, and with no better guard than a knot of firemen, he found her—like a quiet spirit beneath the Ægis of trust.

At the moment when Mr. Raynor entered the room, water and smoke were for a time triumphant, and the sudden darkening almost prevented his finding her; but a word or two which she spoke to some one else had brought him to her side before the red blaze again sprang forth. Her attention was fixed upon Hulda, who now hid her eyes in her sister's neck, and then as by some strange fascination opened them long enough to give one fearful look towards the front windows and about the room; but never moving her arms from the one to whom she looked for safety on all occasions. At the first sound of her friend's voice however, Hulda started up, and stretching out her arms to him she sobbed out,

'Won't you please take us home, Mr. Raynor? because Thornton isn't here, and I'm so frightened.' And she was instantly in a new resting-place.

'Will you persuade your sister to come, Hulda?'

'O yes, she'll come,' said the child, whose little heart was beating quieter already for the strong hand laid upon it. 'Won't you, Rosalie?'

But Rosalie did not answer; for something in Hulda's salutation, or in the way it was met, or in the sudden relief she felt, let not word and thought work together.

'Won't you, Alie?' she repeated, stretching her little face down towards her sister, but by no means loosing her hold of Mr. Raynor.

'I will let you go, love, very thankfully. Hulda has kept me prisoner here,' she said, 'so that I could do nothing.'

'And I am come to put you in closer ward. I shall not think you safe until my mother has charge of you.'

'Take Hulda if you please, Mr. Raynor, but I am not in the least afraid. Perhaps we shall have no more disturbance, and if—at all events I am better here.'.

'I shall not go until you do,' said he quietly.

Rosalie hesitated and again repeated her request.

'There are some things here that would need my attention if the fire should cross the street—I had better not go,

If you will only take Hulda away where she will be safe and unfrightened, I will thank you very much.'

'You will not thank me, for I shall not go,' he said with a slight smile which by no means helped her irresolution. '*Your* being frightened is I suppose of no matter, but who shall assure me that you will be safe?—I do not want to be frightened myself.' And wrapping Hulda more closely in her shawl, he added, 'I shall wait for you,—therefore please Miss Rosalie give your orders as soon as may be, and let us be off before we have any more light on the subject. Then will I come back and see your brother and do anything you want done.'

The roof of the burning house fell in as he spoke; and though the brilliant light soon darkened again, they saw that the fire was walking along the block with no tardy step, and the engines redoubled their play upon the front windows.

'Make haste, dear Alie!' said little Hulda, again hiding her eyes from the sight.

'Hulda,' said her friend, 'will you let me put you in the carriage first, and will you stay there while I come back for your sister?'

'Who is in the carriage?' said Hulda, raising her head to look at him.

'Caleb Williams is there with the horses.'

'The man in the grey coat?' said Hulda.

'Yes. You would not be afraid to stay with him for five minutes?'

'No,' said Hulda laying her head down again. 'Not if you want me to.'

And her friend carried her out. It was well he had but one to take care of. The way to the carriage was not long, but it was all he could do to pass through the crowd. At least with his hands so full—the way back was much quicker, but confusion had thickened inside the house.

'Gracious me! Tom Skiddy,' said Martha as she knelt in the hall; 'do you suppose folks has no feelings because the house is afire?'

'Ha'n't got time to suppose,' said Tom, as he went up three stairs at a time on some errand for his mistress.

'And I'm sure I don't know how a person can pack with men flying over their heads at that rate,' said Martha. 'And the Captain away too—it's a miracle houses can't catch when people are home.'

'Where is Miss Rosalie, Martha?'

'My!—She aint in this basket, Mr. Raynor—if that's what you mean. Like enough she's up in the skylight—it's a firstrate place to look at fires, if you can get the first chance. Pretty good powers of come and go!' said Martha to herself, as the young gentleman went up stairs much after the example of Tom Skiddy. 'If he's one third more of a witch, he can take a flying leap with her out of the window.

Rosalie was up-stairs, quietly giving directions to Tom and the firemen,—they, swarthy, smoky, black-capped and red-shirted figures,—she in one of the wrappers which Thornton admired so much,—delicate, white-handed; and white-cheeked too, for that matter, with the fatigue of excitement.

'If you have any doubts left,' Mr. Raynor said as he approached her, 'I will resolve them. You are not responsible for being carried off against your will. And I cannot let you have any more time here. These things shall be cared for, but you first.'

And before Rosalie could attempt any organized plan of resistance it was too late,—she was out of the house and passing through the crowd, and then in the carriage by Hulda. Or rather by her conductor, for Hulda had taken her old place on Mr. Raynor's lap, and they were driving rapidly away. In two minutes Hulda was asleep ; nor did she give other note of the change than a sigh, when Mr. Raynor laid her—a softly breathing and sleeping little figure, upon the sofa in the library at the 'Quakerage.' He stayed only to place Rosalie in an easychair at her side, before he sprang up stairs.

Rosalie felt in a kind of maze,—so swiftly had the last hour sunk down, and the little heap of sand seemed of such strange particles. She looked about her. The room shewed no trace of modern things—unless the flowers deserved that name—and the fire which had evidently been lately replenished, shone upon oak and black walnut embrowned with exposure to the light of a century. It rose and fell once or twice, flickering fantastically about, and then a quick step was on the stairs and her dream vanished. And immediately she heard a door open and the words,

'Henry Raynor! thee is not going out again ? Thee must not!'

He stopped and spoke a word or two, but Rosalie did not hear his answer; and in a moment the front door opened and closed. In another moment Mrs. Raynor was in the library.

'Thou dear child!' she said. 'How glad I am to see thee! how glad to have anything bring thee here. Sit thee still, child.'

'And how sorry I am to do anything to give you any trouble,' said Rosalie as she returned her friend's greeting.

'Trouble ? bless thee,' said the good quakeress, 'I would I could keep thee here always! Wilt thou be persuaded to stay ?' she added anxiously, bending down to look at the sweet face that was looking up at her.

But Rosalie's eyes fell again, and she shook her head. The quakeress stood gently smoothing down her hair.

'Well love, thee knows best,' she said. 'But now come away to bed, and trouble not thyself about thy house—Henry has gone back to see that all be done.'

'O I am very sorry! He should not have gone!'

'None could hinder him—not even thou,' said the quakeress smiling. 'He thought thy brother might return—and Henry knows thou art a thing to be asked for. But come, love, and trouble not thy mind about anything.'

Rosalie carried her little charge to Mrs. Raynor's dressing room, and covered her up on the sofa there; and when Mrs. Raynor had left her she sat down on a low seat by Hulda, and laying her head on the same sofa cushion she fell asleep; with the first streaks of daylight falling across her face.

CHAPTER XXI.

Come, says Puss, without any more ado, 'tis time to go to breakfast; cats don't live upon dialogues.—L'ESTRANGE.

THE morning rose fair and still, with that ever fresh look from a night's repose, full of hope, promise, and expectation. As yet that day and the world had not come in contact; and with a child's eye the morning looked at the dark city beneath—wondering and fearless. At present all lay peacefully quiet, and the early light found no cause of complaint except that it could not see everything. Would ever drops lie heavier than the morning dew? could there ever be darkness which the risen sun should not dispel?

As yet the morning glanced only at the chimneys with their upward curls of household smoke,—at the tall steeples that stood like finger-posts to the Celestial City, lest any man should think the way lay near earth's level. At these —but most of all at the sunrise clouds, with their bewitching shapes and colours,—those castles in the air at which so many days have looked; to see some swept away by the strong wind of circumstance, and some dried up at mid-day, and some to pour down their artillery upon all beneath.

So comes the morning with its first look, and the noon with its clear-sightedness that burns as fire, and dries up all springs not fed by the fountain of living waters and shadowed by the Great Rock; and so man goeth forth unto his work until the evening—with its weariness, its repose, its hope of a better day.

"*These all died in faith.*"

"I desire grace and patience," says Samuel Rutherford, "to wait on, and to lie upon the brink, till the water fill and flow. I know he is fast coming."

No such thoughts accompanied Thornton Clyde in his morning walk to Mrs. Raynor's. He had promised to come there to breakfast for certain good reasons *not* very well known to himself; and now in fulfilment of the promise he walked leisurely along—for it was yet early. He had visited the scene of last night's bonfire, looked at the smoking ruins of the destroyed houses, and at the blackened and defaced appearance of his own; and had stood musingly about the spot until the city tide-gates were opened, and its population poured forth. Thornton stayed until a half dozen boys had come to the ruin, to pick up nails and charred wood; and then turning away with a feeling of disgust he walked swiftly on.

I say no such thoughts possessed him,—and yet the blackened home with its destroyed surroundings looked too out of keeping with the fresh beauty of the day, not to stir up some bitter fountain within him. A fountain that murmured of lost precious things; while the water in its basin gave back pictures that he had no wish to see nor remember. Thornton walked faster and faster.

'Will you tell Miss Clyde that her brother is here?' he said, when James Hoxton and he had brought their very different qualities to bear upon each other.

'Truly friend, I think not,' replied the quaker with a cool survey. 'It may well chance that thou shalt see her first. She hath not yet arisen.'

And leading the way into the library James Hoxton gave a grave and sagacious kick to the fire, and left the room.

Thornton thought to himself that one of last night's events would have been quite enough for him without the other. That to have either sister or house spirited away was as much as a man could reasonably expect upon one occasion; yet here they were both. Rosalie established among the quakers, and the house made uninhabitable. Moreover he was at Mr. Raynor's himself—gloomily standing before the library fire,—a thing the sunbeams did not know what to do with. They played about a shawl which lay on the sofa, in a kind of loving way as if they rejoiced to see it there—which Thornton did not. It was Rosalie's shawl, lying just where she had thrown it off the night before, and looking as her brother fancied, just like her. Why was it there? and why did he dislike to see it? Thornton felt as if his canary bird's cage was broke, and she away in her natural element. From a rather vexed mood he went off into one more softened and befitting the subject, which held him till Penn Raynor came to take its place.

'Curious coincidence, wasn't it?' said Penn, with a happy choice of subject.

'What?' said Thornton.

'Why—' said Penn,—'that is, I was thinking how Harry happened to come by your house just when it took fire.'

'He did not—unfortunately for your coincidence.'

'O then I misunderstood,' said Penn. 'But he came by when he did—I suppose you won't deny that; and I say it was lucky, wasn't it?'

'I must be excused for having a keener perception of the night's evils than of its benefits,' said Thornton.

'I declare,' said Penn laughing, 'the fire has done its work upon you!—mere ashes and piecrust—a remainder biscuit—or anything of that sort. Not a drop of the milk of human kindness left.—The Clyde runs dry this morning.'

What sort of a reply Thornton might have made is uncertain, for the master of the house came in; and claiming Mr. Clyde's attention by a hand laid on his shoulder and by his pleasant greeting and welcome, forced the young man into at least outside politeness. Not the true polish of the wood, but varnish; and very susceptible of scratches.

'You are standing here,' Mr. Raynor said, 'as if you were tired of rest—or despised it—which?'

'I am not apt to take rest at this time in the morning,' replied Thornton.

'Not such as a chair can give?'

'I can tell you,' put in Penn, 'that you will gain nothing by your attempts in that quarter. For all the world like the Dead Sea apples,—looks well enough but don't taste good.'

'How long is it since you turned cannibal, Penn?' said his cousin. 'Has the want of breakfast enraged your appetite to that degree?'

'Sure enough,' said Penn, 'what *has* become of breakfast?'

'I have just learned,' said Mr. Raynor looking towards his guest, 'that we must wait yet a little longer.'

'You have delayed it to favour my sleepy sisters?' said Thornton.

'Not I—' said Mr. Raynor. 'My oversight of the household is in a somewhat different line.'

'But lines cross occasionally.'

'His does,' said Penn,—'isn't a line in the house it don't touch somewhere.'

'Lines may touch without entanglement,' said Mr. Raynor. 'The many tinted members of the light make but one white ray of beauty and usefulness.'

'At that rate,' said Thornton, 'each member of a family is incomplete without the rest.'

'No, but the family is incomplete without each member.'

'How full of brilliancy you would make the world to be,' said Thornton somewhat scornfully.

'The world does not make itself so, if I do,' was the quiet reply. 'Those people who shine with a clear and unmixed light are rare.'

'Rare!—I should like to see one!'

Mr. Raynor smiled, and Thornton's memory quickly corrected itself.

'Did you ever take notice,' said Mr. Raynor as gravely as before, 'how beautifully the ideal halo of the old painters is sometimes borne out? They put a visible glory about their saints; and I think you may see a glory around the heads of some saints that do walk this earth. Or as in Bunyan's portrait of a gospel minister, where a "crown of gold did hang over his head."—" And they that sat in the council, looking steadfastly on Stephen, saw his face as it had been the face of an angel!"'

Thornton had seen enough to verify the remark, though he did not say so, and silence followed, until the door of the library opened softly to admit little Hulda.'

'Here comes one little ray,' said her friend turning round.

'What is a little ray?' said Hulda, whose greeting of the two gentlemen was meant to be strictly impartial.

'A little ray is a very, very little piece of a sunbeam.'

Hulda laughed, and keeping hold of his hand she stood leaning her little face against it, and making grave remarks upon various subjects.

'Isn't it pleasant here, Thornton? O Mr. Raynor! I didn't wake up once after you put us in the carriage last night, and this morning I didn't know where I was at first. O there's the cat! Pussy! pussy!—see Thornton, what a nice cat.'

'Where is your sister?' was Thornton's response.

'O she's coming right down, and so is Mrs. Raynor. But you see Rosalie was awake last night, and so—pussy! pussy!'

'And so she slept this morning?'

'What an unconscionable creature you are, Thornton!' said Mr. Penn emerging from the newspaper. 'Routing Miss Clyde out of bed at any time of day, when she's been burnt out over night. I should think she'd run away from you, if that's your prevailing temper and disposition.'

'Should you?' said Thornton drily.

'Yes I should,' said Penn. 'I should do it too, if anybody asked me to get up in the morning—if I was a woman. Because they haven't the resource of knocking people down as men have.'

'But she is up,' said Hulda, 'and coming down.'

And there she came—not looking as if the morning had paid off the night; though the colour came back a little when she first met her brother, and then from his side shook hands with Mr. Raynor and answered his grave enquiries. Thornton felt very proud of her. So did Hulda; and looked from Rosalie up to Mr. Raynor's face without in the least knowing what an appeal she brought, nor how readily it was answered.

'Well,' Thornton said, when they had exchanged a few words about the last night's work; 'and what are you going to do with yourself now?'

'Stay here until I know your plans.'

'And then?'

'Do as a shadow does—' she said, raising her bright eyes to his.

'You are a little like a shadow,' Thornton said with a sobering face, as his arm went round her and felt what a slight creature was within its clasp. 'We were comparing you just now to something about as unsubstantial, though rather more bright.'

'Were you?' said Penn—'it passes my wits to find out what. I do assure you Miss Clyde, they talked of nothing but breakfast and rays of light—O yes, I believe Harry did speak of an angel.'

'And I never spoke the name of any friend of mine in such a commonplace connection,' said Mr. Raynor quickly.

'Connection?' said Mr. Penn turning over the newspaper,—'it is rather a far off connection, and commonplace, as you say. That's the difficulty of running to the top of the language at once—then you've nothing to do but come down—which is the reverse of climactick.'

'Thornton Clyde,' said Mrs. Raynor as she came in, 'thee is almost as welcome as thy sister. But does thee hold her so tight always?'

'"We be all honest men here—we be no thieves,"' soliloquised Mr. Penn from the recesses of his armchair and paper.

'Penn,' said his aunt, 'I pray thee to use fitting language.'

'Certainly ma'am,' said Penn,—'if I could attain that desirable point I should be most happy. But I've tried two or three kinds and they don't any of 'em fit. And as that respectable author whom I just quoted is supposed to have universal powers of adaptation——'

'Can thee be quiet now for a time?' said the quakeress.

'Just let me tell Miss Clyde about the old woman that spoke in meeting, first,' said Penn jumping up. 'Miss Clyde, this old woman was unfortunate enough to lose command of her tongue in church—as I do occasionally out of it'—

'Thee cannot well lose what thee never had,' said the quakeress.

'The fruit of her efforts was that she became dumb, however,' said Penn—'which illustrious example I shall immediately follow. "Mum, mum, without a plum."'

Mr. Raynor prevented all strictures upon this speech by ringing the bell; and such of the servants as scruples would permit, came in and took their seats. But Thornton stood motionless; and though when his sister had placed her chair near him, and Hulda climbing into her lap had assumed the most comfortable position possible, he felt half inclined to join the group,—something withheld; and he remained standing while the chapter was read, and the prayer uttered from a full heart, that they all might be "kept by the power of God, through faith unto salvation." Was it for him?—had he any part in it?

From one hasty glance at the speaker, a glance in which his old prejudice melted away very fast, Thornton's eyes came back to Rosalie's bowed head; on which the sunbeams rested with no fear of defilement. Not words could speak the mind's enwrapped earnestness as did every line of her figure. It was his guardian angel, there at his side, and praying for him. And not Hulda's little arms were twined closer about her than was Thornton's heart, as the witness-bearing drops rose up into his eyes, and he brushed them away that he might see the clearer. But when they arose from their knees he stood there as before, grave and unmoved.

They gathered thoughtfully about the fire in silence for

a few minutes; the mind yet borne up on those spirit wings with which it had been soaring, the heart yet swelling with its last petition. Even Thornton and Penn Raynor were quiet, against their will; and when Hulda slipped away from Rosalie's side, and stooping down on the rug began to stroke the cat,—her little hand went softly from head to tail, and the knight's loud responsive purr was rather startling. At last Hulda looked up.

'Mr. Raynor, I think the cat's very hungry.'

'I doubt it exceedingly,' said her friend sitting down by her. 'What makes you think so?'

'Because just now she looked up at me and mewed.'

'By that rule you must be hungry too,' said Mr. Raynor.

'Why I didn't mew,' said Hulda laughing.

He smiled, and clearing a place for his lips on her forehead, told her she might be as hungry as she pleased, for that breakfast was now ready. And as if he meant to claim his full prerogative as host, Mr. Raynor gave no one else a chance to take Rosalie to the breakfast-room. An arrangement to which Thornton submitted with small inward graciousness; only consoling himself with its banishment of what traces of fatigue the night had left on her cheeks, and the quick return there of the exiles of the House of Lancaster. But if he could have had his will as he walked along behind her, Rosalie's hand would have been quickly dislodged from its resting place, and she and her companion put anywhere in the world but side by side. Thornton was even jealous of the very light hold her hand seemed to have,—why could she not take his arm as she would that of any one else?

As for Hulda, she was beholden to Mr. Penn's good offices; but though she laughed very much as he danced with her along the hall, in her private mind she preferred a quieter rate of progress; and quite agreed with Mrs. Raynor's remark,

'Penn, thee does make an astonishing noise.'

'Very glad if it astonishes any one, ma'am,' said Penn.

'But see! if thee upsets the coffee pot the cat may be scalded,' said the quakeress with a mild reprehension of flourishes.

'Wouldn't accompany Sir Brian into hot water for much greater fun than the overthrow of the coffee pot, ma'am,' said Penn.

'Thornton Clyde,' said Mrs. Raynor, 'thee had better all stay here until thy plans are formed.'

Thornton expressed his thanks, and a polite assurance that his plans were in the last state of forwardness.

'Then stay until you are quite ready to carry them out,' said the master of the house.

'My staying here would effectually prevent their being carried out, Mr. Raynor.'

'And cannot thee leave thy sister, then?' said the quakeress with a wistful look at Rosalie.

'My sisters ma'am,' said Thornton with some emphasis, 'must decide for themselves.'

'My dear Miss Clyde!' said Penn Raynor, 'if you will only take up your abode in this house you will lay me under everlasting obligations.'

'I will not run such a risk,' said Rosalie,—'I shall certainly go at once.'

'No but—dear me!' said Penn, 'I'm sure I didn't mean—that is I wouldn't for the world insinuate—At least I haven't the least idea what I did insinuate, but I didn't mean to discompose anybody.'

'Thee talks a little too fast, either to know what thee means or to say it, Penn,' said his aunt.

'But everybody must know what I mean,' said Penn,— at least Harry ought, for I've talked to him about it dozens of times.'

'Mother,' said Mr. Henry Raynor, 'here is little Hulda waiting with all patience for some kind hand to give her a glass of milk, and Miss Rosalie's cup is in like need of attention. If you know what you mean, Penn, you had better inform us; for Mr. Clyde at least, is perfectly in the dark.'

'Is it possible?' said Penn,—why it's as clear as daylight.'

'As it was to the little boy who his father might be, in your favourite story,' said Mr. Raynor.

'Yes, that is my favourite story, certainly,' said Penn. 'It's so hard to explain things that people ought to understand without explanation.'

'You must try for once, Penn,' said his cousin smiling. 'I am afraid you are one of the things.'

'Never shall believe it without better evidence,' replied Mr. Penn.

Rosalie laughed and Thornton confessed he was in the condition of the storekeeper.

'Why—' said Penn, 'if you'll stay here Miss Clyde, I, as being a noisy member of society should at once depart; and if I were sent off to seek my fortune maybe it would come. Not that I shouldn't enjoy your presence immensely, of course, but then I'm sure you would enjoy my absence a great deal more. If you could only content yourself.'

'O she would be very contented, Mr. Penn,' said Hulda, who thought the silence gave her leave to speak; 'but then you see Thornton couldn't do without her.' And the grave little face and childish voice that spoke as if the subject were quite disposed of, made even Thornton laugh, and relieved the one most concerned from all further reply.

But though Rosalie steadily refused to go to Mrs. Arnet's, or indeed to stay anywhere but with her brother, she must stay where she was until he should find rooms.

10*

And resting quietly in a great chair before the library fire Thornton left her.

'I shall be back in an hour, Alie,' he said, 'and until then—'

'Until then what?' she said looking up at him.

'O nothing much,—take care of yourself, that's all.'

She smiled and told him she was safe enough there, with a look so clear and sweet, that he would almost have given her carte-blanche to do what she liked.

CHAPTER XXII.

The ladies were greatly concerned; but being told the family received no hurt, they were extremely glad; but being informed that we were almost killed by the fright, they were vastly sorry; but hearing that we had a very good night, they were extremely glad again.—*Vicar of Wakefield.*

IF Rosalie had left a clue by which her friends could find her, she would have had little time to rest that morning. As it was Thornton had been gone but half an hour before James Hoxton presented himself and Miss Arnet's card.

'Will thee see her in here, or will thee not see her at all?' said the quaker.

'See her? certainly.'

James Hoxton walked off as if he had expected or would have approved a different answer; and hardly had it reached the carriage before the lady herself swept past him and into the library.

'Why child you look charmingly!' was her first salutation. 'I think being burnt out agrees with you. But how *do* you stand it here among the quakers!—that man be-*friend*ed me till I was nearly out of my wits. To which you would probably reply that your wits are less volatile. But to come to the point—may I fly away with you now? or at least will you fly away with me?'

'Can't, my dear.'

'Won't—I told mamma so before I came. I should have been here an age ago, but mamma got one of her nervous fits when she heard of the fire, and of course I had to stay. I'm sure I was as nervous as she was.'

'And you are also convalescent?' said Rosalie.

'Also convalescent. Only Thornton nearly gave me another fit in the street. Do you know he would *not* tell me where you were? only said that when you were settled anywhere he would let me know—many thanks to him! And I told him he need give himself no trouble, for that I would find you before I was an hour older,—which I have.'

'Many thanks to you,' said Rosalie smiling.

'Not many,' said Marion,—'there is now and then a search that rewards itself; of which I think some less volatile wits than mine may be aware. Where are mine host and hostess?'

'I know not,' said Rosalie. 'I have been here alone since Thornton went.'

'Pretty house, isn't it,' said Marion smiling—'and pleasant people. Satisfactory—don't you think so?'

'Very.'

'Where is Hulda?'

'She went with Mr. Raynor into the greenhouse after breakfast.'

'How comes it you are not there too? I thought you had as strong a *penchant* for roses as Beauty in the fairy tale.'

'I tell you I was here with Thornton for some time.'

'Well he couldn't play the part of Beauty this morning,' said Miss Arnet. 'Such a mood as he was in!—savage. I think I could have exchanged shots with him with pleasure.'

'I presume you did,' said Rosalie.

'No, he wouldn't even stop to fight; which is a degree

of savageness unprecedented for him. I wish Mr. Raynor would come!—I want to see him.'

'He cannot save you the trouble of looking, Miss Arnet.'

'And he needn't save me the trouble of hearing,' said the lady turning round. 'What a police officer you would make! Now I like to have my attention arrested first.'

'You know I was brought up in a quiet persuasion,' said Mr. Raynor.

'My visit here this morning reminds me strongly of a story I once heard you tell,' said Miss Arnet. 'Is that your flower, par excellence?'

'This?' said Mr. Raynor, looking down into the depths of a rose which he held in his hand. 'A queen is rather public than private property, methinks.'

'That depends a little upon the bounds of her jurisdiction,' said Miss Arnet. 'You remember what the song says—

"And my heart should be the throne
For my queen."'

'The peculiar throne of this queen is a somewhat prickly rosebush,' said Mr. Raynor with a smile.

'"Like jewels to advantage set,
Her beauty by the shade does get."

You could not imagine a rose in clover.'

'What an idea!' said Miss Arnet. 'But are roses then always bound to be miserable?'

'Nothing can be that whose chief end is the happiness of others,' said Mr. Raynor. 'And a true rose looks up at the sunshine that comes from heaven—not down at the thorns which spring from earth.'

'And so she bears her discomforts—'

'Like her blushing honours.'

'I give up,' said Miss Arnet. 'I see you have studied the case. If you would only explain the philosophy of thorns, by way of conclusion, I should go away satisfied.'

'The literal and figurative thorns came in together,—"thorns also, and thistles shall it bring forth to thee," was a curse for the mind as well as for the body.'

'That is the fact—not the philosophy,' said Miss Arnet. 'And I suppose you will tell me there is no philosophy about it—which will leave me as unsatisfied as ever. I wonder what you look so satisfied about, child—and you smile, Mr. Raynor,—do you think that is a pleasant doctrine?'

'I think this is.

'"*And he shewed me a pure river of water of life, clear as crystal, proceeding out of the throne of God and of the Lamb. In the midst of the street of it, and on either side of the river, was there the tree of life, which bare twelve manner of fruits, and yielded her fruit every month: and the leaves of the tree were for the healing of the nations.*

'"*And there shall be no more curse.*"'

Marion pulled up her gloves and fitted them carefully for a few moments, in silence which no one else broke.

'Why didn't you come to our house last night, Rosalie?' she began at length.

'I could go to only one place at a time,' said Miss Clyde.

'Clear and conclusive,' said Marion. 'I should have come for you in the night, if I could have been a man for the nonce,—failing that I stayed at home and fretted. Well, I shall not offer you the comforts of my house a second time, having just learned that roses befit not a clover field. I know what a 'thorny path o' care' you will tread in this house. If ever anybody was born to smooth away the sorrows of life, I think it is Mrs. Raynor. I always feel an immediate lull in her presence.'

'We have varieties of weather,' said Mr. Raynor, as his mother walked in by one door and Mr. Penn by another.

'Isn't that remarkable?' said Penn. 'I was wondering this morning what Miss Clyde *would* do, moping here in this castle of silence; and now here is Miss Arnet come to wake us all up.'

'I thank you,' said Miss Arnet,—'I shall not undertake that office for you, Mr. Penn. And the reveillé is quite as like to arouse me as anybody.'

'But cannot thee stay here to-day?' said Mrs. Raynor. 'We will bear thee company if awake, and sleeping Rosalie will give thee hers.'

'I will go away and give her a chance,' said Miss Arnet. 'No I thank you Mrs. Raynor—mamma will expect me.'

'If you are walking Miss Arnet, and will permit me to attend you, I shall think myself too happy,' said Penn.

'You may go as far as my carriage—I suppose that will make you just happy enough,' said the lady, taking a graceful leave of the others.

So audible was the rustling of Miss Arnet's dress, so brisk Mr. Penn's attendant steps, so gay and laughing the voices of both, that a quiet little foot along the hall was not heard, even when it reached the library door; for as James Hoxton had at that moment both rottenstone and the front door knocker in his hands, he permitted this visiter to announce herself. Which however she hesitated to do; and there is no telling how long she might have waited had not Hulda accidentally come to her relief.

'O yes Miss Morsel, Rosalie's here, in the library,— why don't you go in?' said the child opening the door and marching in herself; while Miss Morsel followed with a helpless air of intrusion, and returned Mr. Raynor's bow and smile as if they had been in the highest degree reproving, and she had deserved it.

'How does thee do, Bettie Morsel?' said the quakeress coming forward to meet her. 'I am glad to see thee. If thee thinks this is the first time thee has had a friend in this house, thee is mistaken.'

'I am sure I never thought such a thing,' said poor Miss Morsel, who having by this time got hold of Rosalie's hand felt encouraged to speak,—' never! I always told ma that if we lost one friend I should know where to look for another.'

'How do you do?' said Rosalie.

'I'm as well as I ought to be, I s'pose,' said Miss Morsel, —'I generally am. And so's ma. Complainin' don't necessarily mean much in our house.'

'Complaints do but chafe thee ill,' said the quakeress.

'I always thought so,' said Miss Morsel,—' ma don't. She looks upon it more in the shape of a plaster. But O dear! to think of your house, Miss Rosalie! I declare it makes me feel worse than if we'd been burnt out ourselves —though to be sure the house aint ours—nor worth a pin, either. But just to *think* of yours!'

'Why our house is not burnt,' said Rosalie,—' it is only scorched and smoked a little.'

'O yes, I know,' said Miss Morsel, 'but then it don't matter—when you've got to a cinder you may just as well go to ashes. Better too I think; and then you know what you have to start with. But I thought ma 'd go off the hooks; for nothing would coax her primarily that it wasn't our own bed-room. Though as I told her, it didn't signify if it was; but she couldn't view it in that light.'

'The light of the fire was stronger,' said Rosalie.

'It was strong enough, I'm sure,' said the little guest, 'and I told ma we ought to be crying our eyes out, and not sit there looking at it. And she said it never did her any good to take physic for other folks' ail—and I suppose it don't.'

'I should be very sorry to have you cry your eyes out for me,' said Rosalie; her lips just moving with the kindly smile that went round the circle. 'And it is very needless in this case, Miss Morsel. I hope we shall have the house in nice order again in a few months.'

'Months! yes,' said Miss Morsel, 'but where are you going to be while the months run over your head? I never wished I had a place of my own as I did this morning—never!'

Rosalie made no reply but by holding out her hand, which Miss Morsel fastened upon with great energy.

'You don't feel like going through fire and water, neither,' she said, giving it a good squeeze. 'And to have it happen so too! now if the blockading gun-brigs had set fire to it there 'd have been some sense.'

'Not much, I think,' said Rosalie.

'But I mean,' said Miss Morsel, 'in time of war when you're liable to be bombarded every minute of your life, you naturally don't expect to have anything else done to you. If anybody was to come and cut my throat you know, I should think it quite remarkable to be blown up in a steamboat at the same time. Ma says it wouldn't surprise her in the least to have forty things done to her at once, but it would me.'

'I fear me thy mother studieth not to be quiet,' said the quakeress, when Miss Morsel paused for breath.

'No, that she don't,' said the little woman with renewed spirit, 'she never did study much of anything. And I suppose it can't be expected she should take it up now. I must go home this minute, or she'll be in a great to-do about me and the dinner and everything else.'

'Well you see that I am safe,' said Rosalie smiling.

'Yes my dear. O I thought you were, but still it's a pleasure to see it,' said Miss Morsel getting up and surveying Miss Clyde intently. 'And comfortable? I may tell ma you're looking comfortable?'

'By all means!'

'Then I'll go right straight home, and be content for the rest of my natural life,' said Miss Morsel. 'And so will ma —as content as she ever was, which is saying less than you'd imagine. However, we all have to do as we can in this world. Sit still dear and I'll carry you away in my eyes just as you are. And please let me go out as I came in and nobody take any notice.'

'Thee has one friend, Rosalie,' said the quakeress, as the door closed upon Miss Morsel.

'But lest she should have more than one,' said Mr. Raynor, 'or to prove that she has more than one—whichever you like, mother,—I wish you would give orders that she is not to see another until night.'

'Where does thee intend to banish thyself to?' said the quakeress.

'I shall be friend enough to go away and leave her to go to sleep,' he answered,—'that is only one of the lighter kinds of banishment.'

And left alone in that pleasant light, one feeling after another folded down like the petals of a veritable rose, Rosalie slept.

And there was no disturbance. Hulda was kept at her play in the greenhouse or elsewhere, and happily neither Thornton nor Mr. Penn made his appearance. Whatever steps came in the library were of the softest, and with the lightest of hands was the fire from time to time replenished. Even dinner was made to wait; and still "Nature's soft nurse" kept Rosalie in dreamless sleep.

She awoke to find Mrs. Raynor bending over her.

'Poor child!' the quakeress said tenderly, 'I knew not thy weariness till I saw thee asleep, and thy cheeks so white. Art thou rested?'

'Yes, I believe so,' Rosalie said, as she sat up, and pushing back her hair discovered that there was another person in the room. The colour came back very fast.

'Why doesn't thee put thy hair back altogether, and shew thy pretty ears?' said the quakeress with a quiet smile.

'And then give you leave to cover them up with a cap, mother?' said Mr. Raynor.

'Nay, I said not so,' she replied; 'but however thee knows white muslin is not very thick. Sit thee still dear Rosalie, while I call thy sister. She is at play yet but hath asked for thee many times.' And as she opened the door and passed out, Mr. Raynor came close to Rosalie's chair.

'How do you do to-day?' he said.

'Quite well—at least I suppose I shall be quite well after another night. Though one would think I had taken extra sleep enough already.'

'No one would think so who watched you sleeping. And I fear you are not putting yourself in the way of rest. If you will stay here Rosalie, I will be as completely out of the way as Penn offered to be; and no one but you shall know the reason.'

'And no one could it trouble as it would me,' she said gently, and looking up but to thank him.

While Hulda came bounding into the room, and establishing herself in her sister's arms whispered confidentially,

'I could be *very* contented here, Alie,—couldn't you?'

Pleasant was the dinner, with its varied talk among characters so different and yet in points so much alike,—with its staid quaker servants and brilliant dishes of flowers,—with its general atmosphere of refinement and good taste; and around all, the freshening influence of a politeness that was not cut and dried and made to order, but which came from the depths of kind and true feeling. It rested Rosalie more than her sleep had done; and half making her forget all painful thoughts of the past or the present, left her free to contribute no small share to the pleasure of the company.

They had left the table, and the twilight fell, and still the pleasant talk went on about the bright wood fire in the library, and no one was in haste for other light. And no one was glad when the door opened to admit Mr. Clyde. *He* was not more light—he was another shadow; and sorrowfully Rosalie's friends marked where it fell.

But Thornton had hardly taken a seat, and had not at all begun what he had to say, before a little running fire of raps announced Dr. Buffem.

'Confound the light in this room—or the darkness, whichever it *is*,' said the doctor,—'here am I laying myself up for life on this chair—none too easy a one for the purpose, neither. Ah friend Raynor, how does thee do? and why does thee not have thy rooms prepared for those people who do not carry pocket lanterns?'

'Thee did not hurt thyself?' said the quakeress.

'Hurt myself? of course I did. How many chairs do you suppose I can kick down and *not* hurt myself? How now, fair Rosalie! methinks the moon suffers an eclipse to-night. Friend Henry give me thy hand. Friend Thornton I will perhaps take thine, when I know what thou art here for.'

'Simply to take my sisters away sir,' said Thornton.

'Hum—' said the doctor, and put both his hands behind him. 'Friend Raynor, is light one of the things you think people should be deprived of because they occasionally abuse it?'

'I think thee is the only person who has abused it to-night, friend Buffem,' said the quakeress quietly.

'Now that's what I call point-blank range—' said the doctor turning to Rosalie. 'Certainly have killed me only that my weak spot is that of Achilles. Came pretty near being killed, that way. But Miss Rosalie how is it that you can sit up to smile?

> '"Thy wee bit housie, too, in ruin!
> Its silly wa's the winds are strewin'!
> An' naething now, to big a new ane
> O' foggage green!
> An' bleak December's winds ensuin',
> Baith snell and keen."'

'There are more houses than one in the world, fortunately,' said Thornton; 'but if you mean to reach one to-night, Rosalie, we had better be moving.'

'There is some sense in that remark—a little,' said the doctor preventing her reply. 'There is this qualification,—you should have been moving some three hours ago.'

'I was on drill and could not,' said Thornton a little stiffly.

'I don't see what your being on drill has to do with your sister's going out at an unseasonable time of night,' said the doctor, taking a pinch of snuff. 'Can't—for the life of me.'

'Unseasonable!' said Thornton. 'Why it's only'—

'I've got a watch,' said the doctor—'and there's a clock on the mantelpiece. Look here—' and taking up a candle he held it before Rosalie's face. '*There's* a watch for you, Mr. Clyde—what time o'night does that say?'

A different hour from the other, Thornton felt; for with the anxious hearing of their talk the weary look had come back again. She was just fit to sit there and be quiet.

'Now listen to me,' said the doctor, 'and be reasonable for once in your life. Take leave of these good people—friends, one or both of 'em—kiss your sister for goodnight and be glad of the chance; and then go home with me. I'll answer for it she'll be forthcoming in the morning, and I'll take as good care of you as you deserve. Come!—I can't stay here fooling any longer.'

'Nor I,' said Thornton getting up.

'Then thee will leave thy sister?' said the quakeress with a gratified face.

'Since she chooses to stay,' said Thornton. But when he turned towards her and saw that she had risen, the generous feeling prevailed. And replacing her in the armchair, he kissed away the words which were on her lips, and told her he was glad to leave her—she was better there.

'My prescription is short,' said Dr. Buffem, as he stood with the door in his hand,—'a mere word, Miss Rosalie.'

"Take thou of me sweet pillows, sweetest bed,—
"A chamber deaf to noise and blind to light,—
"A rosy garland and a weary head,"

—you know what follows.'

CHAPTER XXIII.

Let me but bear your love, I'll bear your cares.—SHAKSPEARE.

THE sky was covered with clouds when Rosalie took possession of her rooms at the hotel, but there were no clouds on her face; and Thornton admired to see how she could bear to lose and to leave what she enjoyed very much, and take up with any sort of a home. If he had spoken out his whole thought he would have added, 'and any sort of a brother;'—he had never felt more inclined to be good company, and never less satisfied with his performance. But Rosalie was satisfied with everything, or seemed so; and had even the skill to hinder all expression of Hulda's regrets for the cat, the greenhouse, and Mr. Raynor.

The rooms were large and handsome, but like other hotel rooms with no individuality of furniture; the windows were too clearly after a public pattern, the doors numbered to distinguish them from those of other people. It was a part of a home, set apart for their use and labelled. Worse still was Thornton's resolve to eat at the public table,—a resolve so fixed, that after some remonstrance Rosalie gave way. But it wearied her exceedingly. Some of her pleasantest times of seeing her brother were lost now; and instead there was the sight and hearing of a crowd of people who came together but to eat and to discuss eatables. Meals over, Thornton was off; and it was just as it happened whether she saw him again for five minutes until the next physical 'reunion.' The first morning and the second he did sit with her for a while, and stayed at home one whole evening after tea; but the good habit fell off and she was as much alone as ever. More alone—for the range of their once pleasant house had been something, where every picture and piece of furniture gave her a word as she went by, and where the whole atmosphere was that of home. Now, whatever made its way to her senses from without her own room, was strange and depressing. How rarely any foot went along the passage with the free tread of one who walks earnestly in a good pursuit! how few voices spoke except from under a burden or a cloud! The children indeed danced up and down, with the gay spring of a nature that must rebound—touch what it will; but Rosalie looked at Hulda at play in the midst of those hotel chairs, and longed to see her in a setting of green grass and dandelions. But that could not be; though messenger winds were beginning to blow, and the skies looked soft and unbending as from a distant glimpse of the coming spring.

'If people was o' *my* way o' thinkin,' said Miss Jumps one day, 'these here hotels wouldn't make much of a livin;' and Rosalie entirely agreed with her.

'There used to be somethin' going on, home,' Martha continued; 'and Tom Skiddy was good enough for to talk to by spells; but here with forty men round you, more or less, you don't know which way to turn. And you're just getting as thin as a rail, Miss Rosalie—and Hulda's as peaked as she can stand. What ails us to go back to the old house and look out of the broken windows? there'd be some air there, anyway.'

'The broken windows are boarded up, Martha: and as soon as the spring opens we must have painters and masons and I know not what all, at work.'

'They won't have *you*,' said Miss Jumps—' not if you don't pick up astonishin' afore fall. And as for pickin' up here, you might as well smother a chicken in a bag o' corn and then tell him to get fat.'

'Patience, Martha,' Rosalie said with a smile. 'We shall love our own home all the better when we get back to it.'

'Don't it spoil your patience to see other folks have too much?' said Miss Jumps,—''cause it does mine. That's what I said to Tom Skiddy last night; and he was up to telling me that the chance was considerable of my keeping what I had as long as I lived, if that was all. He's stropping his wits a little *too* much, lately, for want of time.'

'What does Tom have to do now, Martha?' said Hulda. 'He don't do anything at the house but sleep there, does he?'

'I guess that's all he ever did, o' nights,' said Miss Jumps. 'And if he got through too much of anything other times it was more'n I could find out. I s'pose he runs round after his muskit now and then. A woman would feel smart at that sort o' work. But men 'll foller a drum most any place,—just as easy as I used to fetch down a swarm of bees with an old tin pan. Only beat hard enough.'

The entrance of Thornton, fresh from his part of the cried-down occupation, restricted all further expression of Martha's mind to the peculiar set of her shoulders as she went off.

'Well, how do you get on here?' said Mr. Clyde as he unbuckled his sword-belt.

'Peacefully,' his sister answered with a smile.

'Which would make an end of me, in short order,' said Thornton.

'How long is it since peace and war joined hands?'

'Only do each other's work upon some people,' said Thornton. 'But can you find nothing else in this way of life? I think it is very good for you.'

She smiled a little to think how much he knew what 'this way of life' was.

'It cannot be like home, you know,—there is more confinement—I see less of you.'

'See enough of me, don't you?'

'Not half!'

'I do not like to quote the proverb, "Un sot trouve toujours un plus sot qui l'admire,"' said Thornton, 'but it really comes up before me.'

'Never mind,' said his sister,—' you know what Rochefoucauld says,—" Si nous ne nous flattions point nous-mêmes, la flatterie des autres ne nous pourrait nuire."'

'*Your* tongue is not often dipped in flattery, to do it justice,' said Thornton. 'A little of the Sweetbrier about that, I think. But I'm afraid if I stayed more at home I should break up the peacefulness.'

Her look told him that his staying away often did, even through the smile with which she answered,

'My dear brother, what do you suppose peace lives on?'

'Can't tell, upon my word, Alie—oyster shells I should think, from their known quietness of disposition.'

'Haven't you got beyond the common idea of peace yet?' said Rosalie.

'What is the common idea?'

She thought a moment, and answered.

> '"Sweet Peace, where dost thou dwell? I humbly crave.
> Let me once know.
> I sought thee in a hollow cave,

And asked if Peace were there.
A hollow winde did seem to answer, No:
Go seek elsewhere."'

'Pretty fair,' said Thornton. 'But before I submit to call that mine, let us have the uncommon version.'

He was sorry he had asked, for he saw in a moment from her changing face where the next answer might come from. But her eyes left his and she was silent.

'Well?' Thornton said a little impatiently, for he deigned not to take the advantage she gave him.

The voice was lower, the tones how different, as she said,

'"*Thou wilt keep him in perfect peace, whose mind is stayed on thee: because he trusteth in thee.*"'

'If ever there could be such a thing as an unconscious Jesuit,' said Thornton, 'I should say you were one. It don't signify what point I set out from—you always bring me up in the same place.'

'Well you lead and I will follow now.'

'Wouldn't make the least difference—I've tried it scores of times.'

She laughed a little, with a half pleased half inquiring look that her brother thought altogether charming.

'I will see what I can do, Alie, about staying more in your cave—I am not sure that it will be much to your advantage.'

The promise was something,—a fair shell and not much more; and so the end of the winter wore away.

Once, soon after the removal to their new quarters, Mr. Raynor had come there; bringing flowers and his refreshing presence where both were needed; and often after that the flowers came without him. They were such regular visitors indeed, that when Rosalie opened the door in the twilight of an early spring evening, she held out her hand for the flowers without perceiving what hand held them, nor guessing who had knocked

'May I come in?' he said.

'Certainly!—I did not see you Mr. Raynor, or at least did not recognise you.'

'I must take another shape next time,' said he smiling. 'Were you ever in doubt about a bunch of flowers?'

'Not often—lately,' she answered.

'What are you doing here this fine evening? if it is a fair question.'

'That most unprofitable of all work—thinking.'

'Unprofitable?'

'I believe I should have said musing; and that seldom gives me much for my pains.'

'It is not the best possible work for you,' said Mr. Raynor. 'Where is Hulda?'

'She has been out all day with Miss Arnet, and came back too tired to sit up an hour longer.'

'Have you been out?'

'No, I have indulged myself with a quiet day at home.'

'Then come and indulge me with a quiet walk. I have been mixing with the crowd to-day till I am tired of earth and its inhabitants, and want some one of them to give me a little refreshment. Come Miss Rosalie, it will do you good.'

But Rosalie hesitated—might not Thornton come home to spend the evening with her? And then she remembered that he had gone to some public dinner and would not get away until very late. So she went.

The hotel was in the very lower part of the city, and a few minutes' walk brought Mr. Raynor and his silent companion upon the Battery and within the sweep of its sea breeze. There was a young moon just travelling down the western slope of the sky, bright and sharp-horned, but with too faint a light to throw more than a narrow rippling streak upon the water; and

> "Silently one by one, in the infinite meadows of heaven,
> "Blossomed the lovely stars, the forget-me-nots of the angels."

The walks were clear of people: many being drawn off to Tammany Hall, either as witnesses or partakers of Commodore Rodgers and the great dinner, and others by other attractions turned elswhere. And it was still enough for the dash of the water to make itself sweetly heard, with little interruption but an oar now and then, or the creaking of the cordage of some vessel as her sails swung round to meet the wind, and her dark shadow crossed the little strip of moonlight. Presently the moon went down, and the evening star 'rode brightest.'

'Do you mean that all the good I am to get must come from the sky and stars?' said Mr. Raynor, when they had sat for some time in almost unbroken silence. 'I thought you were to talk me into a better state of feeling.'

'Did you think that?'

'Not exactly, to speak truth,' said he smiling,—'at least not if you could help it. Did you see how the water closed behind each vessel that crossed the moonlight, and how the bright line was soon as straight and as clear as ever?'

'I watched it constantly.'

'And what did it make you think of?'

'"*The vision is yet for an appointed time, and though it tarry, wait for it; because it will surely come, it will not tarry,*"' she said.

'And this—"*Sorrow may endure for a night, but joy cometh in the morning.*"'

'Yet men see not the bright light which is in the clouds,' said Rosalie.

'They are not called upon to see it—only to believe that it is there. *The Lord* is the light of them that sit in darkness.'

'I did not know you ever felt tired of the world, Mr. Raynor,' said Rosalie after another little pause.

'I do not often—should never, if my place in it were better filled. A little weariness of oneself is a great help towards weariness of other people. There is the strong and sad contrast of the great work to be done, with the poorness and weakness of the machinery; and dissatisfaction says, "*Lord, they have slain thy prophets and digged down thy altars,*"—and hears not the answer of God, "*Yet have I reserved unto myself seven thousand men that have not bowed the knee to the image of Baal.*" But I did not mean to do myself good at your expense. Do you expect to stay here all the summer?'

'I suppose so,' Rosalie said. 'If Thornton should go away for a few days I might go with him. Not else.'

'You cannot bear it.'

'O yes—perfectly. I was here last summer.'

'Yes, you were,' he answered gravely. 'There is but a shadow of you here now.'

'Shadows should not throw shadows,' said Rosalie smiling.

'They keep people in the dark sometimes,' said Mr. Raynor.

'If the people will stay there.'

'I wish the law covered all one's rights,' said Mr. Raynor with a voice that was both earnest and playful. 'I have a defrauded feeling which is a little rampant sometimes. Give me leave to say where you shall be this summer, and see if all your wishes will not be as well furthered. Sometimes I think they would, better.'

'I cannot think so.'

'And you will not put yourself in my hands?'

'I could not be happy to do it, Mr. Raynor—not now.'

'It would go hard with me but I would make you happy, if I once had a chance to try.'

'It would do much towards it if you would make yourself so,' said Rosalie in a low voice.

'That is reserved for somebody else to do.'

There was no answer to this—unless the lower bend of the head were answer; and suddenly rising up, Mr. Raynor drew her arm within his and walked slowly two or three times up and down without speaking a word. Then he stopped at the outer edge of the Battery where the water came swashing up at their feet, one wave following another with its little burden of noise and foam, like the days of human life. If Mr. Raynor thought as he watched them how many such days had rolled on and broken at his feet, without bringing the one thing he most desired, he let not the thought appear. And when he spoke it was in the magnificent words of the prophet.

"Fear ye not me? saith the Lord: will ye not tremble at my presence, which have placed the sand for the bound of the sea by a perpetual decree, that it cannot pass it: and though the waves thereof toss themselves, yet can they not prevail; though they roar, yet can they not pass over it."

There was strong spiritual as well as literal comfort in the words,—there was rest in the mere thought of overruling strength. Rosalie felt it; and stood more easily and breathed freer.

The clocks of St. Paul's and Trinity were striking the hour, the hum of the city every moment receded and softened and died away; and when the last iron clang had sounded forth, the ebbing tides of that day and of the world went each its course in silence.

'That blessed thought of infinite power!' Rosalie said.

'Joined with infinite goodness and wisdom—where should we be without it! Are you tired dear Rosalie? have I kept you here too long?'

The voice was grave, but she knew it would say nothing more to trouble her.

'O no, I am rested.'

He walked with her a while longer, talking brightly and amusingly of different things of interest; and before he left her once more in her own room, she *was* rested, and felt better than she had done in a long time.

CHAPTER XXIV.

Mat. I understand you, sir.
Wel. No question, you do, or you do not, sir.
Every Man in his Humour.

IF anything could have reconciled Rosalie to the thought of leaving town, it was that as the spring went on little Hulda was evidently pining for what the town could not give. The hotel life to which she was now shut up by no means replaced her old life at home; and the April days were not more languid than Hulda.

'Give her a strawberry for her breakfast, and then set her on a chicken's back and let her hunt grasshoppers,' was Doctor Buffem's advice. 'And hark ye, Miss Rosalie, I would recommend another winged horse for yourself—only don't get thrown by endeavouring to fly away from earth altogether, as did Bellerophon.'

The one prescription was hardly more needed than the other. Rosalie knew not how the workings of the mind were refining away the body,—how the anxious watch over one and another was softening down her colour, and chiselling a little too close the fair outlines of her face; nor how very, very delicate the hand was become on which Hulda laid her weary little face for rest and refreshment. No one knew it in fact, but the person whose eye she rarely met, often as it rested on her.

'Thornton,' said Mr. Raynor one night, as they walked home together from the evening drill, 'I wish you would take your sister into the country.'

'Hulda do you mean?' said Thornton, when the first little start of surprise had passed off. 'Yes—I believe she does look rather so-soish.'

'There is no question of that. But I meant Rosalie.'

If the progress of Thornton's mind might be measured by the ground his feet went over, it was tremendous.

'Rosalie!' he said. 'And pray Mr. Raynor, what do you wish me to do with *Rosalie?*'

'Take her into the country, as I said before.'

'But what—what upon earth have you to do with the matter?' said Thornton, whose words and ideas were knocking their heads together after the most approved fashion.

Mr. Raynor smiled a little, but waving the question he only said,

'She is not well, Thornton,—she needs the change even more than Hulda.'

Mr Clyde strode on as before, swinging his sword, and looking very much like a wasp in a cobweb.

'And has she requested your intercession to that effect?' he said.

'No—' replied his companion coldly.

'Then I cannot see, I really cannot imagine what you have to do with it, Mr. Raynor.'

'Neither is that the point. My words are true. She is not the same person for strength that she was a year ago.'

'You have been observant, Mr. Raynor,' said Thornton, though the words half choked him. 'Rosalie will be glad to hear that there are such watchful eyes abroad.'

'You will hardly be repaid for the trouble of telling her; but about that as you please.'

And it will be as I please about taking her into the country I presume,' said Thornton stiffly.

'There would be no question of your pleasure on the subject if you knew how ill she is looking,' said Mr. Raynor with the same grave, undeclarative manner. 'But one who sees her every day becomes accustomed to the change as it goes on.

'And how far out of town would you recommend?' said Thornton with a glance at his companion's face.

'So far, that the town and that place should never be named together.'

'To those woods where the belle and the wild flower met, in short,' said Thornton drily. 'Well—I will think of it. But how will my sister do there without the considerate friends she has in town?'

In absolute silence Mr. Raynor walked on, the calm lines of his face not changing in the least; while Thornton at his side was inwardly working himself up to the boiling point recommended by Dr. Buffem. At last the words came—as come the first drops from the heated spout of a tea-kettle; sputtering forth in great commotion, and almost dried up on their way,

'What the *deuce* have you to do with this matter, sir? What concern can it possibly be of yours?'

'I do not wish to bring a third party into our conversation unnecessarily,' was the quiet reply; 'therefore if you please we will leave that out. As to what concern it is of mine—look at Rosalie yourself, Thornton, and then remember that your eyes see but half in her what mine do.'

It was no longer boiling water,—it was one of those substances which when perfectly hot become perfectly quiet. Thornton even slackened his pace; and while his eyes were outwardly measuring blue flag-stones, in reality they were following Mr. Raynor's advice—and finding it to the last degree disagreeable.—They walked in silence for some time.

'The man who counsels a friend to take care of his bird, is not of necessity intending to steal it himself, Thornton,' said Mr. Raynor as they neared the hotel.

'That is a most unnecessary idea on the part of anybody,' was Mr. Clyde's gracious reply. 'Do you mean to insinuate that my sister is in a cage, Mr. Raynor?'

'A sort of one—in this hotel.'

'The wonder is,' said Thornton breaking forth, 'the most astonishing thing of all is, that you don't relieve me of all responsibility in the matter.'

'Is that the most astonishing thing? Well—be it so. And yet I will not waive all right to entreat for the bird purer air—a bower of leaves to sing in instead of this one of bricks. And rest, and quiet, and sunshine.'

'The bird is much obliged to you,' said Thornton haughtily, 'but I may waive the right if you do not. Assume the charge if you will,—only let it alone while it rests with me.'

'The dove has fed from your hand too long,' said Mr. Raynor quietly.

'Nonsense!' was on Thornton's lips, but it came no further. A something rose up and stayed it there; and though he strode on more vigorously than before, his eyes saw but that one sweet vision, and saw it not clearly. Those few words, the name, the image, had reached the very inner springs of his nature.

And what did the words mean? Was that shadow the truth or his own imagination? He could not decide and he could not ask. No—if the dove would fly he would not hinder her,—he could not bid her go. And even with the thought she was enfolded to his very heart and the heart's own bitterness wept over her in secret.

Not another word was spoken until they paused at the steps of the hotel.

'I shall follow your advice Mr. Raynor,' Thornton said then;—'the more because you have told me the cause of it.' His friend smiled, and gave him a parting look and clasp of the hand that were never forgotten. Thornton went up stairs more completely conquered than he had ever been in his life.

The scene there was not such as to do away the impression. Rosalie and Marion sat near the window talking earnestly, and Hulda with a hand on the lap of each was jumping lightly from side to side; now laying her head upon Rosalie to see how Marion looked, and then leaning upon Marion to try the effect of Rosalie; while the two gave her an occasional glance and smile, but without seeming to come back from their conversation. How completely their different characters were worn on the outside, Thornton thought, as he stopped and looked at them, the twilight and their own preoccupation keeping him unseen; for while Marion's warm quick nature excited itself for every trifle, kept head and face in earnest motion, and gave the little hands many an excursion into the air when Rosalie's lay perfectly quiet,—there were times and subjects that called forth a light and energy in this one's face, before which the other sobered down, and took the listener's part with an air subdued and almost tearful. A manner to which Thornton gave both understanding and sympathy.

The window was open, and the spring wind stirred the curtains with a fitful touch; sometimes sweeping their folds back into the room with its soft gale, and then just playing with their fringe, and softly tossing and waving the hair on the brows of the two ladies.

The twilight was falling softly, mistily, and lights began to glimmer in heaven and on earth; and the city din was murmuring itself to sleep. Footfalls now were individual, and wheels rolled on with monotonous distinctness; and still the air came in with freshening breath, and still the ladies sat and looked and talked. Looked with grave eyes, and talked with quiet voices. Now and then the air wafted up a strong whiff of Havana smoke; or the slamming of the hotel doors, or loud footsteps in its hall broke the silence. But they hardly interrupted the murmur, which seemed to the listeners like the distant beat of the ocean of life about the cave of their own thought.

'And you think, Alie,' said Marion with a tone as if she had been pondering some former words; 'you do truly think that one can learn not to fear death? Death never seems to me a reality but in these mimic ebbings away of life. One's spirits do so ebb away with it, that one naturally asks, will they ever return? I don't love to sit and think at this time of day—it makes me gloomy. And you look as bright as that evening star.'

Rosalie smiled.

'It is so resting to me—so soothing, to think and remember!'

'Yes, at floodtide.'

'If the tide carry not all my treasure it matters little whether it ebb or flow. I shall not lose footing till the commissioned wave come, and then—" The other side of the sea is my Father's ground as well as this side."'

'You speak so assuredly,' Marion said.

'" I know in whom I have believed,"' Rosalie answered with a little bit of that same smile. '" It will be hard if a believing passenger be casten overboard."'

Marion leaned her head against the window frame with

a dissatisfied air and was silent. And wishing to hear no more such words, Thornton came forward and laid a hand upon each.

His sister looked up with a bright welcome, while Marion after one glance and word looked away out of the window, her shoulder half withdrawn from his touch.

'Did you see my carriage at the door, Captain Thornton?' she enquired.

'I did not even look, not knowing you were here.'

'Do you never see a thing without looking?' said Marion a little impatiently.

'If you can see me at present, then doubtless I might have seen your carriage if it was there.'

'O but it isn't there,' said Hulda, trying to get her chin over the window sill; 'so you'll *have* to stay to tea, Marion.'

'I can wait for my tea, pet.'

'But won't you stay?' said the child coming back disappointed. 'Because we want you to very much.'

'And because Rosalie is going out of town in a few days,' observed Thornton.

'Out of town!' said his sister. 'You have had but one word to that bargain yet.'

'I have had as many words as I want.'

'With whom?' said Marion with a keen look. But as Thornton chose to answer the look first the question was not repeated.

'Will you go along and take care of her?' he said.

'That duty would appear, to unsophisticated minds, to devolve upon somebody else.'

'Very likely. But sophisticated minds can see that men have something else to do.'

'It is time they hadn't then,' said Marion.

'I should be very happy to leave you in command of my company, if you prefer that sphere of action.'

'Well I did forget certainly, that just now you *have* something else to do,' was Marion's rather pointed reply.

'But I thought,' said Rosalie, 'that if I went at all you were to go too. I thought you meant to get leave of absence for your own good.'

'For just so much good as it will do me to put you in clover, my dear—no more.'

She shook her head.

'Then I will not be put in clover, and we will stay here quietly together.'

'We will do nothing of the sort,' said Thornton. 'You are to stay all summer at a farmhouse; and I am only waiting to find one that is far enough off.'

'O will you *really* take us away into the country?' cried Hulda, who had stood listening with intense interest. 'O how glad I shall be! Won't it be delightful, dear Alie?' she said, leaning on her sister's lap and looking up.

Rosalie was silent. There had been words just waiting their chance, but at the flush that came over the pale little face raised so eagerly to hers, all power to speak them failed. It was hard to choose between such alternatives. And Thornton saved her the trouble. Never had she seen him so set on anything as upon this plan; and his strong will and Hulda's silent pleadings carried the day. Rosalie quietly made her preparations.

'I s'pose you'll forget all about this here town o' York when you get away once, Martha,' said Tom Skiddy, the night before the journey.

'Like enough I shall,' replied Miss Jumps. 'I'm a first rate hand at forgetting. Lost sight o' more things in my life than you could shake a stick at,—people too.'

'Well remember and come back, will you?' said Tom.

'Can't say—' replied Martha. 'If it should seem to be

advantageous for me to stay there, there's no telling what I may do.'

'Sartain!' replied Tom. 'There's no telling what I may do neither. 'Taint a sort of a world for a man to keep track of his own mind easy.'

'The surest way to keep track of a thing is to run on afore it,' said Martha.

'And then it don't always foller,' said Tom thoughtfully. 'It's a pity things is so easy forgot—it's kind o' pleasant to remember.'

'Well you can always recreate yourself in that way when you've a mind to,' said Miss Jumps, with a somewhat relenting air.

'That's true enough,' said Tom with a similar demonstration. 'So can you.'

CHAPTER XXV.

> On the seas are many dangers,
> Many storms do there arise,
> Which will be to ladies dreadful,
> And force tears from wat'ry eyes.—*Spanish Ladye's Love.*

It was in a corner of the Bay State that Thornton decided to place his sisters. Partly from the fine country and the wholesome air, and partly from the peace and security which could be found there more surely than in New York. But he abhorred stage-coaches; and determined that at least one part of the journey should be pleasant, he would go as far as New Haven by water, and in a sailing vessel—which in those days of Steam's apprenticeship was far better.

The Old Thirteen was a pretty little sloop, neat and trim built; worthy of the sea as well as sea-worthy; and despite her name had seen but just enough service to prove her an excellent sailer. Her canvass was new, with only the unfledged look of newness worn off; her mast white and tapering; her hull painted of a deep dull red half way above the water line, and from that to the bulwarks of a dark olive green. Her flag was of the largest, her streamers of the longest and brightest; her figure-head was the Liberty of the old coins with the thirteen stars for a crown. In this sloop Mr. Clyde saw fit to take passage for New Haven,— not truly because of the beauty of her equipments, but because she was reputed swift and her captain the 'right sort of man.'

He had spent his life in trading vessels upon the Sound,—generally running out as far as Point Judith and taking up a little of the shore trade on his way. For some time indeed, the Sound had been too closely blockaded to permit unarmed vessels much freedom upon its waters, and the shipping trade was rather dull. But Captain Pliny Cruise being of the mind that a week on shore would certainly kill him, continued to brave the enemy's guns as offering a much more desirable death; and by a system of dodging, running, and out-sailing, which was always successful, he carried on his trade with Rhode Island as though no Squadron were in the way.

The Old Thirteen then, lay at her pier in the East river; and the May morning acted the part of Macbeth's witches, and said,

"I'll give thee a wind."

But when Mr. Clyde and his companions appeared, there sprang up a breeze of another kind and not quite so favourable. For Thornton with characteristic carelessness had merely engaged 'the best accommodations there were, for four people;' and the idea of a lady passenger had never entered the Captain's head.

'Bonnets!' he said as Thornton's party emerged from the carriage,—'one, two, three on 'em—what on airth!' And Captain Pliny Cruise at once walked off to the other end of his vessel, took a seat and looked into the water. There he sat until Thornton touched his shoulder.

'Good morning, Captain Cruise.'

'How are you, Mr. Clyde?' said the Captain, looking round and showing a very discomfited face.

'Is this where you commonly receive your passengers?' said Thornton.

'No,' said the Captain, returning to his gaze at the water,—'not commonly. I do' know where the place is, no more.'

'If you are not particularly engaged,' said Mr. Clyde, with some emphasis, 'I should like to know where to put my sisters!'

'So should I,' said Captain Pliny. 'Give a' most anything I'm master of at this present.'

But he rose and walked aft; and being formally presented to Miss Clyde he welcomed her with,

'Right sorry to see you here, ma'am.'

'Sorry to see me?' Rosalie said.

'Exactly,' said Captain Pliny. 'Always sorry to see a cargo come aboard I do' know how to stow.'

'Don't know how to stow!' said Thornton impatiently. 'Why you said you could take half a dozen.'

'Sort not specified,' said the Captain. 'You never said the first word about bonnets—and the Old Thirteen aint a bandbox, though she do come near it.'

'You will not want much room in which to stow me,' said Rosalie with a smile.

'Always give chena particular packing and soft quarters,' said the Captain. 'And if you aint labelled 'Glass with care,' never trust me with another crate. Then there's another thing, Mr. Clyde; afore the vessel heads off into the stream, you'd maybe as well take a look at my chart; but that's between you and me;' and leading the way into the little cabin he made Rosalie understand, that if by the use of the whole or any part of the Old Thirteen she could make herself comfortable, it was at her service.

'Now Mr. Clyde,' he said, 'come and take a look at my chart.'

'I don't know anything about charts,' said Thornton.

''Taint too late, yet,' said the Captain. 'Know where you're going and how to go, and you're half there. Come sir.'

And Thornton went, though laughing both at himself and the Captain; but when once on deck the manner of the latter changed.

'The thing is just this, Mr. Clyde—and I wouldn't have such a cargo aboard, not for a sloop load o' prize money. The Sound's full o' rough customers, sir; and like enough we'll fall in with some of 'em. And they don't speak no softer to ladies' ears than to others.'

'They'll never get a chance to speak to us,' said Thornton,—'they're too far down the Sound.'

'We'll hope that,' said Captain Pliny, 'and yet they might. They've found out there's Eastern people most every place, doubtless. Never run a feminine craft into rough weather sir, if you know it aforehand. They aint just built for it.'

'O,' said Thornton laughing, 'my sister can stand fire like a soldier.'

The old Captain shook his head.

'Ay sir! like and not like! better and worse! And she don't look as though she'd seen much salt water—not o' the genuine.'

'She'll see more if we ever get away from this wharf,' said Thornton. 'You come and go, Captain Cruise,—where's the danger to other people?'

'Ay,' said Captain Pliny,—'I come and go. What of that? This here mainmast's my post, sir—that's why I stand by it. It aint yours. And all the rest o' my fleet is at anchor sir, long ago,—safe moored in the harbour. There's none to look in the papers and see whether Pliny Cruise is arrived, or only cleared for a better country.'

'Well when shall we have our clearance from here?' said Thornton, who was not fond of meeting Rosalie's opinions where he didn't expect them.

'I've said my say,' was the Captain's reply. And in half an hour, during which three or four messengers had been sent in as many different directions for fruit and other lady-like comforts, the Old Thirteen glided off into the channel and set her sails before the wind.

By that time Rosalie and Hulda came on deck again, and took seats there to enjoy the fresh breeze. View there was not, at least that was very well worth looking at; though spring colouring made even those low shores look pretty, and the river in its blue windings shewed many a curl and crest over its rocky bed. The sloop went smoothly on, and her Captain busied himself with his own judgment of her passengers. There was no disagreeable observation of them, but now and then a few words or a look—chiefly at Rosalie; and each time his eyes went back with increased vigilance to the reaches of the river that lay beyond. But the afternoon passed quietly and the night fell with no disturbance: and if Rosalie failed to sleep with absolute forgetfulness, it was for no such reason as made Captain Pliny pace the deck all night over her head.

The morning broke with light airs from the north, and the vessel made small headway. The Sound began to open out now, and the prow of the little vessel pointed to a horizon line of sea in the far distance; lying blue and sweet as if no disagreeable thing had ever crossed it. Yet thither were Captain Pliny's eyes directed, as if at every moment he expected to see the whole British fleet come in sight; while the same watchful glances raked the coast on both sides.

'How fair everything is this morning,' said a voice at the Captain's elbow.

'Yes—all is fair—sartain!' said Captain Pliny rising with a surprised look at his visitor. 'Sartain!' he repeated softly as his eye took another observation of that delicate face. 'Fair and softly goes so far into this twenty-fifth of May. But Madam we don't all keep watch aboard,—and they that watch for the morning had ought to be the strong and not the weak.'

She smiled—partly at the rough and kindly mingling in his speech, partly at the 'sweet English' which as she truly said the Bible always was to her ear; and she repeated—

"*My soul waiteth for the Lord more than they that watch for the morning.*"

'Ay, ay,' said Captain Pliny, 'I thought that was in your face, from the first you come aboard. But if you'd ever been where I have—on deck in such a hurricane as you couldn't stand for one minute, young lady; with the rain coming down whole water, and the waves flying to meet it like a thirsty caravan,—I say if you'd ever done that, you'd know what the verse meant! And it seemed as if I 'waited for light and behold obscurity.''

Did she not know? had she not watched through those long nights of stillness in a sick room which precede the storm and the wreck? She was silent and Captain Pliny went on.

'Waiting's a hard thing somewhiles—that's true. I've seen times when I would do the worst day's work I ever did, sooner than wait. And yet "*blessed is he that waiteth,*" and "*he that waiteth shall not be ashamed,*"—that's true too, on land and water. Even for things of this world.'

'Yes,' Rosalie answered; and half to herself she went on.

"*For since the beginning of the world men have not heard, nor perceived by the ear, neither hath the eye seen, O*

God, beside thee, what he hath prepared for him that wait eth for him."

'True, true,' said Captain Pliny; 'I believe that. And this heavens and earth shall not come into mind, for the glory that excelleth. And yet that's sort o' handsome,' he said after a little pause, raising his weather-browned hand and pointing forwards. The wind was blowing quite fresh, and beneath its influence the water rose and fell in large, deep green waves, each with its white cap lit up with a thousand sparkles. The vessel dipped and rose on the undulations with a graceful submission to circumstances; and now and then one of her opposers came full tilt against her prow, and was dashed to pieces on the little Liberty figurehead.

'The Old Thirteen takes the waves pretty much as her namesake did the British,' remarked Captain Pliny as the spray flew over the deck. 'How do you like that, young lady?'

'I like it well,' she answered with a smile.

'Craft running t'other way has it smoother,' said the Captain; 'but the wind's dead ahead for us, and we take the waves which way we can get 'em. Slow work too. But an honest voyage is always just the right length.'

Their progress was indeed slow. Long tacks from side to side made it rough as well, and every puff of the wind was charged with spray; but still the Captain's unwonted cargo remained on deck, and even Hulda enjoyed without fear the salt water and the fresh breeze. There had been little in sight all the morning,—few white wings abroad but sea gulls, and what there were mere specks. By dinner time two or three of them were nearer, but the Captain knew them for American coasters, and having pointed out Hart Island to Rosalie, and told her that at this rate she would be in New Haven before she knew it, they went to dinner.

'You have spent all your life in this way, Captain?' said Rosalie.

'Set afloat afore I knew a painter from a buoy,' returned Captain Pliny; not at all aware that his hearers had not yet attained that knowledge.

'And what sort of a life do you call it?' said Thornton.

'First rate!' said Captain Pliny. 'Can't be beat, if you go the world over and try your hand at everything.'

'Tedious enough, I should think,' said Thornton.

'Why as to that, young gentleman,' said Captain Pliny, 'there's many a one I do suppose, too fresh to like salt water. But no man who does his duty has a right to call his life tedious—or I might say, a chance; for those very things are just what he was put into the world to do. If he will ballast his ship according to his own fancy, not for her build and cargo, no wonder if she don't sail well.'

'One might have a bad cargo though,' said Thornton.

'Not without you've got sense to match,' said the Captain. 'The best cargo's what'll fetch most where you're going.—The end of the voyage, young gentleman, and the profits—keep your eye on them,—then load your ship and make sail.'

'Now here were you only yesterday getting a bad cargo, said Thornton.

'Bad? no,' said Captain Pliny with a smile—'just a thought too good; and I won't say that feminine bills of lading are always made out true. Put 'em in another hull's the best way—let them have their craft and keep your own, —keep at a safe distance and you may sail on together 'most'—

'Sloop ahoy!

The words rang through the Old Thirteen as if she had been a speaking trumpet herself. Before they had died away Captain Pliny stood on the deck with his own trumpet in hand.

'Old Thirteen—New York—Pliny Cruise, commander,'—the words almost knocked each other down with the rapidity of their egress.

'Put about—' came from the other vessel, which was one of the Government coasters. 'Enemy below.'

'What force?' returned the Captain.

'Frigate—38'—was the reply.

'How far?'

'Four miles.'

Captain Pliny laid down his trumpet and turned to confront his passengers, who stood close behind him.

'I told you so, Mr. Clyde,' he said. 'I shewed you a Squadron laid down in my chart, as plain as the old Point herself. Never launch a feminine craft on no sea but the Pacific.

'What is to hinder our running for New Haven and outrunning the Frigate?' said Thornton.

'Might fall out that we shouldn't win the race,' said the Captain.

'But you run past these frigates continually?'

'Just so,' said the Captain,—'I do, sartain:—hope to again,—when there's only Pliny Cruise aboard it don't signify. I'd rather be shot through than have the Old Thirteen turn tail this fashion.'

'Sloop ahoy!' came from another coaster that was bearing down upon them.

'Ay, ay!' said Captain Pliny catching up his trumpet to reply.

'Frigate ahead—38 guns—run!' was shouted out as the vessel swept by.

'Now there's a few of the unpleasant'st words!' said the Captain,—'though I've heard it all afore. Not a gun—'cept for salutes,—I'd like to give 'em a kiss once!—Must be done.—Put about there!' he shouted,—'haul down her colours!—all sail for New York!' And as he walked off the Captain tried to console himself with,

'Can't run a feminine craft into danger—*can't*—it goes agin my conscience.'

And as one sail after another spread out in its place, until near all were set that she would carry, the Old Thirteen changed her course and went scudding up the Sound. But as if to shew his good inclinations, the Captain seated himself with his face in the other direction and sailed backwards.

'Pliny Cruise,' he said to himself, 'never engage a cargo again without knowing what it is.'

The wind held on its way and the vessel on hers without interruption; but the passengers took their tea alone and Captain Pliny would not leave the deck. There Thornton found him when he went up at nine o'clock, but Rosalie and Hulda remained below.

Captain Pliny was on his feet now, standing motionless at the stern of the vessel; his eyes doing what eyes could to pierce the darkness on all sides, but especially in the wake of his own sloop.

'Dark night,' said Thornton as he came up.

'If we don't get more light on the subject afore another hour, be thankful,' said the Captain. 'You see them lights astarn? they're after us, as sure as my name's what it is; and whichever of us gets in first 'll have the best of it.'

'After us?' said Thornton. 'The frigate?'

'Something less than that,' said Captain Pliny,—'nothing more than a sloop, I take it. But she follows us. I've veered once or twice to try her, and when she turns you can see eight mouths on a side.'

'Lights?' said Thornton.

'Ay—at her ports,' said the Captain coolly. 'I can't tell yet which of us gains.'

'Hoa! ship ahoa!' came faintly from the pursuing vessel.

'There you are!' said Captain Pliny. 'Mind your own business and leave Yankees to ask questions. Make sail!' he added, turning quick about. 'If we've got to shew the white feather it shall be a good one!' And as more and more canvass was spread and filled there came another hail borne down on the night wind.

'She'll speak louder next time,' said Captain Pliny,— 'and we've got no more canvass. Go below Mr. Clyde, and take care of your glassware. What man can do has been done—what the Lord will let him do.'

But Thornton stood still.

Two or three port-hole lights appeared now, and presently a brilliant flash shot out into the darkness, and a ball whizzed through the mainsail of the little sloop which was spread out before the wind.

'Plain speaking,' said Captain Pliny, almost leaning over the stern of the vessel in his interest. 'There comes another;—and a third;—right through her sails, both on 'em.'

But the fourth shot fell astern.

'We gain now,' said the Captain with a voice less clear than before. 'I doubt Mr. Clyde there's something stronger than wind helping us on.'

And as if impelled by some new power the Old Thirteen sped along, until even the lights of the pursuing vessel grew dim in the distance. Not until then did Thornton quit the deck.

IN THE CABIN.

Rosalie sat by Hulda's bed, so motionless that her brother at first paused lest she might be asleep. But she looked up, and as he came and sat down by her she laid her head on his shoulder, and neither spoke nor moved till the day broke. Captain Pliny's advice needed no further repetition.

CHAPTER XXVI.

> O blessed nature, "O rus! O rus!"
> Who cannot sigh for the country thus,
>   Absorbed in a worldly torpor—
> Who does not yearn for its meadow-sweet breath,
> Untainted by care, and crime, and death,
> And to stand sometimes upon grass or heath—
>   That soul, spite of gold, is a pauper!—HOOD.

'IT's an astonishing thing how much it takes to kill folks!' said Martha Jumps the morning after their safe arrival in Massachusetts. 'Beats all my arithmetic. Now here we are, just as 'live as can be,—nobody'd guess to look at us that we'd been chased and run over and shot through.'

The scene was the kitchen of the farm house where Rosalie was to spend the summer; and as Miss Jumps looked out of the open window over a pleasant expanse of green meadows, cows, chickens, and corn fields, agreeably diversified with a red barn and a fair little brook; the perils of the sea appeared in strong contrast. Peace was the atmosphere around everything in sight. The cattle cropped their grass in a quiet leisurely way, secure and satisfied; the shadows crept softly down the green slopes, aware of the sun's pursuit but with no fear of being caught; and in the uncut fields the grass waved to and fro with the very motion of repose. Swift of wing and light of heart, the feather-clad tribes bestirred themselves for breakfast; and filled up that hour of the day with a merry song and chatter which did honour to their good sense and to their business habits. No such morning songster would ever build his nest ill, or talk while it was a building, or tire on the wing when seeking food for his family. Such joy with a day's work before it, said the work would be done well.

Some chickens were already in the cow meadow, circling about the cattle as they nosed the rich herbage and started a thousand insects; and others sauntered along wherever a chance grasshopper or a fly-away butterfly might lead them. And the little brook murmured of freshness, of coolness, of no work but rest. And yet its work was to run—and it ran, —tumbled too, occasionally, but not as if it thought it hard work. Clearly the brook took things by their smooth handle. It ran not by the road, upon which opened the kitchen windows, but through a dell at the back of the house—which oddly enough was also the front. For the house with singular good taste had set its face to the dell, and into that cool shade looked the best windows and the best door; leaving the kitchen and wood shed in full possession of the road, its dust, and its passing wagons. Even the well with its boom of a water-drawer, stood by the road-side; and visiters arriving in that direction had their choice of a walk through or a walk round the house.

'This is a queer place o' yours, Mrs. Hopper,' said Martha Jumps, when she had looked out of the window for the space of one minute. 'It sounds dreadful quiet after York.'

'Don't say!' replied Mrs. Hopper. 'Why there's a noise here sometimes to that point, with the chickens and the dog and the children, that I can't hear myself think.'

The voice issued from a dark blue calico sunbonnet, plentifully sprinkled with white spots, the apex to a tall and slim pyramid of the same. Two brown hands, hard and sunburnt, but nervous and capable withal, rested on the window sill; and that was the outward display of Mrs. Hopper.

'I s'pose you're used to doin' with such noise as you can get, and makin' the most of it,' said Martha.

'I guess I ought to be used to 'most everything here,' said Mrs Hopper. 'All the fetching up I ever got come off o' this farm, and my forbears lived here longer'n I can count. It's a right good one, too.'

'Looks enough like it,' said Martha. 'How come you to get your house wrong side before?'

'Didn't get it,' said Mrs. Hopper, as if the words implied some mistake on the part of the house builder. 'It was sot so a'purpose.'

'What for?' said Martha.

'He was a thoughtful sort of a man that did it,' said Mrs. Hopper, 'and he kind o' fancied the brook looked lonesome. Kitchen winders he said ought to have the sun on to them,—didn't make no odds about the company side, for that warnt never used unless there *was* company. When a man's alone he wants everything done to him, and round there he said you couldn't hear a wagon go by once a week. That's what they say he said—them that's gone now.'

And Mrs. Hopper took off her sunbonnet, and having carefully bent it into shape, she put it on again; thereby giving a short view of her hair, which had much the colour and appearance of dried corn silk, and of a face strong and weatherbeaten—useful but not ornamental.

'Sunbunnits is dreadful smothery, aint they?' said Miss Jumps as she surveyed the operation.

'Why my, no,' said Mrs. Hopper. 'I don't never feel as though I had a stitch o' clothes on about my work without I have a bunnit.'

'Well I think likely you don't,' said Martha, 'and I knew what that was once myself, but I've got out of the fashion. I haven't been in the country since I was fifteen.'

'The land sakes!' said Mrs. Hopper. 'How the goodness did you get along? That's just Jerushy's years. Jerushy's real smart too, though you wouldn't think it to look at her; but she's always enjoyed such ill health. She faints away so easy,—a little scare or anything of that sort'll keel her right over. I wouldn't wonder now if she'd drop if you told her Abijah was coming.'

Miss Jumps naturally inquired who Abijah might be.

'Abijah?' said Mrs. Hopper—'why that's my son— Abijah Hopper. Five foot nine in his stockings and as handsome as a pictur'. He's off to some fur'n country now, fighting for his'n.'

'How old is he?' said Martha.

'Just in his two and twenty,' replied Mrs. Hopper. 'He was first and then Jerushy; but Jerushy never see her father to know him.'

'She didn't!' said Martha.

'No,' said Mrs. Hopper taking off the sunbonnet and giving it another bend.

'Well who are the children you tell about?' said Martha.

'Not mine,' said Mrs. Hopper—'The neighbour's saplings come in here whiles and raise Cain with Jerushy.'

'Got pleasant neighbours here?' said Martha.

'Pleasant enough as folks run—' said Mrs. Hopper,— 'and that's pretty much like a flock o' sheep. There's some fine families. But this won't make my child a frock,' she added, tying her sunbonnet with great vigour and tightness 'What time does your folks breakfast?'

'O just when they take a notion,' said Martha imposingly.

'That's the time o' day, is it?' said Mrs. Hopper. 'Then I'll tell you what, they'll have to get it without me. I have to pour out coffee bright and early for the men folks, and it saves time to eat as I go along. And two breakfasts in a morning is one too many for my appetite.'

'I guess they'll all be glad o' the spare one,' said Martha. 'I'm hungry, for one.'

'You look as if you was used to that—stall fed,' said Mrs. Hopper. 'But Jerushy can fry the eggs as good as I can, every bit—whenever they do get up,—and there's bread and butter enough in the pantry—cheese too if they like it; and pies, real good ones. Tell 'em to eat all they can lay their hands on.'

'They always have their eggs boiled,' said Martha.

'Then they don't know what's good,' said Mrs. Hopper. 'But it's nothing to me if they eat 'em raw. There's eggs enough, and water enough, and kettles enough—fire enough too, for that matter; but if I'm not up to the store in a jiffy Squire Hubbard 'll be off with my quarter of mutton. He owes me two now.'

And Mrs. Hopper departed; leaving Martha in great admiration of her smartness and liberality, to get breakfast with Jerusha, who was a chip of the same block. Or rather a *whittling*—with very faint blue eyes and a tongue that was strong in proportion.

With this young lady's able assistance and conversation, Martha prepared both table and breakfast admirably; and Rosalie found but one thing wanting to her comfort. Now that the time was come for parting with her brother, she felt the old painful doubt of it grow stronger; and often wished that she had refused to leave the city. Sometimes she half resolved to go back with him; and then a look at Hulda's face, already brightening in the pure air, kept her silent. And silent the whole breakfast time was. But after breakfast, when the table was cleared and Hulda had gone out to inspect clover heads, Thornton spoke.

'I hope you feel satisfied with your farm house, Alie?'

'I should be, if you were to be in it.'

'I thank you my dear—I am afraid I should not.'

'I have been wishing this morning that I had not come or that I was going back with you.'

'Thank you for that too,' he said, drawing back her hair and kissing her, 'but I do not join in the wish.'

They stood silent again; and the little wagon that was to take him to meet the stage came slowly out of the barn, and was attached to its locomotive.

'What commands, Alie?' said Thornton then. 'I must be off, my dear, in five minutes.'

She turned and laid her hands on his shoulders after her old fashion, and looked at him, and did not speak. Her heart was too full, each word that came to her lips seemed too weak; and without words the brother and sister parted.

'"*He is able to keep that which I have committed to him*,"' Rosalie thought, as she saw Thornton drive off and caught the last wave of his hand. And quitting the window she sat down and took her Bible. Not to read, but to turn over leaf after leaf; catching here and there a word of comfort, a word of hope, a word of strength; until the promises had done their work. Her lips lost their nervous trembling, and with a few long breaths the heart beat easier; and laying her head down upon the closed book Rosalie cried herself to sleep.

'Well this is a pretty state of things!' said Miss Jumps when she came in to set the table for dinner. 'Here's everything ready—and the mutton 'll be rags, and no living creature can tell what the potatoes 'll be. Pickles 'll keep —that's one thing, and so 'll bread,—and she wants it bad enough in all conscience.' And softly closing the door at the end of her soliloquy, Martha retired.

CHAPTER XXVII.

> But my good mother Baystate wants no praise of mine,
> She learned from *her* mother a precept divine
> About something that butters no parsnips, her *forte*
> In another direction lies, work is her sport,
> (Though she'll curtsey and set her cap straight, that she will,
> If you talk about Plymouth and one Bunker's Hill.)
>
> FABLE FOR CRITICS.

How lovely it was! how fresh, how sweet!—with what a fair face did Massachusetts welcome the summer. Ceres followed close on the steps of her labourers, and the young grain with its vivid green hue was fast shooting up into perfection. The potato fields with their long alternate lines of brown and green, the corn fields with their tufted crop; and meadows in the mowing stage, and others that were one spread of red clover blossoms; swelled upon the hills and sloped down into the valleys, and were dovetailed into each other as far as the eye could reach. Everything about the farms and about the houses had that perfectly *done up* look, which shewed the owners quick of eye and hand. The fence rails were up, the bar-place stood steady, the gates swung freely and shut tight. And vines were trained, and wood sheds full, and barns and outhouses in good order. The cattle too looked sleek, and the many-coloured droves of horses gambaded about the fields with the very friskiness of freedom and good living. Content was the very atmosphere of the region.

But Rosalie found it hard to get used to her new way of life. She loved its quietness with all her heart, but it gave her more thinking time than was quite good for her. For with a heart in itself perfectly in tune with all the sweet sounds and influences that were around her, she wanted a little of Hulda's untouched joyousness to take their full benefit. As it was they often set her a musing,—as often perhaps made her grave as gay. Constantly the image of Thornton would present itself; and 'what is he doing?' was no resting question,—she wearied herself with asking what there was none to answer. She tried to throw the burden off, and yet the shadow of it remained; and like a fair plant deprived of the sunlight, her colour grew more and more delicate. Little Hulda was every day gaining strength and health, and her gambols were almost her sister's only amusement; but even from them Rosalie sometimes turned away, with a sickness at heart that refused to be forgotten.

For a while after Thornton left her, he wrote long letters, for him, and often; but then they dwindled, and became angel's visits only in the length of time between. Yet his sister craved even them most eagerly, and each time hoped to find more words and those more comforting. The change was the other way; and well she felt that they would have been longer had the writer been better satisfied with himself, —that if the stream of his daily thought and action had flowed in a purer channel, it would have turned with a fuller gush towards her. He was going on then just in the old way, and she was not there to use even her weak efforts. And sometimes unbelief was ready to ask why?—and when faith bade her wait,—then came back the old Captain's quotation—" It seemed as if 'I waited for light and behold obscurity.'"

'It aint none o' my business, I do suppose,' said Mrs. Hopper one day, when she had followed Rosalie out to the edge of the ravine and stood within three feet of her for some time without being observed; 'and 'taint likely I'll get many thanks for speaking; but it does appear to me, Miss Clyde, that you want shaking up.'

'I!' said Rosalie starting.

'Why yes,' said Mrs. Hopper, 'you. What's the use o' coming out here to stand'n look at that brook—jus' as if it hadn't been running as hard as it could ever since the deluge.'

'But it's a pretty thing to look at,' said Rosalie.

'Maybe it is—' said Mrs. Hopper,—'I'm not in that line o' business myself. *I*'d rather look at a mill tail. Do you more good too. Don't that everlasting spattering down there make you think of all the friends you ever had or expected?'

'What makes you imagine such a thing?' said Rosalie.

'Looked as if you'd been talkin with half of 'em, to say the least. Now I've always got too much to do for my friends to sit'n think about 'em.'

'Suppose there was nothing else you could do, Mrs. Hopper?' said Rosalie.

'Then I'd take good care of myself for 'em—besides there always is something—one thing or 'tother. Folks that can work, can work; and folks that can write, can write; and folks that can pray, can pray, one would suppose,—and believe too.'

But Rosalie turned to her a face so submissive to this last reproof, that Mrs Hopper had no heart to give more.

'Now I'll tell you what it is,' she said, 'my tongue's as

rough as a card, I know, but it don't want to stroke things the wrong way; 'n it makes me feel queer to have you gettin' thin on the place—and payin' so handsome too—which nobody ever did afore, nary one. To be sure you do run round after that child all day, but it's a question which way that works.'

'What would you like to have me do?' said Rosalie smiling.

'Will you do it?' said Mrs. Hopper.

'I will try.'

'Just let Hulda run round by herself a spell then,' said Mrs. Hopper—'I'll have an eye to her—and you get on one of the farm horses and trot off to seek your fortune. I tell you old Lord North 'll shake up a person's ideas so you wouldn't know 'em again afterward!'

'Is Lord North one of the farm horses?' said Rosalie.

'Why yes,' said Mrs. Hopper, taking off her sunbonnet and straightening the edge; 'Stamp act and Lord North—he called 'em so because he hadn't no patience with Lord North. However the horse behaves better 'n *he* did, by a long jump, and so does Stamp. Will you try him?'

'If I can get a saddle and skirt—and find a day when the horse is not ploughing.'

'He won't plough with you on his back,' said Mrs. Hopper, 'and you might do worse if he did. The saddle 's easy enough—what ails the frock you have on?'

'O it's too short,—I will get some stuff and make one.'

'That's long enough, for gracious,' said Mrs. Hopper—'you might as well not have tops to your feet, now; but fix it any way you like. I'll get some Indian willer and twist you up a first rate rattan. See if that don't put a little genuine red in your cheeks. All you've got now just makes you look whiter. Don't you want to go up to the sewin' meetin this afternoon? they'd be tickled to death to see you, and if you can't knit you can look on.'

'I will go anywhere you have a mind to take me,' said Rosalie, with a hearty appreciation of the good will of her hostess.

'Well now that's clever,' said Mrs Hopper. 'I like to see folks that have got some reason into them. And I s'pose you won't mind your Martha's going along,—times when all the men fight together 'twon't hurt the women to knit, I guess. But I don't believe now you'd be a bit stuck up in the best o' times—I'll say that for you, and you're the first city body I ever did say it for.'

The sewing meeting—which might more properly have been called a knitting meeting—met that afternoon in a tall white house by the roadside, which having neither porch nor vines nor piazza, nor even a wing, presented a singularly bare and staring appearance. It being generally supposed however, that juvenile seats of learning should be as unattractive as possible, this was quite in order, and might be claimed as a model. Straight, square, the windows drawn up like the multiplication table, the doors at either end,—the building was highly fitted to inspire its tenants with a love for irregularities of any kind. Even the white paling was angled by rule, and equally distant from the house on every side.

At twelve o'clock that day the school had been dismissed for the usual Saturday afternoon holiday; and so soon thereafter as dinner could be eaten and cleared away, ones and twos and threes of the feminine population of White Oak, began to approach the angular schoolhouse paling. Some few in straw bonnets with knots of gay ribbon, but the most in calico sunbonnets,—made it is true after very different patterns—ruffled and unruffled, corded, pasteboarded, and quilted; but each with its long depending cape, and its somewhat careworn and hardfeatured face beneath.

Hardfeatured not by nature but by work,—staid, and combed down, as their hair was combed back; and with a certain mingling of sober, subdued, wide awake, and energetic, in the general look and mien, which spoke a life of work and emergency that each one must meet for herself, and could. The mere walk of these women as they converged towards the schoolhouse, spoke energy and independence,—there was freedom and self assertion in the very gait; yet more of the feeling which says 'I am as good as you are,' than of that which would say 'I am better.' Neighbours of very different standing indeed (as to wealth and name) exchanged most affable salutations; though always with that same air of gravity which seems chosen by our country people as more dignified than a smile.

Some—especially the younger women—carried fanciful and gay coloured workbags, from the top of which stuck out bright knitting-needles; but more had their work in their pockets or merely wrapped together in their hands, just as it had been caught up from the window sill, with perhaps a twisted skein or two of yarn to bear it company. One or two were even knitting as they walked along.

'I wouldn't wonder a bit if we were late,' said Mrs. Hopper, as they went up the little slope down which the boys used to rush with accelerated speed the moment school was let out. 'Mis' Clipper's bunnet's gone in, and she aint apt to be the first apple that falls.'

A steady murmur that issued from one of the end doors seemed to confirm this suspicion, and when they entered the room it was quite full. That is it was well *lined*, for everybody sat back against the wall,—and there was a perfect glitter of knitting-needles. Knit, knit, knit, knit,—

here a grey sock and there a blue mitten and there a scarlet comforter; while the knitters went carelessly on with their talk, looked out of the window and at each other's work, got up and crossed the floor and came back again, and never stayed their fingers for an instant. Eyesight seemed needless—except to examine Miss Clyde when she appeared, and to form an exact opinion as to her dress. One or two of the younger ones, who had worn straw bonnets to the meeting, laid down their work for a minute till the new arrival had taken her seat, but the others knit on as fast as ever; with merely a 'Hope you're well Miss Clyde,' from those who felt best acquainted.

At the further end of the room a large wheel flew round and round, under the hands of a brisk young lady who stepped back and forth with very creaking shoes; and the bright little spindle whirr-r-red! off the yarn with consummate neatness and speed.

'What will you set me about?' said Rosalie, when she had found a place—not of rest—upon one of the hard wooden chairs. 'Shall I wind some yarn?'

'A person can do that for himself about as handy,' said one of the company, who with her right knee a rest for the left had elevated her left toe into the air, where it did duty as a reel.

'What then?' said Rosalie. 'I am afraid I do not knit fast enough to be of much use in that way.'

'Every roll makth one leth, Mith Clyde,' said the brisk little spinner, stooping as she spoke to take another from the bundle that lay across the wheel.

'Yes, if I could turn them off as fast as you do,' said Rosalie.

'Maria Jane does spin fast,' observed Mrs. Clipper.

'But look a here,' said Mrs. Hopper, 'there's just that

one wheel—and I don't s'pose any one here's got spare knittin' work.'

Nobody had.

'There's nothing for her to do but look on then,' said Mrs. Hopper.

'What ails her to read the news?' said the postmaster's wife producing a paper from her pocket. 'This only just come from York; and he brought it when he came in this noon and then went off and left it after all. So thinks I I'll take it along—the children won't get it anyway.'

This motion was much approved; and with exemplary patience and distinctness Miss Clyde read the paper for the benefit of the meeting. Nor without interest to herself; for there was much that she wanted to know.

A few paragraphs read, such as 'Battle of Bridgewater' —'Truly British account,' &c. then came,

"Phœbe and Essex—before the capture of the latter."

'*Before* the capture of the latter!' said Mrs. Hopper dropping her work. 'Why when on earth or on water was the Essex taken?'

'It does not say,—it refers to some former account.'

'We lost our last paper,' remarked the postmaster's wife.

'Then Abijah Hopper's a prisoner and I knew no more of it than a baby!' said his mother.

There was a pause, even of the knitting-needles, and then Mrs. Clipper vouchsafed to say,

'He mayn't be took, Mis' Hopper—he might ha' got away.'

'Got away!' said Mrs. Hopper contemptuously—'skimming over the ocean like a sea-duck! And what did he go to sea for, I should like to know?'

'Didn't go to be took, did he?' ventured Mrs. Clipper.

'Yes he did,' said Mrs. Hopper—'when his time come and he couldn't help it.'

"'Taint worth while to fret till you *do* know, Mith Hopper,' said Maria Jane from her wheel.

'I should like to see myself at it,' said Mrs Hopper, the little burst of indignation having been eminently useful in keeping down her anxiety. 'Read straight on Miss Clyde—don't stop for half a piece of news.'

Rosalie read straight on.

"Fortifications at Brooklyn."

"On Tuesday morning last, the artillery company of Capt. Clyde (reinforced to the number of about 70 by volunteers from the seventh ward) with the officers of the third brigade of infantry under Gen. Mapes, repaired to Brooklyn for the purpose of commencing the additional fortifications for the defence of this city. They broke ground about 8 o'clock under a salute from a 6 pounder of Capt. Clyde's, on the heights southeast of the Wallabout. Gen. Swift superintended their construction, attended by alderman Buckmaster, of the corporation committee of defence; and Major Raynor, commandant of the district, with others, visited and remained with them through the morning. The weather was extremely fine, the situation airy and the prospect beautiful and commanding; and the labour was begun with a degree of cheerfulness and alacrity highly honourable to the gentlemen concerned.

"The societies of Printers, Cabinetmakers, Tanners and Curriers, Cordwainers, Butchers, House-carpenters, Pilots, officers of the 10th brigade infantry, of the 3d regt. artillery, students of medicine, sixty hands of the wire factory, and many others not mentioned, have already volunteered one day's labour to the construction of these works."

"The Printers being employed yesterday at Brooklyn

'Make the bread, Martha?—what upon earth for should you spoil a batch of flour? I've got my hands yet—feet too,—if I haven't got every else.'

And with the pent-up torrent whirling her in its grasp, she would go round the house and do two women's work at once. But if perchance Rosalie came to seek her—or without seeking came in her way; and she met the sweet look that had known its own sorrow, and felt hers,—Mrs. Hopper gave way at once; and dropping whatever she had in her hand would sit down, and as she expressed it 'have her cry out'—then and there.

'I aint a bit better than a fool when I come across you,' she said on one of these occasions, when the tears were spent for the time, and she had looked up and saw Rosalie still standing by her.

'It isn't best to keep up always,' said Rosalie gently, and sitting down by her on the stairs.

'Oh my!' said Mrs. Hopper, leaning her head back against the wall—and there was a world of expression in the words. 'I have to keep up out there, or that child would drive the life out of me. She feels pretty much as Noah did when the flood come and took all away. She aint used to trouble yet, poor thing—and 'twon't do her no good to get used to this sort. There's no more brothers to lose for her.'

Rosalie almost shivered at the words, and for a moment she did not speak. Then her hand was laid softly upon Mrs. Hopper's.

'When the flood came and took all away, those that were in the ark were safe,' she said.

The hands, toil-worn and toil-hardened, closed upon that little white messenger of sympathy; and Mrs. Hopper leaned her face down upon them, the tears again streaming down her cheeks.

'Don't you fret yourself,' she said, looking up after a while. 'I'll feel better when he's come and I've done all I can for him. And I've got to go see to things afore this day goes over my head. Would you mind going too? It sha'n't be anywhere to hurt you.'

Rosalie readily promised her company.

'Then I'll come for you when I'm ready,' said Mrs. Hopper, 'and we'll slip out o' the front door and down the brook,—I don't want Jerushy to go.' And hearing a step she started up and went off.

After dinner as Rosalie sat alone in her room, Mrs. Hopper came softly in, with her sunbonnet held down by her side; and the two went out of the front door and were soon hid in the trees that hung over the dell.

'I sent 'em all off into the garden to look for a hen's nest,' said Mrs. Hopper, as they descended towards the brook, 'so we've got ten minutes clear, and that's enough. Miss Clyde, you aint one of the folks that's easily frighted, be you?'

'I never was much tried,' said Rosalie, 'but I think I may say no.'

'Some is so 'feerd o' death and all that sort o' thing,' said Mrs. Hopper, 'that they'd only ha' plagued me.' And without further explanation she began to follow the brook in its course, with an air of business determination that seemed a relief to her mind,—bestowing no more words upon Rosalie, but never failing to give her a hand in the difficult places.

It was rough going but beautiful. The large moss-covered stones, dripping with the spray of the brook, stood in and athwart its bed; now turning the course of the bright water, and now shining beneath its rush as through a transparent veil. And at every turn almost, the stream broke

'Make the bread, Martha?—what upon earth for should you spoil a batch of flour? I've got my hands yet—feet too,—if I haven't got every else.'

And with the pent-up torrent whirling her in its grasp, she would go round the house and do two women's work at once. But if perchance Rosalie came to seek her—or without seeking came in her way; and she met the sweet look that had known its own sorrow, and felt hers,—Mrs. Hopper gave way at once; and dropping whatever she had in her hand would sit down, and as she expressed it 'have her cry out'—then and there.

'I aint a bit better than a fool when I come across you,' she said on one of these occasions, when the tears were spent for the time, and she had looked up and saw Rosalie still standing by her.

'It isn't best to keep up always,' said Rosalie gently, and sitting down by her on the stairs.

'Oh my!' said Mrs. Hopper, leaning her head back against the wall—and there was a world of expression in the words. 'I have to keep up out there, or that child would drive the life out of me. She feels pretty much as Noah did when the flood come and took all away. She aint used to trouble yet, poor thing—and 'twon't do her no good to get used to this sort. There's no more brothers to lose for her.'

Rosalie almost shivered at the words, and for a moment she did not speak. Then her hand was laid softly upon Mrs. Hopper's.

'When the flood came and took all away, those that were in the ark were safe,' she said.

The hands, toil-worn and toil-hardened, closed upon that little white messenger of sympathy; and Mrs. Hopper leaned her face down upon them, the tears again streaming down her cheeks.

'Don't you fret yourself,' she said, looking up after a while. 'I'll feel better when he's come and I've done all I can for him. And I've got to go see to things afore this day goes over my head. Would you mind going too? It sha'n't be anywhere to hurt you.'

Rosalie readily promised her company.

'Then I'll come for you when I'm ready,' said Mrs. Hopper, 'and we'll slip out o' the front door and down the brook,—I don't want Jerushy to go.' And hearing a step she started up and went off.

After dinner as Rosalie sat alone in her room, Mrs. Hopper came softly in, with her sunbonnet held down by her side; and the two went out of the front door and were soon hid in the trees that hung over the dell.

'I sent 'em all off into the garden to look for a hen's nest,' said Mrs. Hopper, as they descended towards the brook, 'so we've got ten minutes clear, and that's enough. Miss Clyde, you aint one of the folks that's easily frighted, be you?'

'I never was much tried,' said Rosalie, 'but I think I may say no.'

'Some is so 'feerd o' death and all that sort o' thing,' said Mrs. Hopper, 'that they'd only ha' plagued me.' And without further explanation she began to follow the brook in its course, with an air of business determination that seemed a relief to her mind,—bestowing no more words upon Rosalie, but never failing to give her a hand in the difficult places.

It was rough going but beautiful. The large moss-covered stones, dripping with the spray of the brook, stood in and athwart its bed; now turning the course of the bright water, and now shining beneath its rush as through a transparent veil. And at every turn almost, the stream broke into little waterfalls, with their mimic roar and tiny eddies of foam and mock wrecks—twigs and dry leaves and acorns; and in one or two places a fallen tree had thought to stop the brook,—but the brook leaped it and went its way laughing. Rich ferns grew in the moist earth at the brook edge; and lichens crept over the rocks, and maiden-hair spread forth its delicate leaf. Fall flowers were there too,—gentian and the pretty lady's tress, and the purple gerardia. But Mrs. Hopper went past them or over them without a look, and did not 'draw bridle' until she reached the foot of the dell and met the yellow light that came streaming in from the open meadow. Then she turned and looked at her companion.

'I do believe I've run you well nigh off your feet,' she said.

'O no—I am not tired.'

'Hold on a bit further,' said Mrs. Hopper, ''taint far.' And crossing the brook she took the diagonal of the broad meadow through which it wandered; its banks gay with autumn's embroidery. The summer crop of grass had long been cut, and over the short after-growth tall cardinal flowers reared their scarlet heads, and rich golden rods bowed and bent over the rippling water; and lady's tresses and gentian had followed it from the dell. A flock of sheep were nibbling about the meadow, and as the two intruders came up went bounding off, taking now one bend of the brook and now another in their way. And straight to the further corner of the meadow Mrs. Hopper pursued her course, and over the rail fence which there went angling about as if to stop her. There was an immediate rise in the ground beyond, into a stony and scantily clad hill; along the base of which ran a little footpath. Slowly taking the first steps on this path, Mrs. Hopper turned again and spoke to Rosalie.

THE STONE-CUTTER'S.

'We're all but there—see, yonder's the place,' and she pointed to a little stone-built habitation, which crouched humbly at the foot of the hill as if asking shelter. A few slow paces, and then resuming her former rapid gait Mrs. Hopper soon placed herself in front of the little dwelling.

It was a stone-cutter's, and samples and materials of his work lay all about. Door stones—slightly smoothed from their original roughness,—a pile of unappropriated flags,— and most conspicuous of all, several tall grave stones standing on end in a finished or half finished state, and sundry slabs of different coloured marble set apart for the same use. Mrs. Hopper gave one quick glance about, and then passed the house and went to the little work-shed in the rear, guided by regular blows of a mallet and the sharp clink of the chisel.

'Good evening, neighbour Stryker.'

The old greyheaded man looked up, and with a little nod of recognition laid down his mallet and pushed back his hat.

'It's done,' he said with another nod. 'Come to see it?'

Mrs. Hopper gave silent assent, while her hands nervously untied and tied again her sunbonnet strings.

Mr. Stryker threw down his chisel, and moving leisurely about among the hard companions that surrounded him, leisurely whistling too, the while; he lifted one and another in examination.

'Here,' he said at length,—'this is it.'

Rosalie saw the mother's hands clasp each other tightly for a moment—then the clasp was loosed and she went forward, and her friend followed.

It was a plain, dark, grey stone—square and severely simple, with the name and age in plain black letters at the top. Then came a rudely chiselled ship lifted up on a wave of its petrified ocean; no bad emblem of the young life-current so suddenly stayed; and below were these words:—

"*Thy servant did descend into the midst of the battle.*"

As if it had been an indifferent thing to her, so did Mrs. Hopper scrutinize every word and letter; pointing out an undotted *i*, and a *t* uncrossed, with a cool decision that they must be rectified.

'Wal, wal,' said Mr. Stryker—'that's all easy enough, though nobody'd ever find it out, after all. The rest suits ye, don't it? pretty clever notion of a ship, aint it? haven't made a better lookin' stone this some time. He was a likely boy though, so it's just as well.'

'Fetch your bill!' said Mrs. Hopper, turning almost fiercely upon him.

'Save us and bless us!' said the old man. 'Why I don't know as it's made out, and '——

'Make it out then,' said Mrs. Hopper. 'How long d'you s'pose me and this lady's agoin' to stand here waitin' on your slow motions? Your goods and chattels is too heavy to be run off with afore you get back.'

Mr. Stryker turned towards the house, muttering a little to himself, and Mrs. Hopper's hands came together again with that quick clasp. She stood looking at the stone.

'"*Thy servant*,"' Rosalie said, in a voice so low that it claimed none but willing attention. 'Those sweet words!'

'Belonged to him if they ever did to anybody,' said his mother shortly, as if to get her words out while she could. 'He didn't serve two masters—but he served one.'

'"*If any man serve me, him shall my Father honour*,"' said Rosalie, in the same tone.

Mrs. Hopper moved her head as if she would have

spoken, but no words came—only again her hands were pressed together, but this time with a joyful difference; and like a flash her look sought Rosalie's face, and again went back.

'Here's your bill, missis,' said the old stone-cutter returning. 'Made out pretty consider'ble quick, too.'

'Let's have it,' said Mrs. Hopper, with her former abrupt tone. 'Now neighbour Stryker, you set this all right the way I told you, and then you take it into the house and kiver it up close. Don't you let a living soul set eyes on to it, and then when I send I'll send the money. But if ary person sees the one, there's no tellin' when you'll see the t'other. Goodnight t'ye.'

And with rapid steps she followed the little path till they had turned the hill and the hut was out of sight, and then went forward to the high road at a more reasonable rate; but with her face set in stern composure, and in perfect silence.

'How thankful I am you could put those words there!' Rosalie said at length, the long breath seeming to bear witness to sorrowful thoughts in her mind as well. 'How thankful! how glad!'

'Yes—I'm thankful too—I s'pose,' said Mrs. Hopper, in a kind of choking voice. 'I'd like to have 'em go on my own!'

And again she quickened her pace, nor changed it till through the gathering twilight they saw the gleam from their own kitchen windows.

'Bless you, Miss Clyde!' she said then, laying her hand on Rosalie's arm, and speaking so low that but for their earnest strength her words would scarce have been heard. 'Bless you a thousand times for going with me!—and more'n all for not talkin' to me, nor plaguin' me with questions.

And for sayin' just the right words—I'd forgot all about 'em.'

And with a firm and steady step she opened the kitchen door, and inquired 'why upon earth they hadn't got supper ready?'

CHAPTER XXIX.

Softly the evening came. The sun from the western horizon,
Like a magician extended his golden wand o'er the landscape;
Twinkling vapours arose; and sky and water and forest
Seemed all on fire at the touch, and melted and mingled together.
              EVANGELINE.

MEANWHILE Rosalie's own causes of trouble began to press more heavily. Thornton's letters had now ceased to come at all,—whether because the camping-out life took more of his time or more of his thought, his sister could only guess. Even one of those short half sheets which were in themselves so unsatisfying would have been most welcome, but none came; and the papers gave her none but general tidings. Sometimes she could almost have resolved to go and learn for herself; but there was Hulda—how could she be either taken or left?

It was near the close of a September afternoon when she stood at the window turning over this question in her mind. Not at the window which faced the dell, but one on another side of her room, which looked askance as it were towards the road and the open country. Everything was very still, only for a little peal of laughter which came every now and then from some unseen place; though the voice itself was well known, and said that Hulda's fountain of pleasure knew nor drought nor hindrance. Save this and a few fall crickets the silence had no break.

The leaves were beginning to make their bright changes, and the beautiful gay tints infringed very perceptibly upon the summer green. Rosalie wondered to herself if changes were once again creeping over her life,—if what had so long been was to be no more. And yet—for the mind loves even surface sparkles on the water rather than its cold depths—she could hardly take up the thought in a sorrowful way. Sober it was, as the long shadows that stretched across the fields; but fair streaks of sunlight lay between, and in them the fall tints looked bright and hopeful: there was even comfort in the thought of such beauty-working cold nights of frost. And when the sun had set, and twilight had taken her place, then arose the rich after-glow,—as in verification of the promise, "*At evening time it shall be light.*"

"*I form the light and create darkness. I make peace and create evil. I, the Lord, do all these things.*" And the quietness of full assent fell on Rosalie's heart.

The glow was brightening now, steadily; as cloud after cloud caught the signal and lit its own fire, or hung out its colours of gold or purple or the ashes of sunburnt roses. And spread over the western sky the purest rose-colour came flushing up, a fair back-ground to the floating clouds. On earth the glow rather pervaded than fell on anything,—it was like looking through a golden atmosphere.

Afar off on the road, where one of its windings stretched away into the distance, there came slowly along a large covered wagon. The glow was about it and over it—it moved through that yellow light—but itself loomed up brown and dark as before. Slowly it came on,—the two brown horses upon a quiet walk, the driver using no means to urge them. It seemed to Rosalie as if darkness fell as they moved on—as if the glow faded because they came. As if the clouds could not keep their bright tinges with that wagon beneath; and as it came on at the same slow pace and halted before their gate, she knew it was the answer to Mrs. Hopper's hopes and fears for her son's return. A startled bird flew twittering past the window, touching Rosalie with its own undefined fear, and hastily she turned away and opened the kitchen door.

She paused on the threshold however, for in the dancing light of the newly made-up fire Mrs. Hopper sat alone, and for a wonder doing nothing. The room was scrupulously put up, the very fire laid with neatness and precision, and every chair in its place; and the mistress sat in the chimney corner with an air of nervous listlessness which became her strangely. At the noise of the door latch she looked up, and instantly rose; standing still then for one moment with her hand pressed to her side, she merely said,

'I felt it, Miss Rosalie;'—and then throwing up one of the kitchen windows which looked towards the barn and outhouses, she called in a voice that went through the still evening air without the ringing effect of an ordinary loud call,

'Jabin! Mr. Mearns!'
then shut the window and came and stood on the hearth again, without speaking or looking at Rosalie who had not stirred from her first position. But when there was heard a low knock at the door, Mrs. Hopper turned and said,

'Don't stop—you can't help me. Go round the house and keep 'em quiet.' And went forward to open the door.

Rosalie closed hers, and passing swiftly to the front of the house glided out in the soft cool twilight, and went round as she had been directed. There was no one to be seen at first; and then hearing Hulda's merry laugh in the direction of the barn she crossed the bit of meadow that lay between, passing the two men as she went, and found Martha

13*

and Jerusha and Hulda playing with bundles of straw and each other upon the threshing floor. Here the men had been at work apparently, for the fanning-mill stood out and a heap of grain shewed duskily on the floor, overlaid with the great wooden shovel; and threshed straw and unthreshed grain were on either side. Through the great wide-open doors came in a silver strip of moonlight and lay softly upon the barn floor; and there Hulda frolicked—like a silver-winged butterfly.

'Alie!' she cried out, and rushed up and threw her arms round her.

'My stars alive!' Martha said,—'if Miss Rosalie don't look just like a ghost in the moonshine!'

'Mother aint sick, is she, Miss Clyde?' said Jerusha timidly.

'No my dear. What are you all about?'

'O we're playing,' said Hulda, darting away with a flying leap to a distant bundle of straw.

Rosalie sat down on one that lay near the door, and looked out and looked in with strange feelings. This door of the barn was toward the house, and she could see its dark outline, softened here and there by the moonlight, and the twinkling of candles from the kitchen window. That was all—the house was too distant to see more, and no sound crossed the space between. And within the barn there fell the same moonlight, but upon what different types of humanity. One little sigh, and another escaped her lips—then somebody softly touched her hand. It was Jerusha.

'Miss Clyde, it looks lonesome to see you sit there so. Sha'n't we go back to the house?'

'I guess I'd as good be going to get tea,' said Martha.

'We shall not want tea till I go,' said Rosalie,' and I am not going yet. The kettle was on some time ago.'

'O yes—it 'll boil by itself,' said Hulda, with another spring into the straw bundles.

'I am a sober kind of person at best, Jerusha,' said Rosalie kindly. 'Nothing else looks lonesome, does it?'

'No,' said the girl in a half whisper. 'Only it frighted me when mother called the men, and I've felt scared ever since. I wanted to go right up, and Martha wouldn't let me.'

'Martha was quite right. But why were you frightened?'

'I do' know,' said Jerusha, her voice sinking again. 'I'm always so 'fraid of—of—I didn't have but one brother, Miss Clyde—and it's hard.'

The same shiver that she had felt before passed over Rosalie. But she spoke quietly.

'Are you afraid to have him come home here to rest?'

'Yes—I do' know,' sobbed the girl. 'It seems so dreadful.'

'Do you remember,' said Rosalie, 'what Jesus has said —"*Thy brother shall rise again.*" That is as true to you Jerusha, as it was to the sisters of Lazarus.'

'Yes,' said Jerusha in the same smothered voice, crouching down by Rosalie and hiding her face against her.

'Poor child—' Rosalie said, and for a moment she paused, her words suddenly cut off. Then softly she repeated—

"*I am the good shepherd; the good shepherd giveth his life for the sheep.*

"*My sheep hear my voice, and I know them, and they follow me: and I give unto them eternal life; and they shall never perish, neither shall any man pluck them out of my hand.*"

The sweet words found their way down to the fear as well as the sorrow of Jerusha's heart, and with a long sigh she dried her eyes and looked up. At the same moment her mother's tall figure stood in the doorway, and the strip of moonlight was cut off.

She did not speak, but stepped aside as if to let the others pass; and when they were all out of the barn she took Jerusha's hand and followed them slowly.

There was a large gathering in the house that night,— friends, unneeded yet not officious, came and went and stayed; though these last but few. Rosalie had given up her sitting room as the best and largest in the house, and retreated for the time to a smaller one up-stairs which she used for a bedroom. And there with Hulda sleeping quietly near her she sat through the long evening, nor even lit a candle. With what feelings of pain she listened to the busy steps that went to and fro, making ready the room, and then to the heavy tread of the men as they brought in the unconscious one for whom all the preparations were made. Then everything was hushed, and the house sunk in profound stillness; and she might sit and think it over. And the weary thought of the afternoon had in part come back, and she questioned with herself if such a trial might be awaiting her.

With the stifled feelings of one who breathes in imagined sorrow, Rosalie went to the window and threw up the sash. The night was perfectly still. A slight frost in the air kept down all dampness, and hushed the many insect voices that were wont to sing; and the stars shone with a perfect light; but the moon had long since dipped her crescent beneath the dark woods of the horizon. Rosalie wrapped herself in a warm shawl and sat down by the open window; and while she looked and listened the hours went by with feet as noiseless and swift as her own thoughts.

Suddenly from the room below there came voices; and in slow soft measure arose this hymn.

"Forever with the Lord!
  Amen, so let it be;
Life from the dead is in that word,
  'Tis immortality."

Untutored though the voices were, unsoftened by practice according to any rules, there was a wild kind of sweetness and force about their music which cultivation could but have hindered. An earnest belief too, a deep seriousness and feeling in the words gave them power. The voices ceased for a while and then began again—this time as it were for themselves; and though Rosalie's tears flowed as she listened, the first gush took off all their bitterness.

"Come let us anew our journey pursue,
  With vigor arise,
And press to our permanent place in the skies.
Of heavenly birth, though wand'ring on earth,
  This is not our place,
But strangers and pilgrims ourselves we confess.

"At Jesus's call, we gave up our all;
  And still we forego
For Jesus's sake, our enjoyments below.
No longing we find for the country behind;
  But onward we move,
And still we are seeking a country above:—

"A country of joy without any alloy;
  We thither repair;
Our hearts and our treasure already are there.
We march hand in hand to Immanuel's land;
  No matter what cheer
We meet with on earth, for eternity's here!

"The rougher the way, the shorter our stay;
  The tempests that rise
Shall gloriously hurry our souls to the skies:

> The fiercer the blast, the sooner 'tis past;
> The troubles that come
> Shall come to our rescue, and hasten us home."

The last words died away on the night air and all was hushed; and in that hush of feeling as well as sense, the rest of the night past to one watcher, and the first few streaks of the morning began to appear. Rosalie looked to the east, and in the opal unearthly light which flickered up from the horizon the morning-star rode supreme—O who that saw could describe it to those who had not seen!

"'A country of joy without any alloy"—' Rosalie thought. 'Yes—where they have "*no need of the sun, neither of the moon to shine in it; for the glory of God doth lighten it, and the Lamb is the light thereof.*"—Where *the bright and morning-star* shall reign forever—"*and his servants shall serve him. And they shall see his face, and his name shall be in their foreheads.*" Then it will come—not here.'

CHAPTER XXX.

Thou com'st to use thy tongue: thy story quickly.—SHAKSPEARE.

TIME went his way as quietly as if he had been about child's play, and his rough wind seemed to have left no trace. Except indeed the stillness which followed that sweep through the house, and the afternoon dress of its mistress. All the morning she went about her usual work in her usual working trim—sunbonnet and all; but the toil of the day once ended, and all sign of it cleared away,—Mrs. Hopper arrayed herself in deep black, with much more particularity and regard to appearances than she was wont to use. The rest of the afternoon was devoted to spinning, and to grave conversation with Martha or Miss Clyde, or with any neighbour that might chance to come in.

There Rosalie would find her, when she went out into the kitchen towards tea time to see if Jabin had gone to the post-office and had come back; the big wheel whirring round, the spindle throwing off its long fine thread, with now and then a break and now and then an added roll.

'Mrs. Hopper, has Jabin gone to the post-office?'

'Haint thought a word o' the post since morning, Miss Rosalie. Jerushy, go see.'

And Rosalie would come and stand with folded hands before the fire.

'What's the good of expectin' letters all the time?' said Mrs. Hopper, running down the long thread of yarn with skilful fingers.

'Not much good,' said Rosalie. 'One ought to come, and so I expect it.'

'Things oughtn't to come till they do,' said Mrs. Hopper.

'No—that is true, in the large sense.'

''Taint worth while to take small sense,' said Mrs. Hopper,—'just as well have plenty while you're about it.'

'There's no letters,' said Jerusha returning. 'Jabin saw Mr. Squill himself, and there warnt but two letters come this morning at all—the bag hadn't nothing else into it; and one o' them was his'n, and 'tother was for the minister.'

'Feel disappointed?' said Mrs. Hopper.

'Yes—somewhat.'

'No need,' said her hostess. 'No news is always good news—firstrate. And you couldn't hope for one o' the letters, when there come but two.'

And Mrs. Hopper spun her wheel round and round with a degree of spirit that seemed to say she was speaking her mind with some force to somebody.

Rosalie thought she could not hope for letters much longer; and in that mood she sat with Hulda at breakfast next morning; giving wistful glances now and then at the bright fire which tempered the cool air within, and the bright sunlight which did the same work without. The night had been frosty, and long streaks of white lay upon the fields instead of shadows between the sunbeams.

'Miss Rosalie,' said Martha presenting herself with hot toast, 'Jabin wants to know if he'll go to the post-office this noon afore he comes home, or if night 'll do?'

'How is your foot, Martha?'

'Here,' said Miss Jumps,—'large as life, if 'taint no larger.'

'Could you walk so far without hurting it?'

'Guess *I* could,' said Miss Jumps. 'Wouldn't like to say what it might do on its own account.'

Rosalie looked out of the window again, and quickly resolved that she would be her own bearer of despatches.

'I will go myself, Martha.'

'Afoot?' said Martha. 'Or will you take Stamp Act along for company?'

'O I will ride of course, unless they want the horse on the farm.'

'Can't have him if they do,' said Martha. 'He's bespoke,—or will be just as soon as I can come at the back door.'

'Stay Martha!' Rosalie called, 'I will go and see about it myself.' And taking Hulda, she went forth to where Jabin was splitting pine knots for Mrs. Hopper's spinning light.

He readily undertook to catch the horse, or at least to try; for Stamp Act was disporting himself in the adjoining meadow with colts and horses of every degree. Jabin however took an old rusty pan of salt and a bridle, and went off; and Rosalie and Hulda stood still to see the fun.

Now it was apparent that the bridle in some degree nullified the salt, for though the horses stretched out their heads and snuffed and neighed and walked about Jabin, till he was quite surrounded; none but the younger ones who had never been caught would approach his offered handful. Jabin whistled and tried all manner of blandishments and conjurations—shook the salt pan and handed out the salt; and the horses looked, and walked round and took up a new position and then looked.

' 'Taint no sort o' use to try 'em here,' Jabin called out. 'If Jerushy and Martha 'll come out and help I'll drive 'em into the barnyard.'

Jerusha and Martha came accordingly, the one to run and the other to stand; for while Martha was to watch at a particular turn of the road and head them off, Jerusha took stand behind her on the chip yard to guard a large expanse of ground between the garden and the barn, in case the first barrier should prove insufficient.

Meantime Jabin had let down the bars, and having gone to the end of the field was now slowly driving the horses before him. Their pace quickened however as they came out into the road and perceived that the barnyard was their destination; and passing that with a scornful toss of her head, the leader, a beautiful black mare, trotted on towards Martha. Here was a pause,—the road was narrow, the barn on one side, the fence on the other, and Martha with her big stick displayed in front. The horses turned and walked back—there was Jabin with his bridle. There was a moment's consultation, the horses putting their heads together: but as Jabin began to draw near, the black mare raised her head and with a loud neigh charged down upon Martha,—plunging forward, with tail thrown out and mane tossed upon the wind, and hoofs beating a rapid and sounding gallop. Martha gave way, and on went the whole drove. The black one first, flinging out her heels as she passed, then a grey colt, then a fine roan, then Stamp Act and Lord North in an overplus of glee, then another black, a bay colt, a sorrel, and so on until seventeen were passed,—after which came a rolling cloud and silence.

'That's what you call kickin' up a dust,' said Martha, as Jabin followed in the train of the horses.

' 'Taint what I call a stoppin' it,' said Jabin, who looked

very hot and dusty with running and calling Whoa. 'If Jerushy don't stop 'em they may run!'

The horses had clustered at the top of the hill before Jerusha's sunbonnet and were again in doubt. Then the black leader wheeled and charged down hill, the whole troop following; but this time into the barnyard,—for with Martha and Jerusha uniting their forces, the array of sticks was too imposing, and the horses submitted to superior force.

It was early yet when Rosalie set forth, and the frost was scarce off the ground, it crisped and cracked beneath Stamp's feet, who probably liked his exemption from farm duty or felt exhilarated with the stampede, for he went along at a good pace.

There was great beauty abroad that morning. The Indian corn fast ripening for the garner, the bright yellow pumpkins gleaming out beneath,—the stubble fields with their grazing flocks of sheep,—the green meadows spotted with cattle, or with a drove of horses grouped about some great tree,—buckwheat and flax in a state of ripening perfection, and the light of plenty and peace upon everything. The brooks had filled up since the summer droughts, and tumbled and murmured along—the only murmur that is not complaining,— the mills were busy—the road filled from time to time with the great farm wagons and their o'ertopping loads of grain. In such a case Rosalie and Stamp turned out, and took no more of the road than its flowery edge, and no more of the grain than a mouthful. Stamp was pretty sure to get that, by some adroit turn of his head. The fall flowers were beautiful by the way side—and when not strictly beautiful very showy. Tall elecampane and golden rod among the yellows, and yarrow and everlasting for the whites; with cardinal flower and blue gentian and pink-tinted snake root. In the boggy places where the brooks now and then spread out and stayed their swift course, tufts of green rushes waved gracefully in the fall wind, and immense green bullfrogs splashed down into the water at the first sound of Stamp's feet.

At every house might be seen marigolds and balm and feverfew in full glory; with now and then a drooping cranberry, loaded with scarlet fruit; and at every back door were strings of drying apples, and sieves of 'sweet corn' and currants, and bunches of onion heads. Chickens trooped about the barns and fattened upon the scattered grain; and the flails beat regular and musical time on the sounding floor. Business, comfort, and beauty walked over the land; and its face wore the smile of a well-fed child—fair and fat. There was more ethereal beauty overhead, in the blue sky and fleecy white clouds; and health and exhilaration in the cool mountain air, which sometimes swept Stamp's mane and tail quite out of the sphere in which they were placed by nature.

Rosalie rode on much at her leisure; partly to please her own mood and eyesight, partly because Stamp's most rapid pace savoured a little too much of the perpendicular; therefore she rather held him in. She was also willing, perhaps unconsciously, to prolong the pleasure of hope, and was in no haste to meet disappointment if one awaited her. And though as she neared the little hamlet that clustered about the post-office she quickened Stamp's pace to a round trot, and reined him up sharply before the office door; there was only enough expectation left to give a keener edge to the words,

'No, Miss Clyde—no letters—sorry to say, if you want 'em.'

And Rosalie turned and rode home as slowly as before, at least for half the way; and then her admonitions were so frequent that Stamp at last understood that a perpetual trot was expected of him.

'For gracious!—how you do come clattering up!' said Martha Jumps who was sunning herself at the back door. 'Fine day, aint it Miss Rosalie?'

'Very fine.'

'Something more'n common, *I* thought,' said Martha. 'And Hulda's out after sweet apples with Jerushy. Miss Rosalie, if I was you I'd take off my skirt here and let me take it up stairs, and not go trapesing through the whole house that fashion.'

'Why not? I always do.'

''T won't hurt you to do something now and then by way of a change,' said Martha. 'Me and Tom Skiddy always took turns runnin' up the back stairs and down the front. I've fetched your other skirt here too—but have it your own way.'

'I am not so fond of this particular way,' said Rosalie as she made the change. 'I believe yours is the most convenient.'

'Look here!' said Martha, as her young mistress moved towards the door leading to the hall, 'don't you go through there, neither. Jerushy's been washing up the front entry, and it's just as wet as sop. Go across the kitchen and through your sitting room—then you won't have to but just cross the wet. Furthest way round's the surest way home nine times out o' ten. This aint the tenth, neither.'

If Rosalie could have seen the little shake of Martha's head which followed these words, her eyes would have been better prepared for the sight which met them as she entered the sitting-room; for Mr. Raynor stood by the window, half leaning against it, with folded arms, and looking down into the dell where ran the brook; he turned as the door opened just to see Rosalie's painful start.

A start of pain—for why had he come? and to tell her

what? She closed the door and stood still as if to gather breath.

'You need not be afraid of me,' Mr. Raynor said, coming forward and taking both her hands. 'I bring you no bad tidings.'

She drew the breath then, long and wearily, and bringing her forward to the fire, Mr. Raynor placed a chair for her and took one himself.

Rosalie untied her hat, as if even those light strings choked her, but she asked no question.

'How long is it since you have learned to distrust my word?' said her companion with a slight smile that was very reassuring.

Rosalie's paleness gave way a little, and she looked up less fearfully, and smiled herself.

'You must forgive me Mr. Raynor. Is Thornton well?'

'No, not quite well: he is better.'

'He has been sick then?'

'Yes, very sick—for many weeks. But he is now so near well that you need feel nothing but gladness.'

'O Mr. Raynor! why did you not tell me before? why did you not send for me?' Rosalie said.

She was answered by one of those rare smiles that needed no words to help its meaning. The eyes went down again and the question was not repeated.

'He has not wanted for care,' said Mr. Raynor quietly, —'he has had what man could do—I will not say that is what woman can. Does that content you?'

'But half.'

'It may as well,' he said after a minute's pause. 'And it were better that you should look a little less pale,—a little more strong. I know not when you will be fit to see Thornton at this rate.'

'Where is he?'

'Not within your reach to-night. If you are well enough you may see him to-morrow.'

'Ah do not talk about me,' she said; and the tears came then. But she sprang up and left the room.

Not for long,—and though when she came back her face wore the sobered and tendered look of long anxiety and deeply stirred feeling; yet the nervous excitement had passed off with the tears, and she could look and speak quietly. And quietly she sat there before the fire while Mr. Raynor gave her the long account; scarce interrupting him unless with a look.

'You may expect to see him to-morrow, Mr. Raynor said in conclusion, 'and I came on before to bring you word. Dr. Buffem advised that he should spend three or four weeks in the strength-giving country air.'

'And then?' said Rosalie.

'I did not ask his further plans—not feeling sure that they would agree with my own.'

There was a pause.

'You say he will come to-morrow?' Rosalie said at length.

'If I find him no worse to night.'

'To-night? are you going back to him to-night?'

'Yes, he will expect me.'

'O,' said Rosalie starting up, 'then I will go too and see him at once!'

'No you will not,' said Mr. Raynor.

'Wherefore?'

'Because I shall not take you,' he answered with a little smile, looking up at her as she stood before him.

'That is a very arbitrary reason,' said Rosalie, her cheeks flushing as she resumed her seat.

'Very—but not to be gainsaid. You are much better here, and I should deserve I know not what, were I to let you go.'

'You are coming back with him to-morrow?'

'No.'

'It seems to me you are all at cross purposes to-day,' said Rosalie.

'No, not cross purposes—very kind ones; or at the least needful.'

'But do you care so little for strength-giving air?' said Rosalie with some hesitation,—'or is your time too precious? Shall we not see you here again?'

'Perhaps,'—he said with that same relaxing of the lips. 'I do not know how it will be. And my time is not too precious to spend here, but it must be given to less precious things. Are you sure you are quite able to give Thornton what care he needs at present?'

'O yes, it will do me good.'

'I hope it will,' Mr. Raynor said more gravely. 'Few things seem to have done that this summer.'

'Why I am perfectly well,' said Rosalie.

'Which puts the health of other well people a good deal above perfection.'

'It is best to rest contented with what one has,' said Rosalie lightly. 'And I have been doing what I could to make myself well,—so do not you put it into Thornton's head that I am not, Mr. Raynor.'

'And I cannot rest contented with what I have, nor until I have you. May I put that into his head?'

'Oh no!'

'Why not?'

She did not say why not, but the fluttering colour in her

cheeks was a little distressful. His next words were spoken in that old tone she remembered so well.

'You may rest—I shall say nothing without your leave. I think you have the warrant of past experience that I will do nought to trouble you.'

Her look in return was very grateful; and if the drooping eyelids could not quite conceal why they drooped, it was no matter of regret to at least one person.

'You are in safe hands,' Mr. Raynor said,—' stronger and wiser and kinder than mine—that ought to give me a sort of rest, and does. But dear Rosalie, take better care of yourself, for my sake. You must let me say so much, and so much you must do.'

She watched him ride off in the fair autumn light as she had watched Thornton so many weeks before. But about her brother fear and sorrow had thrown their shadows—now she looked through an atmosphere of perfect trust. Probably she did not recognize the rainbow which this sunshine made from the lingering tear-drops in her eyes, but it was there, nevertheless.

CHAPTER XXXI.

*His sweetness won a more regard
Unto his place, than all the boist'rous moods
That ignorant greatness practiseth.*—BEN. JONSON.

'You have seen her!' was Thornton's exclamation, when Mr. Raynor entered his room about eight o'clock that evening.

'Certainly—for an hour.'

'And what did she say? is she well?'

'She said she was well.'

'Does she want to see me?' was Thornton's next question, but put in a different tone.

'You do not deserve to see her, for even asking,' said his friend. 'How are you? let me feel your hand.'

'O I am well enough,' said Thornton, throwing himself into the other corner of his easy-chair—' or should be, if my head would stop turning round. But after all, Henry, what makes you say that? you know as well as I do that I don't deserve to have her care whether I am alive or dead.'

'Then go further back, and say that you do not deserve to have such a sister. Never ask me whether Rosalie is herself still. What is the matter with your head?'

'Turns round, that's all,' said Thornton. 'Waltzes—seeing my feet have not the power. How cool your hand is! a very quaker touch, and my head stops waltzing.'

'What machinery set it agoing?'

'I dont know—' said Thornton with another fling. 'Or at least it is not worth while to inquire.'

'Very worth while, for you. In the mean time sit still. I have quaker prejudices against a general waltz.'

'Well you keep your hand still then,' said Thornton laughing. 'Now tell me every word that Rosalie said. And in the first place, Sir Henry, I think quite as highly of her as you do.'

'I should be glad to think so,' said Mr. Raynor quietly.

'Well think so then!' said Thornton with an impatient gesture. 'You are not obliged to admire her any more than I do, at all events. Was her conversation so sweet and pleasant that you have scruples about repeating it?'

'On the contrary the words spoken were mostly my own, and Rosalie said but little.'

'Rosalie again!' said Thornton. 'Why will you always call her so?'

'Merely because it suits me.'

'But other people do not.'

'Other people have their way and I have mine.'

You have it in most things, to do you justice,' said Thornton. 'Well will it suit you to tell me what she *did* say?'

'She asked how you were, and why she had not been sent for; and wished very much to come directly to you to-night.'

'The gypsey!' said Thornton looking pleased. 'Well why didn't she?'

'Because my wish was different.'

'What do you mean by that, Mr. Raynor?' said Thornton facing round upon him.

'The simple truth.'

'Very peculiar truth to my ears,' said Thornton. 'What had you to say about it?'

'I did say that I should not bring her.'

'And she submitted?'

'Certainly,—she could not well come alone.'

Thornton kicked off his slipper to the furthest corner of the room—then subsided.

'You are so excessively cool!' he said—'and slippery to match. Do you never congeal in the course of a conversation?'

'Not often,' said Mr. Raynor—

——"He that lets
Another chafe, may warm him at his fire."'

'What else was said?' inquired Thornton abruptly.

'I gave your sister a very particular account of your weeks of illness, the beginning thereof, and the state in which they had left you: told her that probably you would be with her to-morrow, and that she need feel neither sorrow nor anxiety about your health.'

'Hum—' said Thornton. 'What else?'

'That is the substance of what was said about you.'

'What about anything else?'

'Nothing that I think it worth while to repeat.'

'But I think it worth while that you should,' said Thornton. 'And I think I have a right to know all that is said to my sister by anybody, or by her to anybody.'

'I think differently.'

'I don't care what you think,' said Thornton starting up from his chair.

'And I care what you do,' said Mr. Raynor, with strong though gentle hands bringing him back to a resting posture. 'Sit quiet Thornton, and throw not away the little strength you have gained.'

'Little indeed!' said Thornton bitterly, as he felt it by no means up to the resisting point. 'But you may take your hands away—I suppose I can sit still without being held.'

One hand still kept its guard however, but the other laid that same cool touch on his forehead, and for a little while there was silence. Mr. Raynor stood motionless, and Thornton tired with the excitement into which he had wrought himself, was nearly as still; a quick breath or two escaping like pent up steam from time to time.

'What do you vex me for, Henry?' he said at length.

'I did not intend it.'

'But you know it always vexes me to see you so cool.'

'I may not vex myself to please you, Thornton,' said his friend.

'And Rosalie—you know I never can bear to hear you talk about her.'

'You insisted that I should.'

'Well but—' said Thornton,—'of course I did, but not in that way. How did she look?'

'I fear any description I might give would be too much in "that way,"' said Mr. Raynor.

'You are certainly the most provoking man I ever had to deal with. Did she look as well as she used to?'

'As she used to when?'

'Why always!' said Thornton.

'Her health has had several phases since I first knew her,' said his friend gravely. 'She is perhaps looking better than she was last spring, and will I hope improve faster now that her mind is at rest about you,—partly at rest.'

Thornton could have been vexed again, but the words touched him on more points than one.

'Did you see Hulda?' he inquired.

'No, she was out.'

'May she always be that when I am there!' said Thornton, his illhumour rushing off into that channel. 'When one cannot walk away from a disturbance, one is glad to have it save one the trouble.'

'I see you are not cured yet, Thornton,' Mr. Raynor said.

'What do you mean by not cured?' said Thornton kicking off his other slipper.

'I did hope that this fever might bear off some other maladies. Meanwhile if you will put on these slippers which stand by your chair, it may be the better for your bodily health.'

'I am not apt to take cold in my feet,' said Thornton, thrusting his toes into the slippers—from which however the whole foot gradually worked in. 'What particular maladies do you suppose me afflicted with?'

'Some much akin to that which befell Christiana's son in the Pilgrim's Progress, when he eat of the fruit of Beelzebub's orchard,' replied Mr. Raynor. 'But he was willing to take the cure.'

The anger which had flushed into Thornton's face at the first words, faded away when he heard the last. And even the show of it was hard to keep up.

'You talk knowingly of the disease, and think the cure easy to get,' he said. 'That is the way with Rosalie—and I suppose with all paragon people.'

'"*Is there no balm in Gilead?*"' said Mr. Raynor's deep grave voice; "*Is there no physcian there? why then is not the health of the daughter of my people recovered?*"'

Thornton could almost have put his hands over his face and wept. For if the cause of all his impatience could have been traced out, it would have been found not so much in his bodily weakness as in those other ailments to which his friend referred; or rather in his consciousness of them. Neither his long weeks of illness nor the living presence of his friend had lost their work; but his mind was only stirred up and roiled—not clear nor at rest. For a half hour he sat there, striving to control himself enough to speak without shewing any emotion; and then it was hid but with a poor veil of carelessness.

'If you feel obliged to stand at the back of my chair all the time, Mr. Raynor, I shall feel obliged to go to bed. You must be tired after your day's journey.'

'It is the best thing you can do,' said Mr. Raynor quietly.

And Thornton went to bed, trying hard to persuade himself that he was a very ill-used person, and by the time he went to sleep was pretty well established in that pleasant conviction; but when he woke up in the night, and saw his friend still watching over him,—sometimes standing at his side, sometimes by the light with that little Bible in his hand which had for Thornton's eyes a strange fascination, —he was forced to change his mind. When he awoke in the morning Mr. Raynor sat before the fire with his head resting on his hand, but at the first movement Thornton made he came to him.

'You are better this morning,' Mr. Raynor said, when he had felt Thornton's head and hand and had taken his usual grave survey of his countenance.

Thornton looked up at him and repeated his last night's question—

'What do you vex me for, Henry?' And for almost the first time in his life Mr. Raynor answered him with a smile.

'Well, why do you?' said Thornton.

'Why do you vex yourself?' said Mr. Raynor, his clasp

of Thornton's hand a little closer. The feeling of last night rose up in Thornton's eyes,—he closed them and was silent.

'I am absolutely sorry to part with you, and to give you up into other hands,' said Mr. Raynor—'even though those be the best possible.'

'Part with me!' said Thornton. 'That is what you shall not do. You are going with me to White Oak?'

'No.'

'You must!'

'It is so short a journey,' said Mr. Raynor, 'and you seem so well this morning—I think you can ride there with only Tom's attendance.'

Thornton began the business of dressing with his mind hard at work.

'But I shall want you there,' he said.

'Not when you have seen Rosalie.'

'I wish she was anywhere else!' said Thornton, with his usual attempt at diversion. 'Such a place to go to for three weeks!'

'Such a beautiful place.'

'The beauties of nature are not in my line,' said Thornton.

'Then you are out of your own,' said his friend.

'As how, Mr Raynor?'

'Something is wrong when the most pure and beautiful things the world can shew give no pleasure. If sweet music seem to make discord there must be discordant notes within.'

Thornton finished his dressing and breakfasting in comparative silence, and even Mr. Raynor said little, and seemed willing to let him muse if he felt inclined. Breakfast over, the carriage came to the door and Thornton set forth on his short journey. For a few miles Mr. Raynor's horse was by his side, and the rider from time to time called his attention to some notable thing in the landscape. But when they stopped for an hour that Thornton and the horses might rest, Mr. Raynor ordered a fresh horse for himself to be got ready immediately.

'Are you going no further with me?' Thornton said.

'No further. This is your road—that is mine.'

'And when am I to see you again?' said Thornton, who looked disturbed at the prospect.

'When you come back to the city I hope,' said his friend. 'And what am I to hear from you in the mean time?'

'O that I am as well as ever again, I presume,' said Thornton.

'And no better?'

Thornton flushed a little, but instead of flinging away the hand he held—as he would have done some months before—he only swung it backwards and forwards, and was silent.

'Are you so unwilling to take up the lightest and sweetest service to which a man can submit himself?' said Mr. Raynor.

'It seems so to you—' said Thornton,—'it does not to me.'

'Nor ever will until you try it. When the doubtful ones asked Jesus, "*Master, where dwellest thou?*" he said unto them, "*Come and see.*" "*If any man will do his will he shall know of his doctrine,*" and of his service. Or as Rutherford says; *Come and see will teach thee more—come nearer will say much."'

'Well—' Thornton said in a very unsatisfied tone.

'Let it be well, dear Thornton, for more sakes than your

own.'· In silence the hands were clasped and parted, and Mr. Raynor rode away.

Thornton looked after him as long as even a dusty trace could be seen, and then returned to the beauties of nature with a mind very unfit for their contemplation. The quiet depth of the blue sky disturbed him, and made his own spirit seem dark and cloudy,—the bright sun threw shadows upon his mind of less fair proportions than those upon the landscape; and the sweet voice of birds and winds and brooks was too pure, too praise-giving,—too much like the children crying hosanna in the ears of the offended Jews. It was an unbroken concert, but Thornton's instrument was not in tune. Everything jarred—he shook hands with nothing; and by turns sad or impatient he drove wearily along, until in the afternoon light Mrs. Hopper's gate appeared before him, and the journey was at an end.

CHAPTER XXXII.

Omission to do what is necessary,
Seals a commission to a blank of danger.—SHAKSPEARE.

IF Thornton had never before seen the perversity of human nature he had abundant cause now. Much as he had wished to be with his sister, often as he had resolved that for the future she should have no reason to complain of him—that he would be at least part of her happiness,—it seemed as if when the trial came every current set the wrong way. He had wished to prove to her that he was as good as other people, and he was worse than himself.

Rosalie spent her strength upon him most unweariedly; though less in doing than in watching,—in trying to amuse him, in hoping that he would be amused. But her efforts met with little success. A cloud of moodiness had settled down upon Mr. Clyde, and he seemed in no mind to come out of it. Indeed his attempts at coming out were rather unfortunate, and were as apt to land him in a fit of impatience as anything. His mind was not fitted to bear up against weakness of body—or was itself out of order; and either craved old associates or the other extreme of something new. Nothing satisfied him, not even Rosalie's watchful love; though he was more ready than of old to appreciate its working; but if he shook off his moodiness at all, it was generally with such a fling as sent a reminder of the mood into the face of every one present—after which he relapsed tenfold. And though quite able to ride or to walk, in moderation, he was with difficulty persuaded to do either; and nature's sweet influences had small chance to try their hand upon him.

'Are you sure it would not do you good to go out?' Rosalie said one day as he sat by the fire. 'I am so sure that it would.'

'What use?' said Thornton. 'I can imagine pigs without the help of eyesight.'

'You cannot imagine sunshine,' said his sister, with a playful attempt to make him raise his head and look out.

'No—nor feel it if I go. There is nothing to see here.'

'But there you are mistaken. There is a great deal that is worth seeing.'

'Probably—to canary birds,' said Thornton.

'O there are a great many birds here,' said Hulda. 'Sparrows, and robins, and '—

'Take yourself off to their neighbourhood then—or keep quiet,' said her brother. 'You must not talk if you stay here. Why don't you go and pick up apples with Martha as you did yesterday?'

'Because Martha's talking to Tom Skiddy,' said Hulda, 'and I don't like to.'

'When they have talked each other into a wedding they will be easy,' said Thornton.

'Ask Jerusha to go with you Hulda,' said her sister. 'Take my little basket and fill it for me, and by and by I will walk with you.' And as Hulda left the room Rosalie came and knelt down by her brother.

'What is the matter with you dear Thornton? You

will never get strong in this way, and it troubles me very much.'

Thornton put his arm round her and drew her head down upon his breast.

'You are not more tired of me Alie, than I am of myself.'

'I am not tired of you,' said his sister weeping,—'you know that.'

'I should think you might be. Why don't you go and take care of Mr. Raynor, and leave me alone?'

She was silent a moment.

'Why do you ask me such a question?'

'For the pleasure of hearing you answer it.'

'That would not make me happy.'

'Then what would?'

There was answer even in the slight movement of her head before she spoke.

'What would?' Thornton repeated.

'To see you what I call happy, I believe,' said his sister.

Thornton drew a long breath—or rather breathed one out—as if that were a thing he might whistle for sooner than get; and for some time there was not a word spoken. Then Thornton began again.

'I used to wonder sometimes, in those long hot nights when I lay sick in my tent, that he did not administer poison instead of medicine. And sometimes I almost wished that he would—then you would be taken care of, and I should be in nobody's way.'

'I am sure he never suggested that last idea,' said Rosalie.

'No, to do him justice,' said Thornton, 'he never mentioned your name unless I did. And he took as tender care of me as if I were his own brother—or perhaps I should say yours. There was no make believe in it though. Yes Alie, I was forced to give up my dislike, and to agree to all the praises you would have spoken had you dared. He is a man to trust.'

There was pleasure in hearing these words,—but for the cold, unenjoying tone, Rosalie would have felt it strongly. As it was the pleasure was qualified; and her quiet

' I am glad you think so,'

told of both feelings. She waited long for Thornton to speak again, but his lips did not move; and slowly she arose and went to give Hulda the promised walk: her voice and eye following the child's merry pranks, and all her thoughts left at home. She could hardly have told whether the walk was long or short, and most like her brother could not; for when Rosalie again entered the sitting-room he had not stirred from his former position—had not even changed the hand which supported his head. Rosalie came up and laid her hand on it, but the soft touch called forth no words, and in silence she sat down to await the coming in of tea. The meal passed with equal taciturnity; Hulda went to bed, and Rosalie sat down as before—her eyes apparently seeking counsel of the little wood fire, which flashed into their bright depths with great vivacity. How grave they were, how thoughtful! catching none of the fire's dance.

' It strikes me,' said Thornton suddenly, ' that you and I have done thinking enough for one night, Alie. What say you?'

' I don't know.'

' Why don't you know ?'

' I suppose,' she said, with one of her fair looks up at him, ' I suppose if we have been thinking unprofitable thoughts, it might be well to give the mind some better refreshment before the body takes its own.'

'What do you call unprofitable thoughts?' said Thornton.

'Fruitless ones—or such as bearing fruit, are yet shaken off too soon, before it be ripe.'

'You have covered the whole ground for me,' said Thornton. 'I had better begin again. I wonder if yours have been worth a silver penny?'

'Not to you—and some of them more than that to me.'

'Suppose you were to indulge me with the hearing thereof,' said Thornton,—'just by way of a lesson in fruitful thinking.'

'Truly,' said his sister, 'my best thoughts were not my own, but drawn from a little hymn of Wesley's.'

'Give us the hymn then,' said Thornton. 'Are you the only alchymist who can fetch gold from thence?'

'The gold is of an ancient stamp,' said his sister sadly, 'and little thought of in the alloyed currency of this world; for it bears the impress of the first commandment—not "*Cæsar's image and superscription.*"

> "Lord, in the strength of grace,
>   With a glad heart and free;
> Myself, my residue of days,
>   I consecrate to thee.
>
> "Thy ransomed servant I
>   Restore to thee thine own;
> And from this moment live or die,
>   To serve my God alone."'

Thornton looked at his sister while she repeated these words,—felt that she had found the gold, that it was in her hand—and knew that his own was empty. And why? He was ready to say it was so because so it was to be; but those words came back to him again—

> "With a glad heart and *free* "—

and to none had Rosalie's face given more strong assent and effect.

'Do you like it, Thornton?' she said, drawing up closer to him.

'Seems like pure metal my dear,' he answered carelessly. 'I presume my ready money would scarce exchange for it without a pretty heavy discount.'

Rosalie looked at him, as if she thought and truly that just then he was counterfeiting; but his face gave her no invitation to speak, and her eyes went back to the fire. When she turned to him again, however, and somewhat suddenly, he was regarding her with a grave abstracted sort of look, as if from her his thoughts had taken a wide range: not into the pleasant regions.

'What can you possibly be musing about, Thornton?' she said.

'There are a great many things about which I could possibly be musing, Alie.'

'Only that you were not apt to muse at all.'

'I doubt I am getting into bad habits then—you are such a muse-inviting little object.'

'Am I?' said Rosalie smiling. 'What ideas do I suggest?'

'Various ones of human perfection.'

'"*The spirits of just men made perfect*,"' Rosalie said. 'That will be a fair thing to see!'

'For those that see it,' said Thornton with some bitterness. But he wished the words unsaid—her quick look up at him was so humble, and at the same time so full of pain.

'What makes you speak so, Thornton?'

'What makes you look so, Alie?' he said with his old light tone. 'It is not possible that you think *all* men need perfecting? The gentleman who took care of me so lately, for instance—how *could* he be any better than he is? I am afraid you undervalue him.'

'O Thornton! I cannot jest with you after such words.'

'Jest! no,' he said, but something in her eye checked him,—he turned away and rested his head on his hand as before. Rosalie came and laid her hand on it again—laid her cheek there too, but he did not move.

'What troubles you, brother?'

'Why do you suppose that anything does?'

She did not answer—as being needless, and he added,

'You had better go to bed, Alie—take care of yourself, my dear, if you cannot of me. I feel as if I had you in trust.'

'Only me?' she said sorrowfully.

'Only you!' said Thornton rousing himself, for the implication was not pleasant. 'You are a reasonably precious trust, some people think. And I shall have to account pretty strictly for all the pale cheeks that you carry back to town.'

'"*And every one of us shall give account of himself to God,*"' she answered in a low voice, her lips touching his forehead. But she waited for no reply, and left the room.

For the first time since he had been there, Thornton went softly in to look at her when he went up-stairs and she lay asleep; as much perhaps because he was tired of himself, and tired of remembering his own existence, as anything. And certainly if contrast could make him forget, the end was gained.

Existence had been no burden to her, and life no failure —what though it was crossed with anxieties and disappointments,—they were all according to that higher will to which hers was submitted. Life could be no failure,—the purpose of God must stand, and she wished none other.

It was a strange point to reach, Thornton thought, as he stood watching her calm face, and felt that whatever shadows lay there came not from discontent. Could he ever reach it? was it not rather of nature than of grace? It was easier for a woman—with her gentler spirit and its few outlets. There came up before him the image of one whose nature was at least as strong as his own, in whom manhood was not better grown than Christianity; but he put it away and looked at Rosalie. And then with a bitter wish that he were like her—or like anybody in the world but himself, he stooped down and softly kissed the lips whose repose he so much envied.

They stirred a little, though he caught no words, and with a long sigh Rosalie folded her hands upon her breast as if she were making a last appeal. Then they relaxed and lay quiet as before, and the lips were still; and Thornton went away with a quick step, feeling that from her his questions could get no answer such as they wished. Any excuse—any belief which would throw the responsibility off himself, he could bear,—he could bear to be unhappy and discontented, so it touched not his own omissions. If he could have persuaded himself that he was *necessarily* restless and ill at ease, it would have gone far towards curing the evil.

'What nonsense!' he repeated to himself again and again —'I never could quiet myself down to her temper, if I tried all my life'—and then he remembered that he had never tried for one day.

This was not the way to get to sleep, however, as he sagely remarked; and having banished all grave thoughts with such vigorous efforts as he would not have bestowed upon acting them out, sleep followed—unbroken till Sunday morning had dawned, and its atmosphere of rest lay over the wide landscape.

There were sounds astir—but all sweet, all soothing. The twittering of the birds, the tinkle of the cow bells as their four-footed wearers wound slowly along the meadow-course of the brook,—a hum of voices from the chip-yard, where Martha and Tom were comparing notes with Jabin,—and nearer still a voluntary from Hulda—who standing out in the sunshine sang her morning hymn with birdlike freedom and enjoyment. When another voice joined hers, and gave strength and clearness to the tune and distinctness to the words, Thornton closed his window and betook himself with great earnestness to the business of dressing.

But though that business was finished with much elaboration, Thornton would not go to church; and Rosalie staid with him. Everybody else went, and the house was left in utter solitude; with windows closed and doors bolted, and Trouncer the old bull-dog lying in the porch with his nose between his paws.

Rosalie persuaded her brother to come out to the edge of the dell and spend the morning there; where the brook's soft rush at their feet and the bird notes up in the air, were all the interruptions. She had her Bible in her hand and sat down to read; but Thornton sat leaning against an old hickory tree, with his eyes sometimes shaded by his hand and sometimes by an unseen cloud. And so they remained; with the sweet Sabbath bell sounding forth in the distance and answered by another still further off, until the last ring floated away on the pure air and all was still.

Rosalie had closed her book for listening, and now sat with closed eyes, as if too many senses were disturbing. Her brother watched her, unconscious of his gaze or that he had even raised his head.

Her face was at rest, as of one asleep after a weary world; for the bells with their suggestions and associations had half done sleep's work. But strong effect was given to the very delicate tinting of her face and its too delicately drawn lines, by those very grave ones in which the mouth was set,—that had not relaxed. Yet as Thornton looked it did relax—and with a slight trembling of the lips there came one of those tearful smiles that just showed itself and passed away.

'Rosalie!'

How the face changed, how the weary look came back, he saw as she turned towards him; her eyelashes yet wet with the drops of that sun-shower.

'Do you see that brook?' Thornton said.

'Certainly.'

'Wouldn't you like to follow its course out into the open sunlight?'

'I have done so many a time.'

'Is it a pretty walk?'

'Pretty and thoughtful both, to me.'

'Take me up the stream of your thoughts from the sunshine that was upon your face just now.'

She looked at him and then down at the brook.

'It would be a more thoughtful walk than the other.'

'No matter—take me. Whence came the sunshine?'

Again she looked at him, and away from him, but the eyes filled as she answered,

'"*Hitherto ye have asked nothing in my name: ask, and ye shall receive, that your joy may be full.*"'

Thornton was silenced. If he had expected Bible words it would not have been these; and he spoke not again for some time. His sister sat looking down at the brook as before; and it rippled and ran along, and flung its foam hither and thither with a wild hand.

'Do you believe that, Rosalie?' he said at length.

'Surely!'

The look was brilliant.

'Have you never asked for what you were wishing yesterday?'

Her eyes fell, and her lips could form no answer.

'Then why is it not done?' said Thornton, with an effort to keep his own firm.

She paused a moment, as if to steady her half-choked voice, ere she answered. 'Because I have not waited patiently, I believe. Because, "*to them gave Jesus power to become the sons of God, even to them that believe on his name.*"'

Thornton was silenced again, and his sister sat still for a few moments with such a wavering play of thought and feeling upon her face, as was like the shadowy leaf-tossed light upon the brook. And then after one glance at him, coming quickly to him and almost before he was aware, her arm drew him down to a place by her side, and her voice spoke words for him that bowed down his heart like a bulrush. And with the belief the power came. He was a changed man.

CHAPTER XXXIII.

*It was autumn, and incessant
Piped the quails from shocks and sheaves,
And, like living coals, the apples
Burned among the withering leaves.*—LONGFELLOW.

'How come you to follow the Capting, Tom Skiddy?' said Martha.

Miss Jumps was enjoying herself in the farm kitchen, her feet stretched out to a huge fire, which crackled and ran away up chimney, and sent forth such a red glow that the room looked as if whitewashed with firelight. The tea-kettle had done its work for that evening, and was pushed off into one corner upon the end of the crane; while the pot of dish-water, in like easy circumstances, kept as far away as it could in the other. And between the two ran up the bright points of flame from a sound foundation of logs, which in their turn overshadowed the glowing bed of coals. The ashes were carefully raked away right and left, and in the cleared space lay the kitchen tongs with its toes to the fire; its iron legs supporting a long ear of corn of the roasting age— full-kernelled, white and delicate. To this Miss Jumps lent a part of her attention, while another share was bestowed upon Tom; who in the very focus of firelight, if there was one, sat paring an apple with his pocket knife and eating slices of it from time to time, as if he rather enjoyed the business than otherwise, and was in no haste to have done. Upon his knee lay a little half-finished boat, on which Tom's knife had been engaged when the fruits of the earth attracted his attention. In the other corner of the hearth, Jerusha with a basket of the same fruit before her and a tin pan at her side, was rapidly skinning the apples by the help of a simple little machine and its crooked knife; and casting now and then a glance of great interest at the two foreigners. Beyond them all, Mrs. Hopper's busy wheel kept its swift whirling, under the skilful hand of its silent mistress. Her black dress made a dark spot in the glowing room, and Mrs. Hopper looked if anything more slim and gaunt and weather-worn than ever. In strong contrast was the bunch of soft white rolls upon the wheel, where the firelight fell after a mere glance at the spindle. The reel stood hard by, and against the wall hung a string of brilliant red peppers, and several bunches of white yarn all knotted and twisted up,—being a part of Mrs. Hopper's day's work of 'two run and a half.' An old cat lay dozing and stretched out at the foot of the wheel—the close neighbourhood of the fire being rather too hot; and a fine tortoise-shell kitten and one of 'gray mixed,' went in frolicksome tumbles about the room.

'How come I to foller the Captain?' said Tom. 'Why because the Captain led on *and* I follered. Just giv' up the business I had in hand and started.'

'Easy business to give up, wa'n't it?' said Miss Jumps, —'don't take common folks long to lay down a muskit. How do you 'spose it 'll manage without you? What sort of a time did you have down there on Long Island, Tom Skiddy?'

'First rate,' said Tom,—' long as the Captain kept about. Didn't do a person's feelings much good to see *him* laid up. I hadn't much chance to look at him neither. How Mr.

Raynor got all *his* work done, and the Captain's, and took care of him beside, *I* don't know.'

'Guess likely he's a smart man,' said Martha demurely. 'Jerushy, don't none o' your corn never stand still to be roasted? does it all go pop-cracking out that fashion?'

'It's only some o' the grains bursted out,' said Jerusha, bending down to look at the corn till her head was in a position almost as fiery. 'It's roasting beautiful, Miss Jumps.'

'It's flying round the world,' said Miss Jumps, stooping down in her turn, and endeavouring to roll the corn over upon its roasted side; to which it responded by rolling into the ashes. Martha seized a fork and tried that persuasion; but after uprooting several grains of the corn, the rest were further down in the ashes than ever, fizzing and sputtering at a great rate.

'Now what's to be done?' said Martha.

'Pick it up, why don't you!' said Mrs. Hopper.

'Tom can—' said Martha,—'he's right in front of the fire.'

'That's just where he means to stay,' said Tom. 'Anybody else may get in that's a mind to.'

'Where upon airth were you all fetched up!' said Mrs. Hopper coming forward, and with one sure pounce restoring the corn to its proper place. ''Taint a bit the worse—ashes won't hurt ye—nor fire neither if you aint too keerful of it. I'm not one of your meltin' away people,'—and Mrs. Hopper returned to her wheel, and spun it round with great energy.

'I thought you could do most any thing, Martha?' said Tom.

'Well?' said Martha with some asperity, 'who says anything against it?'

But Tom wisely forebore to answer, and occupied himself with a particularly large slice of apple.

'It's astonishing how much people can have to do with muskits and not learn to stand fire,' remarked Miss Jumps rather scornfully. 'If I was some folks I'd get up and look at myself.'

Tom paused in the munching of his apple just long enough to blow one of its black seeds off his finger, and then fixed his attention upon the old cat; who now aroused from her sleep by the wheel, came forward slowly and stretchingly, and evinced a wish to shield Tom by taking up a position directly in front of him. And Tom's foot accordingly gave her a push which a little more would have converted into a kick.

'Tom Skiddy, stop!' said Martha. 'I won't sit still and see you.'

'Hop up then,' replied Tom, taking aim at the cat with a long apple paring.

'No I won't,' said Martha,—'and you sha'n't kick the cat, neither—that's more.' And the cat found a safe resting-place in Martha's lap.

'Real Malti' that cat is,' observed Mrs. Hopper; 'and a better couldn't be.'

'The apples aint bad,' remarked Tom. 'Captain Thornton says he'd like a barrel or so on 'em to take home.'

'He can have 'em,' said Mrs. Hopper, bringing forward the little reel and beginning to 'click' off her yarn. 'We've got as many apples as most things this season.'

'Well now—' said Martha,—'let's we go pick 'em up. What's to hinder?'

'Take the cart along, and the bar'ls,' said Mrs. Hopper, 'and it aint bad sport, I can tell you.'

'Miss Rosalie 'll go, I'll venture,' said Martha; 'and all the rest.'

'I wouldn't venture too much, if I was you, Martha,'

said Tom. 'Catch Captain Thornton out in the field picking up apples, and you'll catch a weasel asleep in a stone wall.'

'Why he aint obliged to pick 'em up, bless you! if he does go,' said Martha; 'and he aint a man to be scared at the thought of pickin' up anythin' so small as apples, any way. I say he'll go if she does.'

'Well, I do' know but he will,' said Tom, 'come to think of it. He does stick to her like wax lately.'

'The better for him,' said Martha, 'and I'll go right off and ask 'em this blessed minute.'

'Better eat your corn,' said Tom. ''Tother thing 'll keep cool, and that won't.'

'See what the day is afore you ask your company,' said Mrs. Hopper; and to that Martha agreed.

The day was as fine as could be, and mellow as one of the many apples that plunged down into the grass from time to time, as the loaded boughs swayed lightly about. The farm work and the fall held on their way hand in hand; but the woods were gayer now, and the wagons carried home pumpkins instead of wheat, and the hard yellow corn went craunchingly to its destination in many a well filled pen. At Mrs. Hopper's back door—that is in the road that ran by the dwelling, and under an old apple-tree stood the great ox-cart,—its patient team with heaving sides and bowed heads drowsily awaiting further orders. Half a dozen of empty barrels stood near the cart; and the driver—a rather thin and sharp-set specimen of the natives—was leaning against the tree, overshadowed by its canopy of fading leaves, and with great diligence was whittling away one stick after another to keep his hand in.

He looked up with a kind of wondering and scornful surprise as the house door opened, and the whole family came filing out; and then merely stooping to pick up a new subject for his knife's sharp edge, he remarked,

'Pity you hadn't thought to ask a few o' the neighbours, and you ha' had quite a muster.'

'I guess you'll find there's enough now,' said Martha.

'How many on ye's going in this here cart?' said the man.

'Forty—more or less,' said Mrs. Hopper.

'Can't do it,' said the man.

'Come now, 'Zekiel Mearns,' said Mrs. Hopper, 'stow away four o' those bar'ls, and be spry,—and don't try to make me think oat straw's buckwheat. Step round, now.'

Mr. Mearns permitted the corners of his mouth to relax a little, shut up his knife, and stepping round—though not precisely in the way Mrs. Hopper meant—he swung up four of the barrels off the ground and into the cart, and bestowed them in close order in that end which was nearest the oxen. Then with a nod of his head he signified that the field was clear for whoso chose to occupy it.

'Get in Miss Clyde,' said Mrs. Hopper.

'Bless your heart!' said Martha, 'she's not going to ride so!' and making a dive into the house, Miss Jumps returned with a low rush-bottomed chair which was then planted firmly against the barrels, and Miss Clyde took possession.

'That's enough,' said Mr. Mearns taking up his long whip. 'Don't want no more on ye.'

'O I must ride,' said Hulda, 'but I can sit on the floor.' And Thornton jumped her in likewise.

'Well, you aint much heft,' said the driver. 'Ge' long! haw!'

'Now Mr. Mearns, stop,' said Mrs. Hopper. 'We're every living soul of us going.'

'You aint going in *this* cart,' said Mr. Mearns, lightly flapping his whip about the ears of the oxen.

'I go mostly after my own team when I *do* ride, said Mrs. Hopper,—' and you don't 'spose we're going to foot it all the way to that orchard?'

'You'll tilt the cart the worst kind,' said the driver, pushing his hat back off his forehead and applying his hand to his hair with a disturbed look. 'You'll tilt it up like Jehu.'

'It 'll be the first thing we ever did do like him, I guess,' said Mrs. Hopper. 'Get right in, Martha.'

And Martha got in, and then Jerusha, and then Mrs. Hopper. Mr. Mearns stood irresolute.

'You'll look well, tilting the oxen into the air!' he said.

'They'll look well,' said Mrs. Hopper, 'so well they'll come down again, pretty quick.' And amid a burst of laughter from the representatives of the lower circle, the party moved on.

Moved on through one meadow after another; by a pretty road, which was indeed but wheel tracks in the green grass—deep enough now and then to jolt the cart and its occupants in a laugh-exciting way.

The fall had laid its hand upon every thing now: there was not a tree nor a bush nor a flower but wore a touch of autumn about it somewhere; and over those things which change not but with the gradual breaking up of many seasons—the fences, the farm buildings, the ponds and little water-veins of the country,—over and about these lay a soft haze, and they were seen through a fall medium. The green grass was set thick with gay forest leaves, strewn over it in every direction; the tufts of fern bent their yellow heads as gracefully as when they wore June's freshness;

the lichens and mosses did their beautifying work as well as ever. There were changes too in the sounds,—flails and fanning mills had taken the place of scythe whetting—crickets instead of grasshoppers sped away from intruding feet; and the bird over head was not a sparrow—it was only a chickadee. Only!—

The orchard field was full before they reached it; first of apples and then of apple-gatherers. The loaded trees bent down with their red and green and spotted and striped fruit, or shewed their round heads against the distant forest sprinkled over as if with roses. The long grass beneath was worth the turning over for the apples it hid; and a drove of white-sided porkers were pursuing that business with grunts which if not loud were deep,—flapping their great ears, and whirling their little tails to make the most of them. In moments of rest they turned to bite encroaching companions, or gave a glance of great wickedness out of their little eyes towards the new comers. The ground sloped gently down to a frisky brook at the hill-foot, just enough to help the momentum of any falling apple that failed to lodge at once in the grass; and at the brook edge the ox cart was now drawn up in state, emptied of all but the barrels and left alone. Beneath it, in the shade, lay Trouncer, as motionless as the oxen themselves; but all other living things had mounted the hill.

There were pretty moss-covered rocks shewing their heads above ground from place to place, and on one of these Rosalie seated herself to watch the play on the hill-side. Thornton sat by her, but Hulda was one of the players.

Mr. Mearns had swung himself up into one of the trees, basket in hand, to pick off such apples as were for barrelling; while Tom on his part had climbed another, and with vigorous foot and hand sent down showers of the ruddy fruit to the ground below. Then came a chase! The apples ran first—had the start—and after running a few steps and getting excited began to bound; and at that pace soon cleared the hill slope, and either plunged into the brook or flew against the oxen or lay still ingloriously on dry land. Then came the pigs in open phalanx,—grunting between dismay and appetite, running over more apples than they pursued; and stopping now and then to munch and enjoy one, and to cast back malicious looks at Mrs. Hopper and Martha, Jerusha and Hulda, who bore down in full tide of conquest and at such rate of speed as bipeds can maintain on a side hill. At this moment Tom would despatch to earth another half bushel of apples, and both pigs and women tried to go up and down at once. Then Martha and a particularly large and flap-eared quadruped having set their hearts upon the same apple, pursued it down hill,—the pig squealing and Martha shouting, the apple bounding along, regardless of bruises, and dousing into the brook. At such a termination the pig gained the prize; for he followed the apple, and stood with his feet in the brook, munching and looking up-hill, whither Miss Jumps was retracing her weary steps. Sometimes just as the chase was near the end, Trouncer roused up from his slumbers, and standing on the alert he seized the flying apple and stood confronting Miss Jumps—his mouth kept open by it as with a corn-cob,—then dropped it as an unprofitable speculation. Of all the trials to Miss Jumps on those occasions, the worst was Tom's laugh from the top of his apple tree.

'It strikes me, Tom Skiddy,' she said, approaching the scene of his activity, 'that of the two you'd be worth most down here.'

To which Tom replied by such a fire of well-directed apples that Martha was fain to run away.

'Come down, will you!' she said from a distance; 'and stop that.'

'There's a firstrater going down hill,' was Tom's answer.

'I'm not going after it, if it is,' said Miss Jumps. But perceiving her old enemy of the large ears addressing herself leisurely to the pursuit—there was no withstanding the temptation, and Martha was off again.

The cart went home at night well loaded with apples, and the little train of gatherers went home well tired. The day had changed too; and now soft grey streaks athwart the western horizon foretold different weather. The wind went sighing through the trees, rising now and then into a chill gust, and rustling the fallen leaves—so brown looking and drear, despoiled of the sunbeams: lights twinkled out from hill and valley; and wood fires and tea and bed became the pleasantest things in prospect.

CHAPTER XXXIV.

*All is but lip-wisdom which wants experience:
I now, wo is me, do try what love can do.*—SIDNEY.

'How long are we going to be here, Alie?' said Hulda as they sat at tea.

'I do not know—you must ask Thornton.'

'How long?' Hulda repeated, looking at him.

'I do not know.'

'But that's very funny!' said Hulda.

'I am not sure but I shall go to New York for a week or so before you do, Rosalie,' said her brother.

'What for?'

'O sundry things. I must see Marion—give the required promise and make her redeem her own.'

'Not till I come?'

'No, not that. But there are other matters to arrange. At what time in the future is the Quakerage to be blessed with a new queen?'

'I am sure I know not,' said his sister as composedly as she could.

'I believe,' said Thornton, 'that in a voluntary change of dynasty it is usual for the reigning power to withdraw to another court,—else might the new comer be branded as a usurper. And I am not sure that it is best for you to give

Marion any lessons in the science of government. She rather needs guardianship herself.'

'She will have it now,' Rosalie said; the warm flush of joy and thankfulness coming over her face.

'Better than she once could, I trust,' said Thornton gravely. 'O Alie! my dear child! what a guardian *you* have been!'

'Not I—' was all she could answer; and Hulda looked wonderingly from face to face, and saw the one not less stirred than the other.

'I was not so selfish as I seemed,' Thornton said, when they left the table and stood musingly before the fire. 'I knew you gave up a great deal for me, but I did not know how much. I could not, without knowing Henry better; and by keeping him at a distance I partly kept off the belief of some things that concerned him.'

'Who is Henry?' said Hulda, who had been watching for some word which she could understand.

'Your friend Mr. Raynor. Of whom his mother justly remarks, there is but one in the world.'

'I wish he would come here,' said Hulda. 'I want to see him very much.'

'So do I,' said Thornton. And bringing a chair to the fire he sat down and took Hulda on his lap.

'How would you like to live with him, Hulda?'

'Live with him!' cried Hulda. 'What all the time?'

'Thornton'—Rosalie said.

'Be quiet Alie, and trust me for once. Well Hulda?'

'I don't know what you mean!' said the child with a very puzzled face. '*I couldn't* leave Rosalie.'

'Put Rosalie out of the question.'

'But I shouldn't want to leave you, now,' said Hulda, her eyes looking up to his with all the enjoyment of trust.

She little knew how straight both look and words went to her brother's heart, nor guessed the meaning of the quick breath he drew in that moment of silence.

'I think we must arrange a compromise, Alie, don't you? How would you like then Hulda, to live half the time with Mr. Raynor and half the time with me? Or would you rather live half the time with Rosalie and half with Marion?'

'But then there'd be nobody to take care of Rosalie,' said Hulda. 'And if I lived with you and Mr. Raynor there'd be nobody to take care of me.'

'You know your lesson sufficiently well,' said Thornton laughing. 'What do you say, Alie?'

She did not say anything; but sat there on a low seat by the fire, reading histories in its bright play, until Hulda was ready to go to bed; and then went with her, and returning softly sat down as before.

'Why don't you answer my question about the Quakerage?' Thornton said, moving his seat close to hers. 'Am I bound to learn it first from another quarter?'

'I cannot tell you what I do not know myself, dear Thornton.'

'Yes, but upon whose decision does your knowledge wait?'

'I cannot decide upon anything to-night—and I would rather talk on some other subject. Rather think of the end of life than of its way.'

'You are not well,' Thornton said, putting his arm round her and drawing her head down upon his breast.

'Not perfectly—or else I am a little tired.'

He stroked her forehead and stooped down and kissed it, and then sat looking at her in silence. But after a few moments she looked up and smiled.

'I believe I am tired—that need not hinder our talking.'

'What shall we talk about, precious one?' he said. 'What were you thinking of, with your eye upon the fire? What did you see there? an ideal presence?'

'No,' she said with a faint colour—'at least not when you spoke to me. I was thinking of the journey through the wilderness. "*Thou shalt remember all the way which the Lord thy God led thee these forty years in the wilderness, to humble thee, and to prove thee, to know what was in thine heart, whether thou wouldst keep his commandments or no. And he humbled thee, and suffered thee to hunger, and fed thee with manna, which thou knewest not; that he might make thee know that man doth not live by bread only, but by every word that proceedeth out of the mouth of the Lord doth man live.*"'

'And then?' Thornton said.

'Not much else,' she answered with that same little flush. 'I was thinking how even Moses desired to see the promised land in this world.'

'What has come over you to-night, Alie?' said her brother. 'When did this world's land of promise ever make you forget the better country?'

'It is easier given up in the wilderness than on the borders of Canaan. But if the Lord hath said, "*Let it suffice thee concerning this*"—good is his word which he hath spoken. "*The Lord is thy life, and the length of thy days*"—how true that is!'

'Rosalie,' said her brother with a look that was both fearful and wondering—for she had raised her head again, and was eyeing the fire in the same intent and abstracted way; 'you are tired, you are not well. Let me carry you up-stairs now, and to-morrow you may talk more of these things.'

'I believe I am tired,' she said again, but without moving,—'my mind feels tired. Tell me something to rest it. Words of comfort are so sweet from you.'

'And my knowledge of them is so small compared with your own, Alie. You must not let even part of this be true of you, dear—it was all true once of me.'

'"My people hath been lost sheep—they have turned them away on the mountains: they have gone from mountain to hill, *they have forgotten their resting-place.*"'

As if a cloud had rolled away from before her eyes, so did Rosalie look up at him,—a child's very look, of quietness and peace.

'I will not forget it,' she said. "*For thus saith the Lord, the Holy One of Israel: In returning and rest shall ye be saved; in quietness and confidence shall be your strength. And the work of righteousness shall be peace; and the effect of righteousness quietness and assurance for ever. And my people shall dwell in a peaceable habitation, and in sure dwellings, and in quiet resting-places.*"'

The words were spoken clearly and strongly, though rather as if thinking than speaking; but as she rose then to go up-stairs the colour faded swiftly from her cheeks, and laying her hand on Thornton with a confused look, sense and strength failed together.

Thornton carried her up-stairs and laid her on the bed, and toil-hardened hands tried their gentlest powers about her; but when at length paleness and unconsciousness yielded to their efforts, it was to give place in turn to a brilliant colour and a fevered sleep.

In silence Thornton sat by her through the night,—remembering with intense bitterness the years of her society that he had shunned, and feeling that whatever might be the effect of this sickness he could not say a word. The women went softly about the room, attending to the fire and bathing the poor sleeper's forehead and hands; but whatever words they spoke were scarce whispered out, and Rosalie's quick breathings fell on her brother's ear without interruption. How he wished her away from there,—with her own physician, in her own home—with other friends within reach. Such skill as could be found in the neighbourhood was called in, and pronounced her disease to be a slow fever; more tedious than dangerous unless it should take some special type, but requiring constant care and watchfulness. And until the day came streaming in through the windows, Thornton hardly removed his eyes from her face.

How cold the daylight looked! how cheerless: and yet the sun shone brilliantly clear, and the tufts of autumn leaves with which the trees were spotted shewed their gayest tints; and the birds sang and twittered their merriest. But the contrast was lost upon Thornton, for his eye and ear took little note of anything but Rosalie; and the morning came on, and the women went softly in and out, and he scarce noticed them nor heard their low consultation.

At length Mrs. Hopper came up to him.

'Mr. Clyde,' she said, 'the very best thing you can do is to go where you can be o' some use. You can't do her the least bit o' good stayin' here, and that poor little soul down stairs 'll cry her eyes out afore long, if there don't some one speak to her.'

Thornton sprang up instantly and left the room, remembering that Rosalie would never have forgotten anybody as he had forgotten Hulda: even in her deepest sorrow.

'How far, how very far she is on the way which I am but beginning to tread,' he thought as he went down stairs.

Hulda was in the sitting-room, crouched down on the floor in one corner, pouring out a flood of sorrow that was exhausted only in its tone,—there was no stay to the tears. And when Thornton raised her up in his arms and tried all his powers of soothing and caressing, the child shook all over in the violence of her grief.

'They won't let me see her!' she cried. 'They won't let me even go into the room! And I wouldn't make the least noise—and oh I know *she* would let me!'

'Do you think you could keep perfectly quiet?' Thornton said, putting his face down by hers.

'O yes! O yes!'

'Then I will take you up there; but first you must wait a little, for Rosalie would be troubled to see all these tears. I am going to write to Marion to ask her to come here, and you shall sit quiet on my lap till that is done.'

'Do you think she will come?' Hulda said, as she watched the rapid tracing of his pen, and tried the while to seal up her tears.

'I am sure that she will.'

And almost tired out, Hulda lay drooping on his neck until more than one letter was written and folded, and he was ready to take her up-stairs.

She kept her promise of quietness,—shed no tears unless silent ones, and sat on Thornton's lap or stood by his side in perfect stillness, as long as he would let her. And when he knew that she ought to be out in the fresh air, and told her so, and begged her to go with Martha,—Hulda's mute distress was so great that, there was no help for it, he must take her himself.

It was a lesson for him, all this,—he began to try his hand at self-denial, and to learn the lesson which Rosalie had so long practised. True his watching eyes could do her no good—both days and nights were passed in the restlessness or the sleep of fever, and often she seemed hardly to know him. But for himself, what comfort anything on earth could give he found at her side. And now he must devote himself to another's comfort—must walk with Hulda and talk to her and bear with her, and keep her as much as possible out of the sick room. He could not in conscience let her be in it, and to send her out with Martha plunged Hulda into the very depths of grief. Sitting on her brother's lap with her arm round his neck, and probing his distress with her earnest questions,—walking with him—hearing him read, and never failing to bring up Rosalie's name at every turn, she was comparatively cheerful. It was something new for him—something against his whole nature and experience. And nature rebelled. But as if they had been stamped on his mind, checking every impatient thought and word, bidding even sorrow and weariness give place and bide their time, these words were ever before him—

"*For even Christ pleased not himself,*"—and "*If ye love me, keep my commandments.*"

If Hulda mourned her sister's illness, it was not because her brother ceased trying to fill her place.

CHAPTER XXXV.

"It will make you melancholy, Monsieur Jaques."—As You Like It.

'HENRY RAYNOR,' said the quakeress to her son, one day when he had come over from Long Island to dine with her; 'isn't thee wellnigh tired of thy present way of life?"

'It is not the pleasantest way that I could imagine, mother.'

'Then why does thee pursue it?'

'It seemeth right unto me,' said Mr. Raynor, assuming as he often did the quaker diction.

'And thee is resolved to follow, even to the end, these unhallowed proceedings?'

'Nay mother, call them not so. The English have not shown themselves so tender of other places which they have taken, that we need wish our own city to fall into their hands.'

'"The Lord will fight for you, and ye shall hold your peace,"' said the quakeress.

Mr. Raynor smiled a little.

'What do you think of this, mother?—the very first words of Deborah's song.

'"Praise ye the Lord for the avenging of Israel, *when the people willingly offered themselves.*"'

His mother shook her head at him, but answered the smile, nevertheless.

'Thee must hold thine own notions, but thee need never talk of Friends being stiff in theirs. Thee will be fonder of peace when thee is married.'

'When—' Mr. Raynor thought, as he stood musingly before the fire,—and yet there did seem some possibility of it now. But he only said,

'That could hardly be, mother.'

'Has thee seen Penn to-day?' inquired the quakeress.

'Not for two or three days.'

'He talketh so fast that one knoweth not well what he saith,' Mrs. Raynor went on, 'but if I mistook not, he hath a letter for thee, and from the north.'

'Where is he?'

'Nay, that I cannot tell. Perchance he may be in his room.'

Mr. Raynor sought him there, but there he was not; neither did he make his appearance at dinner.

'Well, trouble not thyself,' said the quakeress; 'when he *doth* return I will send him over to thee.'

And with that promise Mr. Raynor was fain to content himself, and to turn his face once more toward Long Island. But it was an unsatisfactory thing to leave the letter behind him; and in a most unsatisfied mood he paced down Broadway, more leisurely than was his wont, and scanned the passers by on either side. The one particularly jaunty and carelessly worn cap that he wished to see, however, was not to be seen; and his search came to an end at the ferry, when his horse had with prettily feigned shyness, carried him on board the boat. He did not dismount, but sat looking off into the distance.

There had been a storm—one of those stragglers from

Summer's troop that sometimes bring up the march in October;—but it was over now, and the growling clouds lay swept together in the east; their angry flashes scarce seen for the sunshine that had followed. Over head was a broad band of the deepest blue, with just a few little dripping clouds scudding across it; and the sunshine had come out with a burst, as if all its unseen light of the last hour had been treasured up for this.

But even as Mr. Raynor sat there in the beautiful light, wondering at its ever new beauty, a low murmur from the west drew his eyes thither. The blue had not changed its depth nor its clearness, but slowly impinging upon it came other cloud heads up from the western horizon, and a light shadow fell over the face of things. Most fine the sight was, and Mr. Raynor was apt to recognize its full beauty; yet now as he looked, his looks grew darker. Half consciously, half unconsciously, he had made the change in the weather a type of other changes—his fancy had been revelling in the sunshine; and these new cloud heads that came on apace seemed to shadow the mind's glow as well. Instinctively his thought took up the beautiful words of the preacher, and he remembered that there is but one time in life " when the sun, nor the light, nor the moon, nor the stars are not darkened, *nor the clouds return after the rain.*"

It was an unwonted thought for him, whose trust was in general so bright, so unmurmuring; and chiding himself almost for the very remembrance, he turned to see again how fairly, how perfectly one storm had rolled away—why should not the rest do likewise?

' Let it, or let it not!' was his next thought; for from one storm and in the face of another, the sunshine had drawn out the token of the everlasting covenant between heaven and earth, and the bow of promise bound both together.

"*My covenant will I not break, nor alter the thing that is gone out of my lips.*" And what was that covenant?— "*Even the sure mercies of David.*" "I will be to them a God, and they shall be to me a people."

"He causeth the cloud to come," Mr. Raynor remembered, "*whether for correction, or for his land, or in mercy.*"

The short October afternoon was already ended when Mr. Raynor reached the little volunteer camp on Long Island, lying quietly there in a mingling of light and darkness; for the moon was shining down between clouds, and the sprinkling of private lights contrasted well with the clear, cold patches of moonshine. Mr. Raynor gave the word, and passing the lines to his own tent, he found there the object of his search. At least one of them. Mr. Penn was making himself as comfortable as circumstances would allow, with three or four camp stools; his back supported by the locker, on which stood a light; his hands supporting the evening paper.

'You don't mean to say you've come back, Major Harry?' was the young gentleman's salutation, as he extended himself a little more at length upon the camp stools.

'You don't mean to say that you are found?' was his cousin's reply.

'Why yes, I suppose I am,' said Penn. 'Absolutely detected in the act of burning your candle and reading your paper. I've brought you something else to read, though.'

'So I understand. Are you sure you have brought it?'

'Why of course,' said Penn. 'At least it would be very odd if I hadn't, when I came over on purpose. I don't know but I should have sent it, only that I saw it was from Captain Clyde; and I should like to hear news of him well enough.'

'How long do you mean that I shall wait for the news myself?'

'Only till I can find it,' said Mr. Penn, despatching several messengers into his pockets. 'It's somewhere, I do presume. Don't be impatient, Harry—you never are that I know of, only you don't just remind one of Patience on a monument, in your present position of uprightness. "Wm. Penn Raynor, Esqr."—*that's* not it. What's this— "To making one" '—

'If you will give me your coat,' said Mr. Raynor, 'I will save you some trouble and myself some time.'

'Take something else,' said Penn—'a book, can't you, till I find it. No trouble at all, thank you Harry. I don't believe it's in this coat, any way. But do take something else in the meanwhile. Now there's a letter would amuse you like anything—from Rutgers—one of my privateering friends, you know, Harry. Capital letters he writes, too.'

'I think I would rather have my own first,' said Mr. Raynor.

'Yes, if you could get it first, but there's the very thing. Do you know,' said Penn, taking his hands from his pockets and lolling back on the camp-stools, 'Rutgers says the queerest thing in that letter!—Absolutely heard in Charleston that I was engaged to Miss Clyde!—as if I ever thought of such a thing!'

'You are quite sure you never did?' said Mr. Raynor, his eyes sending forth a little flash into the dusky gloom of the tent. Then subsiding again, he said, 'My letter, Penn!'

'Why *can't* you sit down and be easy?' said Penn. 'I tell you I can't find it. Maybe I left it at home in another pocket—you know I might have changed my coat. You shall have it in the morning.'

'I must have it to-night.'

'Then I *must* find it in this coat,' said Penn;—'can't

go over and back again—out of the question. Here it is this minute—slipped into that letter of Rutgers'—if you'd only taken that as I wanted you to—'

'If you will give me one of these camp-stools, Penn,' said Mr. Raynor, 'and a small share of the light, I will let you take anything else that you can lay your hands or your feet on.' And so far accommodated he sat down to read his letter.

Penn watched him for a while, but the pages were long turning over and the face unreadable.

'What news?' he said, when at length the letter was folded up.

'Nothing that would interest you particularly.'

'All well, I hope?' said Penn.

'Not all,' said Mr. Raynor.

'Not?' said Penn. 'Well, it's good they're not all sick. Best to take the bright view of things, you know. But I shall be really glad to see Miss Clyde back again—she's always so agreeable and '—

'Hush, Penn!' said his cousin almost sternly; and in wondering curiosity Mr. Penn held his peace.

Only for a time; then he began again.

'How do you suppose that letter got delayed, Harry?'

'Delayed?' said Mr. Raynor raising his head.

'Ever so many days,' said Penn carelessly,—'didn't you look at the postmark?'.

He looked now, and at the date—both told the same story. Mr. Raynor started up and began to put on the overcoat which he had just thrown off.

'You're not going out in this weather?' said Penn. 'Just hear the rain, once!'

'I shall do that to better advantage out of doors—' and he was gone.

Penn looked and wondered, and then slept. When he awoke, Mr. Raynor sat in his former place with his head resting on his hand.

'I had the queerest dream!' said Penn rousing himself,—'that you rushed out into a pouring shower in spite of all I could say. And now here you are, and there is the moon. What a nice place you have here, Harry—quite enviable.'

'To look at,' said his cousin. 'I doubt whether you would like it upon further acquaintance?'

'Yes I should,' said Penn. 'I should like to live here amazingly. I wouldn't have staid in New York another day if I could have got officer's quarters here.'

'How should you like to take my place here for a while, Penn?' said his cousin looking up.

'Like it? of all things! But where are you going?'

'Out of town for a few days.'

'To-morrow?' said Penn.

'No; I find I cannot get away to-morrow. But whenever I do.'

'Of all things, as I said before,' repeated Penn. 'I wish you had a dozen such places, that I might fill them all.'

'I think you will find one answer your turn,' said his cousin.

'But where are you going?' said Penn, his pleasure half-swallowed up in curiosity.

'Out of town, as I said.'

'I shall be very happy to do any thing I can, then,' said Penn, 'but I can't conceive what should take you away.'

Which however Mr. Raynor did not tell him.

'Everybody is going away I think,' said Penn. 'I stopped at Miss Arnet's to-night, and *she* was out of town.

Gone off quite suddenly, the waiter said. Sent for—he didn't know where. Harry, you look sober—what's the matter? Certainly *you* don't care about Miss Arnet?'

'Not much,' said his cousin.

'Then I say what's the matter?'

'" *There came a great wind from the wilderness and smote the four corners of the house, and it fell,*"' Mr. Raynor answered as he turned away.

Penn looked after him, but seeing the Bible which Mr. Raynor had now taken up, he thought that possibly it had been in his hand before, and that he had but read aloud.

CHAPTER XXXVI.

O nuncle, court holy-water in a dry house is better than this rain-water out o' door. In, nuncle, in.—King Lear.

There was no clock in Mrs. Hopper's house to strike the hour, but stillness did the work as well and said that it was very late; past midnight, the stars would have added, had they been visible. But it was raining heavily though with little wind: the rain came straight down from the clouds and dripped straight down in double measure from the trees. One little stream of light shot out into the damp air from an upper window of the house, but below all was dark and shut up and silent; and even the old house dog, who early in the evening had howled a little for low spirits, now indulged in a sounder sleep than usual, lulled by the badness of the weather. But as he lay stretched at length in the little back porch—which was indeed a small shed—there worked into his dreams a pattering that seemed not wholly of rain-water. And Trouncer first raised his head, and then uttered a short gruff 'Ough!'—after which he got up and walked to the shed door to take an observation.

There was not much to be seen. Night's curtains were all let down, with a fringe of mist and a thick lining of rain-water. And in that steady pour one would have said there was little else to hear; but Trouncer clearly perceived that horses' feet were coming along the road, and soon caught the glimmer of sparks from their iron shoes; and again he growled and pointed his ears and bristled up. But when the horses stopped just before him he stood absolutely still, with only that same smothered and gruff ejaculation. He seemed to have made up his mind that a beggar on horseback did not exist in real life, and that thieves would be more wary; therefore when two dark figures presented themselves at the entrance, Trouncer did not fly at them, but merely gave the closest personal attendance. And bestowing an honest sort of pat upon the dog's head, one of the strangers passed through the porch and knocked at the inner door,— a single rap, not loud but given with great distinctness.

The knock aroused Mrs. Hopper; and immediately her window went up and her nightcap went into the rain.

'Who's there in the shed?'

'Two men in the rain,' said a comfortable voice—a little disturbed withal; though its owner was stamping softly about the shed and whistling until disturbed by the question.

'Well, they'll have to stay there till morning,' said Mrs. Hopper. 'Night's the time for folks to sleep in.'

'This aint the place,' said the voice. 'Therefore let's in.' Then as if to some one else—'"Thou'dst shun a bear, but if thy flight lay toward the raging sea, thou'dst meet the bear i' the mouth." To her again.'

'Friends for Mr. Clyde,' said another voice from the darkness, going back to Mrs. Hopper's question and answering it anew.

'Friends for Mr. Clyde,' she repeated; 'well, I dare say he wants 'em bad enough. Who are they?'

'Come, come!' said the first voice, 'open your doors. It's damp here, good woman. "In such a night to shut me out!"'

Mrs. Hopper closed the window.

'Jerushy!' she said, 'start right up and clap somethin' on to ye—here's visiters at the door; and afore I open it do you hide in the passage, and if they get the upper hand o' me, you kin rouse the house. Hope they won't rouse it themselves, knocking.'

The strangers however seemed as cautious as she could desire, and stood in patient silence while she raked open the bed of coals on the kitchen hearth, and tried to light a candle. But either the coals were poor, or the dampness of the night had found its way down chimney; for though Mrs. Hopper picked up one coal after another with the tongs, and presenting her candlewick blew till she saw unknown colors in the darkness; nothing came of it but a shower of sparks, and they fired nothing but her patience.

'Of all nights in the three hundred and sixty-seven!' she said throwing down the tongs, as a second knock made itself heard, but softly as before. 'Fetch the gun, Jerushy.'

'Mother,' said a half-stifled voice from the passage, 'are you there?'

'Where on the face of the airth should I be?' said Mrs. Hopper. 'Fetch the gun!'

'Aint you scared, mother?'

'I do believe you'd shy at your shadder, if there was light enough!' was the reply. And marching past her daughter with as swift and steady a step as though it were noonday, Mrs. Hopper soon returned with the gun, and kneeling down in the faint glimmer which the dying embers sent forth, she as soon had out the flint and therewith struck a light. That done she opened the door.

The strangers entered with no leave asked, without even throwing off their dripping cloaks; though indeed it had been difficult to bestow them in the outside darkness. Mrs. Hopper the while scanned them earnestly with her light, and was not long in finding out that she had seen one of them before; though as she afterwards told Jerusha, 'she couldn't tell when nor where, if her life was to pay.'

He repeated the inquiry for Mr. Clyde.

'Of course he's home,' said Mrs. Hopper; 'most folks is, this time o' night and weather. Who shall I say wants him?'

'Don't say any thing to anybody till we have a fire,' said the other stranger. '"It's a cold world in every office but thine, good Curtis, therefore fire."'

Mrs. Hopper gave him a look which certainly implied that her name was not Curtis, but she set down the candle, and applied such stimulants and remedies to the fire that in a few minutes it blazed to the chimney-top.

'Ah! that's worth while,' said the last speaker, drawing near the fire and spreading himself out before it, to dry as it were. 'Friend Henry—"when the mind's free the body's delicate,—" "the tempest in *thy* mind doth surely from thy senses take all feeling else, save what beats there!" Art thou insensible to fire as well as to water?—a salamander as well as a merman?'

His companion came forward at this remark, but as if the fire were matter of very second-rate importance; and the flickering light which played upon his face awoke no gleam of recognition and enjoyment.

'You want Mr. Clyde woke up then?' said Mrs. Hopper.

'Not on guard—' soliloquised the older man. 'No, don't wake him if he's asleep—which I know he isn't. Give us two shakedowns here on the floor, and no more about it till morning.'

'Likeliest shakedowns you'll get in this house'll be your two selves,' said Mrs. Hopper. 'There's the floor, but where the beds are I don't know. 'Tain't particularly hard, for a floor, I have heard them say as have tried it.'

'Hum—don't think I'll qualify myself for an indorsement,' said her questioner. 'And so Mr. Clyde is asleep. And how's his sister?'

'Little to boast of, except her good looks,' said Mrs. Hopper. 'They stick by her yet.'

'Is she no better?' said the other stranger, turning round.

'Can't be much better'n she is, to my thinking,' said Mrs. Hopper. 'The fever's strong yet, and she isn't—if that's what you mean. Come to, I believe they did have some hopes of her to-day, though.'

'Wake Mr. Clyde at once, will you my good lady?' said the older man in a different tone; drawing forth his snuffbox the while, and taking an immense pinch, as he roused himself up into an attitude of more business and less enjoyment. . 'And harkye, don't let the grass grow under your feet; it's too late in the season for that.'

And for a moment the two stood alone in the light blaze of the fire. But Thornton was not asleep, and came down instantly. The greeting was silently earnest. The doctor then had recourse to his snuffbox, but the two younger men stood with hands yet clasped.

'I must see her at once,' said the doctor, laying his hand upon Thornton's shoulder. 'Come, leave him to take care of himself—always does.'

And as with quiet steps they left the room, Mrs. Hopper returned, and advanced to mend the fire and improve its light as a medium of observation. But for such an object the medium mattered little. Mr. Raynor was impenetrable. Standing there with one shoulder braced against the tall wooden mantelpiece, he had watched the two gentlemen as they quitted the room; and when the door alone met his gaze in that direction he still looked, as if his thought had gone further and the eye but tarried where it must. There was nothing to be read in that look however, or if there were, it was writ in a language unknown to Mrs. Hopper; and he answered all her questions, and refused all offers of supper, with such clearness and self-possession, that she could not suppose him to be 'taking an abstraction' of any thing. She left him to his thoughts at length, and with them he held deep discourse; with but the rain and the rising wind for a refrain.

Meanwhile Thornton had prepared Rosalie for the sight of her kind physician and friend; and the doctor walked in and took his seat at her bedside, forbidding her to speak by a peremptory motion of his finger.

'Now why couldn't you get sick in town, like a Christian?' said Doctor Buffem, as he took Rosalie's hand in his, and examined her countenance with his practised eyes. 'Sending for me into the backwoods at this time of year! it's unendurable. Yes, it was very good of me to come, and all that sort of thing; of course it was. And you didn't send for me; certainly not. I'll tell you what, my young lady, there aren't many people could play the magnet with me this fashion. This was such a desired and pet job of mine, and one of my assistants was so very pressing—pet of his too. Couldn't well refuse to come when he offered to show me the way. Hum—eyes haven't lost much of their brightness. Just put that light a little more out of sight, Mr. Clyde. Now how do you feel yourself, Miss Rosalie?—well and happy?'

'Happy, sir—not quite well.'

'Cart before the horse,' said the doctor,—'no right to feel happy.'

'Not much right,' said Rosalie, with a little smile. 'That is true.'

'Just as bad as ever, I see,' said Doctor Buffem. 'Won't own it, neither.'

He made some further inquiries, left with Miss Arnet both directions and medicine, and taking Thornton's arm walked across the hall into his room. There the doctor sat down and took snuff as usual. Thornton waited in silence.

'The most thing I'm anxious about is myself,' was the doctor's first remark. 'I don't know how you are off for sleep, Mr. Clyde, but I've had none these three nights. Never saw such a power-press as that man is, in my life! Can't form half an opinion upon unsatisfied organs of sleep; therefore if you will permit me at once to retire to this bed, I will with pleasure resign to you my half of the kitchen fire.'

'You think Rosalie is better?' said Thornton.

'Don't know how she was,' said the doctor. 'How can I tell whether she's better? Keep yourself quiet, and don't fret her, above all things. And just tell Mr. Raynor that he needn't come waking me up every half hour to go and see how she is,—I'll wake up myself and no thanks to him.'

And silently Thornton went down stairs. He met Mr. Raynor's look, and repeated the doctor's precise words by way of answer. And then laying one arm on his friend's shoulder, he rested his head there, with the look and action of a weary mind and body laying off their own fatigue upon some one else. Neither spoke, until a half hour had passed; and then Mr. Raynor insisted that Thornton should have in the couch from the next room, and upon that take some more substantial repose. But he himself went back to his old stand at the fireplace.

CHAPTER XXXVII.

Phe. Thou hast my love; Is not that neighbourly?
Sil. I would have you.—As You Like It.

BEFORE morning, or rather before morning light, the weather changed. In place of the falling rain there was now only a gentle drip from the eaves, and the wind had risen, and blew in soft and freshening gusts around the house. Cocks were trying their voices, and a dim perception that was neither light nor yet darkness, stole in through the kitchen windows. Within doors there was no change, no stir. Thornton slept heavily upon his hard couch, and not the footfall of a mouse broke the silence overhead.

Mr. Raynor felt weary with the close, still air of the house—nothing doing, nothing to be done; but he did not move, unwilling to lose the first word of tidings that might come. It seemed to him as if till it came he must stand where he was. And yet in one moment after this feeling had crossed his mind he walked to the door, softly drew back the great bolt and passed out. And Trouncer roused up to follow him.

It was beautiful out of doors, even in that darkling light. The wind waved the leafless branches in a shadowy, fitful fashion, and blew away the clouds as fast as the northwest could gather them up. Overhead they came flying, a perfect rabble of clouds; and in every clear space between them, the stars shewed their bright eyes and winked at the fact that it was near sunrise. Wet, wet, everything was: the very air seemed washed and sweetened; and the advancing light glimmered in long strips of water in the road, with now and then a broad pool.

'Ough!' said Trouncer—but it was only at the impatient kick of a horse in the distant stable; and by turns the cock-crows were contrasted with a cheery, helpless little twitter, low and sweet, from some sleepy bird. Fearless if it was helpless—joyous too, and trustful. '*They neither have storehouse nor barn, yet your heavenly Father feedeth them.*'

Mr. Raynor stood listening, taking the full effect of every sight and sound, yet knew not clearly that effect until the Bible words began to come into his mind—those words which dumb Nature could but point out.

"As the mountains are round about Jerusalem"—so came the first—"*As the mountains are round about Jerusalem, so the Lord is round about his people, from henceforth even for ever.*"

Was not that enough? Could not all be left to that most excellent loving-kindness and tender mercy which could not err? "*Behold, he that keepeth Israel shall neither slumber nor sleep!*"

O human blindness, and weakness, and want of trust! Mr. Raynor thought, as still he stood looking, and heard 'the feathered people' begin their morning song, and remembered: "*Are not two sparrows sold for a farthing? and one of them shall not fall on the ground without your Father.*" "*Fear not therefore*"—that was what everything said. "*Shall not the Judge of the whole earth do right?*"

So constantly had he watched the progress of things, so gradually had it come on, that it was with almost a start that he perceived the first gleam of sunlight which had darted into the world, and lit on the vane of the little village church in the distance. Mr. Raynor turned at once and went back into the house. No change there yet; but hardly had he resumed his stand at the fireplace, before the stifled creaking of shoes was heard and the hall door opened.

If any traces of sleepiness remained about the eyes of Martha Jumps as she entered the kitchen, they all vanished when she saw Mr. Raynor there and Thornton asleep on the settee. But Thornton awoke instantly, and starting up, exclaimed,

'How is your mistress, Martha?'

'She's better, praise be blessed,' said Martha, as she walked up to the mantelpiece and set down her candlestick.

'Who says so?' said Thornton.

'I ought to know, if anybody did, for I've just come from seeing her sleeping like any kitten,' replied Martha. 'Miss Arnet says so, too. There's nothin' whatever to hinder our having breakfast at the usual time.'

Thornton went up to see for himself, and was too well satisfied with seeing to come down again until breakfast was ready. Then he and Doctor Buffem appeared together.

'All right and sweet and comfortable,' said the doctor. 'I may go back to New York as fast as I came; or now I think of it, more leisurely—being at my own risk. You do not go with me, friend Henry?'

'No, sir.'

'I think you will be equal to any emergency which may arise,' said the doctor. 'And now, my dear sir, breakfast! It's ill travelling without the staff of life.'

'And if Rosalie goes on steadily improving, when would it be safe for her to return to New York?' said Thornton, as they took their seats at the table.

'New York? fal de rol!' said the doctor. 'Don't bring her back to brick walls till she's able to climb 'em. She's seen enough of New York for one while. The minute she can stand alone take her off for change of air and scene—jaunt about a little—go South, if you like; but don't let her see New York these three months.'

The doctor mounted his horse and rode away, and the other two gentlemen stood somewhat thoughtfully looking after him. Mr. Raynor spoke first.

'What are you thinking of, Thornton?'

'Doctor Buffem's orders.'

'I will see them carried out,' was the next grave remark.

'You shall, if I have any voice in the matter.'

'Say nothing about it now.' And nothing was said, even before Mr. Raynor went back to New York himself for a week.

But one afternoon at the end of that week, when Rosalie was well enough to sit up in a great chair by her wood fire, and all the rest had gone out for a walk; that peculiarly quiet step might have been heard on the stairs—if indeed it had made noise enough.

Quietly he went up, and quick, for that was his custom; but his foot slackened its pace now on the upper stairs, and as it reached the landing-place stood still, and his breath almost bore it company. Martha had gone down a few minutes before, leaving Rosalie's door half open; and thinking all human ears far away—with the perfect stillness of the house—she was singing to herself in the fading sunlight. Singing softly, and in a voice not yet strong, but with such clear distinctness that the listener caught every word.

He waited till the hymn was finished—waited for another, but it came not; and still he lingered, as if there were a halo about her he liked not to break. Then a quiet knock at the open door, a quiet word of admission, and whatever effect he charged upon his presence the room looked no less bright to her.

'Does thy song betoken strength?' he said.

'Only weakness—of that kind which craves a strong support—and rests in it, and delights in it.'

'Wilt thou make use of my strength, such as it is?' said he smiling. 'I would fain bestow it upon thee.'

'Having more than you want?'

'A little surplus, which I should like to see invested.'

'I should think business might call for it all,' said Rosalie. 'How are affairs on Long Island?'

'In the old state of quiescence. I have left Penn in charge of my department.'

'For the present, I suppose.'

'For the present and future, both. I am going South.'

'South!' said Rosalie. 'You?'

'Yes,' said he, smiling. 'Not without you.'

She looked quickly up at him, then down again, but she heard the same smile in his next words.

'Will that direction suit you?'

'Are you so intent upon journeying, Mr. Raynor, that you can talk of nothing else?'

'Question!' he said with the same tone.

'The first letter of a new alphabet is not to be lightly spoken.'

'That was the second letter; this is the first—When do you expect to come down stairs?'

'I shall have to consider of that,' she answered.

'Let not the consideration be too long, or I may take you away before it comes to an end.'

'I think you are merry to-night, Mr. Raynor.'

'With reason.'

'But if you take up my words so,' Rosalie said, 'I shall not be able to say what I wish.'

'I do not wish you to say anything,' said he laughing 'I merely came to say something to you. For the rest of the evening you may think and not speak. It is always well to know beforehand what one has to do; and this dear Rosalie is not to be reasoned against nor reasoned away,— therefore think not so much as may trouble thee. Goodnight.'

Tom Skiddy stood out in the chip yard next morning, and Miss Jumps in her old position with her hands behind her, stood leaning against a tree and watching him. The frost lay upon every chip and blade of grass to which the sun had not yet paid his morning visit; and lurked in corners and by fences, secure for some time from his approach. The trees were in the poverty-stricken livery of November— some thinly clad, the most not clad at all; and with every rustle of the wind there fluttered down some of the remaining leaves, crisped with last night's frost.

Tom was elaborately dressing out a knitting-needle from a strip of red cedar, while the companion strip lay on a log hard by.

'How would you like to go South, Tom Skiddy?' said Martha.

'Fur south as Connecticut I shouldn't object to,' replied Tom.

'That aint South,' said Martha,—'Connecticut's north when you're in York. I mean South that aint north nowheres.'

'Guess likely I shouldn't care about it,' said Tom.

'Well what'll you do supposen the Capting goes?'

'He won't,' said Tom.

'Now how do you know, Tom Skiddy?' said Martha.

'I tell you he won't,' repeated Tom.

'And I heard the doctor say, "Take her South," with

my own ears,' said Martha. 'You don't s'pose the Capting'd make any bones about it after that?'

'Can't he send no one else?' said Tom.

'He might, I do suppose,' said Martha,—'that's smart o' you, Tom Skiddy. O' course every body knows what *he's* stayin' here for. But then if Miss Rosalie's goin' in for the Quakers, I aint agoin' with her—that's one thing. Couldn't—not for nuts.'

'You can find somethin' else to do, I s'pose?' said Tom, taking up the square stick of cedar.

'Most like I can—' said Martha,—'spry folks like me don't want for work generally.'

'I should think you might,' remarked Tom, measuring the two pieces. 'Nice fit, aint it?'

'Sort o'—' said Martha,—'one of 'em's rough enough for two, and big enough.'

'That's all along o' what's been done to t'other,' said Tom, beginning to work at the square stick.

'Some odds in the stuff, aint there?' said Martha.

'Not much,' said Tom. 'Both out o' one stick. One was further out and t'other further in—that's all.' And Tom whittled away assiduously, while Martha looked on in silence.

'Goin' to make 'em both alike?' she inquired.

'Just alike,' said Tom,—'being knittin'-needles. They're different shades o' red though. I don't care about seein' two things too much alike, if they *have* got to go together.'

'Such as what?' said Martha.

'Horses,'—said Tom,—'and folks. You and I always worked better, Martha, for having such a variety between us.'

'Well, I do' know but we did,' said Martha musingly.

'Just about what you call a fine match, we are, I think,' said Tom.

'Are!' repeated Martha, with a little toss of her head.

'Well, might be, then,' said Tom.

'I don't know about that,' said Martha. 'It mought, and it mought not, as folks used to say where I was raised.'

'So they did in my town,' said Tom, 'but then they always fetched up with "and then again it mought." I shouldn't mind making the experiment, for one.'

'I wouldn't be venturesome, Tom Skiddy,' said Martha, with her head a little on one side and leaning against the tree.

'I'll risk it,' said Tom.

'Well now!' said Martha.

'What's come over you to be so skeery?' said Tom. 'You're as bad as our white colt, that used to always shy afore he went through the bar-place.'

'I might be worse'n that,' said Martha. 'I might shy and not go through the bar-place after all, Tom Skiddy.'

'That aint the fashion o' colts,' said Tom. 'They wouldn't get paid for their trouble.'

'Well suppos'n I shouldn't get paid for goin' through?' said Martha.

'You would,' said Tom, shaving off thin slices of the red cedar.

'Sure?' said Martha.

'Sartain,' said Tom.

'Time I was in the house, I know,' said Martha; and in a very deliberate way Miss Jumps picked up her sun-bonnet and walked off towards the back door.

'Goin' through the bar-place?' said Tom.

'Maybe'—returned Martha. 'You're so good at making up things—s'pose'n you try your hand at some more.'

CHAPTER XXXVIII.

Shall I never see a bachelor of threescore again ?—Much Ado About Nothing.

IF anything could have made Mrs. Arnet deeply unhappy, a letter which she received from her daughter early in November would have done it. Fortunately nature had placed her beyond much risk of that sort, but discomposure she did feel in abundance.

'You must come here if you wish to see the grand ceremony of my life, mamma,' Marion wrote; 'for here it will take place. Thornton wishes it, and so does Rosalie; and I am but too glad to be spared the great New York fuss which you would think indispensable were I there.'

Indispensable!—the word came back from the very bottom of Mrs. Arnet's heart; which was however not so far off as it might have been. But married up there! in a country kitchen!— for what had any farmhouse but a kitchen;—the idea was overwhelming, and yet there was no help. There was time for her to reach them, but not to make them change their plans; and on the whole Mrs. Arnet concluded she had better stay at home. The mere ceremony was not much, and if she went away there would be no prepared fuss against their return; whereas by a diligent use of the time between now and then, she could do much to repair the mischief. Therefore she would not go.

Neither could Mrs. Raynor be present. So she wrote; the journey at that time of year and of her life seemed too much.

'I give thee up, dear child,' she said, 'as fully and freely as if there. I always thought thee too good to be mine alone. But go to thee I cannot: therefore come not for me.'

And so the night before that morning in November there was 'nobody but just their four selves,' as Mrs. Hopper said, in the sitting-room. Hulda had been there to be sure, in such a mixture of pleasure that she was to be with Marion for a while, and sorrow that Rosalie was going away, and joy to think of living always part of the time with her and Mr. Raynor too; that she was sometimes absolutely still, and sometimes flitted about like a very spirit of unrest. But now she had gone to bed and all was quiet. Quiet but for the sweeping remarks of the wind; and they were so general that nobody thought of answering them. The brother and sister were much in each other's thought; and could the thoughts have been read they would have told of

> —" All that fills the minds of friends
> When first they feel, with secret pain,
> Their lives henceforth have separate ends,
> And never can be one again."

Perhaps the faces revealed so much; for of the other two present, one was unusually grave, and the other at least as usual. But he was the first to speak: not in a particularly grave way, but rather playfully—as if willing with a light hand to attach and wind off the long threads of thought in which his companions had enwrapped themselves. And thus he spoke :

> ——' " Knowledge dwells
> In heads replete with thoughts of other men ;
> Wisdom, in minds attentive to their own." '

' Which would prove us all sages,' said Miss Arnet.

' Not all—' said Mr. Raynor. ' My attention at least was not turned within.'

' Nor mine,' said Thornton.

' No,' said his friend ; ' you have come near disproving the other line—

> " And whistled as he went for want of thought." '

' Why ? ' said Thornton laughing.

' You have given the fire so much, so meditative, and so needless attention.'

' So fruitless also,' said Rosalie.

' Very well,' said Thornton ; ' but I have not been so lost in meditation as to miss the glances stolen at us all from under cover of your eyelashes, little Sweetbrier.'

She smiled, but the playful lines quickly composed themselves into graver fashion than before.

' I am thinking, Alie,' said Thornton, ' what you will do without some one to take charge of.'

' She may take charge of me,' said Mr. Raynor.

' You ! ' said Thornton.

' Well ? ' was the quiet reply.

' It is such a comical idea to imagine anybody's presuming to dictate or even advise any line of conduct to you.'

' Presuming—yes,' said Mr. Raynor. ' I should scarcely call the idea comical.'

' Well doing it at all, then.'

'" He that hath no pleasure in looking up is not fit to look down,"' said Mr. Raynor. 'You are making me out very unfit for my trust.'

'I recant then,' said Thornton, 'and am quite willing that you should be perfect after your own fashion. I am certainly afraid she will lose the pleasure of fault finding—but I suppose she can live without it.'

Her lips parted in a little smile as if about to speak, but they closed again silently.

'I am afraid my old simile of the lock of hair must stand, Alie,' said Marion. 'But child you are tired, and in my judgment ought to go to bed.'

'My judgment does not say that.'

'And mine says must,' said Mr. Raynor.

She coloured a little, and Marion smiled, and Thornton said laughing,

'You see, Alie—he endorses my words. I am afraid your judgment will stand but a poor chance, after all.'

Even as he spoke, a little stir was heard in the kitchen; and the opening door shewed them not indeed any part of the stir, but the cause of it,—Mrs. Raynor—a very twilight spot of grey silk against the glow of the kitchen firelight. With as little excitement and bustle as if it had been her own parlour, so did the quakeress come in; and was met at the third step by her son, his motions as quiet though rather more quick.

'Thee sees how much impatience human nature hath yet Henry,' she said. 'I could not wait to see thy wife till she was ready to come to me, therefore am I here.'

'And she will not be here until to-morrow,' he said, leading his mother to where Rosalie stood supporting herself by her arm-chair. 'The next best thing is visible.'

The heart of the quakeress had but imperfectly learned

the quaker lesson; for in silence she embraced Rosalie and softly replaced her in the great chair, and in silence held out her hands to Thornton and Marion, and gave them most cordial though mute greeting. Then her hand came back to Rosalie and rested caressingly upon her head, and once again Mrs. Raynor stooped down and kissed her.

'Mother,' said Mr. Raynor, 'you forget that Rosalie is not a quakeress.'

'Nay surely,' she said. 'Wherefore?'

He answered only by a glance at the transparent hand on which Rosalie's cheek rested, its very attitude speaking some difficulty of self-control; but his mother understood, and removed her own hand and took the chair he had placed for her: answering then his questions and putting forth some of her own. Thornton and Marion meanwhile exchanged a few words but Rosalie said nothing.

'Why does thee not speak, love?' said the quakeress presently. Mr. Raynor answered.

'We were talking a while ago upon your favourite theme of silence, mother. What were those lines you used to quote in its defence?'

'It matters not, child,' she said,—'the lines were mayhap written by one who seldom held his peace save in a good cause.'

'Yet they were good, and you used to say them to me?'

'It may be I had done better not,' she said; 'therefore urge me not to say them again.'

'You will let him say them himself?' said Rosalie.

'If it liketh him—' said the quakeress. 'He thinketh not with me on all points.'

His hand laid on hers seemed to say those points were few and unimportant, as with a smile he said—

> '"Still born silence! thou that art
> Flood-gate of the deeper heart!
> Offspring of a heavenly kind!
> Frost o' the mouth and thaw o' the mind!"'

'Spring and winter are struggling for the mastery here to-night,' said Thornton. 'I wish the thaw would extend itself.'

'No,' Mr. Raynor said, 'not to Rosalie's lips. Do not set her talking to-night. Let her sleep—if to that she can be persuaded.'

'"He hath a will—he hath a power to perform,"' said Rosalie with a little smile as she rose from her seat; nor did she look to see the smile that her words called forth, although it were more than her own.

It was a pretty morning's work that Mrs. Hopper's best room saw next day, and a pretty company was there assembled. Only 'their four selves' again,—with just the set-off of the grey dress and cap of the quakeress, and the wonder and interest in every line of Hulda's little face,—with only the back-ground of country walls and hard country faces,—with no lights but the wood fire and the autumn sun. And the room had no ornament but themselves, unless the splendid red winterberries in Marion's hair. But it was rarely pretty and picturesque; and even the fact that Rosalie must sit whenever she need not stand, rather heightened the effect. Mrs. Hopper said it was the prettiest sight *she* ever saw, and Tom Skiddy quite agreed with her, with only one reservation,—'he wouldn't say that he couldn't see a prettier.'

CHAPTER XXXIX.

*Behold I see the haven nigh at hand,
To which I mean my wearie course to bend;
Vere the maine shete, and beare up with the land,
The which afore is fayrly to be kend,
And seemeth safe from storms that may offend:
Where this fayre Virgin wearie of her way
Must landed bee, now at her iourneye's end:
There eke my feeble barke a while may stay,
Till merry wynd and weather call her hence away.—Fuërie Queen.*

It is a melancholy fact that the end of a voyage cannot be as picturesque as the beginning thereof,—whether it be a voyage in earnest, or merely the 'wearie course' above referred to. There is no momentary expectation of either storms or sea-sickness, and both are an old story. The waves do not gradually run higher and higher, but 'contrarywise,'—there is very little sea *on*—if one may borrow a steam phrase, and the water becomes ingloriously tranquil. Unless indeed the fictional craft is to blow up with a grand explosion—and that in Sam Weller's words, 'is too excitin' to be pleasant.' In fact the voyage is over *before* the last chapter; and the only thing that can do, is to pilot sundry important people over the bar and through the straits, and land them all too safe, on the shores of this working-day world.

Not that, as somebody says, 'people begin to be stupid

the moment they cease to be miserable';—but still, when the course of true love, or of any other small stream, doth run smooth,—its little falls, and whirls, and foam, and voluntary beating against the rocks—its murmurs as a hard-used and thwarted individual—must of course be dispensed with. There is nothing for it, on either hand, but smooth water.

Mrs. Raynor sat alone in her library. Absolutely alone; for though the cat was enjoying himself on the rug, Mr. Penn was enjoying himself elsewhere; or it might be was attending to his duties on Long Island. Even the invariable knitting work was laid aside, and yet Mrs. Raynor busied herself with nothing else,—unless her own thoughts, or the general appearance of the room—for so might be construed the looks that from time to time went forth on an exploring expedition. With never failing recollection she replenished the fire, even before such attention was needed; and once or twice even left her seat, and with arranging hands visited the curtains and the books upon the table. Then returning, she took a letter from her pocket and read the beloved words once more. It was all needless. The words—she knew them by heart already, and the room was ordered after the most scrupulous quaker exactness.

The sharp edge of this was taken off by exquisite flowers, an eccentric little wood-fire, and a bountifully spread tea table; where present dainties set off each other, and cinnamon and sugar looked suspicious of waffles. The silver glimmered with mimic fires, the plates and cups shone darkly in their deep paint and gilding; and tall sperm candles were borne aloft, but as yet unlighted. Even the sad-colored curtains hung in softened folds in the soft fireshine, their twilight tints in pretty contrast with the warm glow upon the ceiling. As for the flowers, they hung their heads, and looked up, and laid their soft cheeks together, after a most coquettish fashion—as if they were whispering; and the breath of their whispers filled the room. A fair, half-revealing light found its way through the bookcase doors, and rested upon the old books in their covers of a substantial antiquity, and touched up the lighter adornments of such novelties as the quakeress or her son approved. The clock in its dark frame of carved wood went tick, tick, with the most absolute regularity, and told whoever was curious on that point that it was six o'clock.

Then Rachel appeared.

'Will thee have the candles lighted?'

'I thank thee, Rachel, not yet.'

'Does thee intend to wait tea even till they come?'

'Surely,' said Mrs. Raynor. 'But ye had better take tea down stairs, if so be ye are in haste.'

'Nay,' replied Rachel. 'Nevertheless, it may well chance that thy waffles shall be for breakfast.' And Rachel closed the door noiselessly and retired.

But while Mrs. Raynor turned her head the door was opened again as noiselessly; and when she once more looked round from a contemplation of the clock face, the very persons whom she had expected stood in the doorway. Rosalie in her flush of restored health and one or two other things, her furred and deep-coloured travelling dress, looking as little as possible like a quakeress; and Mr. Raynor, though bearing out his mother's words that he would have made a beautiful Friend, yet with an air and manner that said if he were one now it was after a different pattern.

'I wellnigh thought the south meant to keep thee!' the quakeress said as she embraced him.

'Nay mother,' he answered smiling, 'it was somewhat from the north that kept me. And you see how my rose has bloomed the while.'

'Fairer than ever! and better loved.'

'Than I deserve to be ——' Rosalie said.

'Thee need not speak truth after thine own fashion here,' said the quakeress with a smile, and laying first her hand and then her lips upon the fair brow that was a little bent down before her. 'Does not thee know that the right of possession is enhancing?'

And Rosalie had nothing to do but sit where they placed her, and let her hands be ungloved and taken care of; while questions and words of joy and welcome could not cease their flow, nor eyes be satisfied with seeing.

Then came tea; but Rosalie drew back from being put at the head of the table.

'That is Mrs. Raynor's place,' she said.

'So I think.'

'What does thee call thyself?' said the quakeress with a quiet smile. 'That is thy name now, dear child, and that is thy place.'

And Rosalie was seated there without more ado; where even Rachel surveyed her with unwonted admiration of colours and uncovered hair.

'Mother,' said Mr. Raynor, as it drew on towards eight o'clock, 'you must let me take Rosalie away for an hour. I know she will not rest till she has seen Thornton and Hulda.'

'This night?' said the quakeress. 'Thee will weary her.'

'That is just what I am trying to prevent.'

'Thee must judge for thyself, Henry,—nathless thee knows that we Friends think much of patience.'

'She is patient enough,' said Mr. Raynor laughing, and laying both hands on his wife's head as he stood by her chair. 'So patient that she requires very particular looking after.' And when the carriage came he took her away as he had said.

What a happy surprise there was! what a joyful hour of talk! How pleasant it was to see the old house again, restored from its fiery damage and with such owners. So much joy, that one is tempted to wonder why nobody ever wrote upon the Pleasures of fulfilment. And if her old sorrowful life came up to Rosalie, it was but to stir the very depths of her heart with wonder and gratitude; till she was ready to say with the Psalmist, "*What is man, that thou art mindful of him? or the son of man, that thou visitest him?*"

An hour had passed, and half of the next one, and still they lingered; until a slight stir arose in the street, and cries and shouts—first distant and then drawing near—broke the stillness. Cries not of fear, as it seemed, neither of disturbance, but of joy—of excitement—of wild congratulation. In a moment the little party were at the door.

All was still, breathless. Then again the murmur came swelling towards them, and foremost among the cries broke forth 'Peace! Peace!' Nearer and nearer the people took it up and cried, 'Peace! the Peace!' From one and another—from deep strong voices and from throats that could hardly raise the cry, it was heard—'The Peace! the Peace!'

'Peace! Peace!' cried out one little boy whose pattering footsteps bore him swiftly past the house. 'Peace! Peace!—I wish my voice was bigger!'

'I wish my heart was,' Mr. Raynor said. And as they rode home lights sprang forth in every window, the city shone as if with daylight; and ever went up that cry, 'Peace! Peace!'

THE END.

Any of these Books sent free by mail to any address on receipt of price.

RECENT PUBLICATIONS

OF

D. APPLETON & CO.,
443 and 445 Broadway, New York.

Mercantile Dictionary. A com-
plete vocabulary of the technicalities of Commercial Correspondence, names of Articles of Trade, and Marine Terms, in English, Spanish, and French; with Geographical Names, Business Letters, and Tables of the Abbreviations in common use in the three languages. By I. DE VEITELLE. Square 12mo. Half morocco.

"A book of most decided necessity to all merchants, filling up a want long felt."—*Journal of Commerce.*

"It is undoubtedly a very important and serviceable work."—*Indianapolis Journal.*

The Mystical Rose; or, Mary of
Nazareth, the Lily of the House of David. "I am the Rose of Sharon and the Lily of the Valley."—*Canticles.* "Many daughters have done virtuously, but thou excellest them all."—*Solomon.* "Blessed art thou among women."—*Gabriel.* By MARIE JOSEPHENE. 12mo. Cloth extra.

"This elegant and charming book has just appeared; it is worthy of a place in every family."—*Bellows Falls Times.*

"Its strong devotional character will commend it to many readers."—*Illinois State Journal.*

Cousin Alice: A Memoir of
ALICE B. HAVEN. 12mo, pp. 392, with portrait. Cloth.

"This is a record of deep interest, compiled with taste, skill, and judgment."—*Christian Times.*

"Exceedingly interesting."—*Eastern Argus.*

"Written with great vigor and simplicity."—*Boston Post.*

A Report of the Debates and

Proceedings in the Secret Sessions of the Conference Convention for Proposing Amendments to the Constitution of the United States, held at Washington, D. C., in February, A. D. 1861. By L. E. CHITTENDEN, one of the Delegates. Large 8vo. 626 pp. Cloth.

"The only authentic account of its proceedings."—*Indianapolis Journal.*
"It sheds floods of light upon the real causes and impulses of secession and rebellion."—*Christian Times.*
"Will be found an invaluable authority."—*New York Tribune.*

The Conflict and the Victory of

Life. Memoir of MRS. CAROLINE P. KEITH, Missionary of the Protestant Episcopal Church to India. Edited by her brother, WILLIAM C. TENNEY. "This is the victory that overcometh the world, even our faith."—*St. John.* "Thanks be to God, who giveth us the victory through our Lord Jesus Christ."—*St. Paul.* With portrait. 12mo.

"A work of real interest and instruction."—*Buffalo Courier.*
"Books like this are valuable as incentives to good, as monuments of Christian zeal, and as contributions to the practical history of the Church."—*Congregationalist.*

Sermons Preached at the Church

of St. Paul the Apostle, New York, during the year 1864. Second Edition. 18mo. 406 pp. Cloth.

"They are all stirring and vigorous, and possess more than usual merit."—*Methodist Protestant.*
"These sermons are short and practical, and admirably calculated to improve and instruct those who read them."—*Commercial Advertiser.*

The Trial. More Links of the

Daisy Chain. By the Author of "The Heir of Redclyffe." Two volumes in one. Large 12mo. 390 pp. Cloth.

"The plot is well developed; the characters are finely sketched; it is a capital novel."—*Providence Journal.*
"It is the best novel we have seen for many months."—*Montreal Gazette.*
"It is marked by all the fascinating qualities of the works that preceded it. * * * Equal to any of her former novels."—*Commercial.*

Chateau Frissac; or Home Scenes

in France. By OLIVE LOGAN, Authoress of "Photographs of Paris Life," etc., etc. Large 12mo. Cloth.

"The vivacity and ease of her style are rarely attained in works of this kind, and its scenes and incidents are skilfully wrought."—*Chicago Journal.*

"The story is lively and entertaining."—*Springfield Republican.*

The Management of Steel,

including Forging, Hardening, Tempering, Annealing, Shrinking, and Expansion, also the Case-Hardening of Iron. By GEORGE EDE, employed at the Royal Gun Factories' Department, Woolwich Arsenal. First American from Second London Edition. 12mo. Cloth.

"This work must be valuable to machinists and workers of Iron and Steel."
—*Portland Courier.*

"An instructive essay; it imparts a great deal of valuable information connected with the making of metal."—*Hartford Courant.*

The Clever Woman of the Family.

By the Author of "The Heir of Redclyffe," "Heartsease," "The Young Stepmother," etc., etc. With twelve illustrations. 8vo.

"A charming story; fresh, vigorous, and lifelike as the works of this author always are. We are inclined to think that most readers will agree with us in pronouncing it the best which the author has yet produced."—*Portland Press.*

"A new story by this popular writer is always welcome. The 'Clever Woman of the Family,' is one of her best; bright, sharp, and piquant."—*Hartford Courant.*

"One of the cleverest, most genial novels of the times. It is written with great force and fervor. The characters are sketched with great skill."—*Troy Times.*

Too Strange Not to be True.

A Tale. By Lady GEORGIANA FULLERTON, Authoress of "Ellen Middleton," "Ladybird," etc. Three volumes in one. With Illustrations. 8vo.

"This work, which is by far the best of the fair and gifted Authoress, is the most interesting book of fiction that has appeared for years."—*Cairo News.*

"It is a strange, exciting, and extremely interesting tale, well and beautifully written. It is likely to become one of the most popular novels of the present day."—*Indianapolis Gazette.*

"A story in which truth and fiction are skilfully blended. It has quite an air of truth, and lovers of the marvellous will find in it much that is interesting."
—*Boston Recorder.*

What I Saw on the West Coast

of South and North America, and at the Hawaiian Islands. By H. WILLIS BAXLEY, M.D. With numerous Illustrations. 8vo. 632 pp. Cloth.

"With great power of observation, much information, a rapid and graphic style, the author presents a vivid and instructive picture. He is free in his strictures, sweeping in his judgments, but his facts are unquestionable, and his motives and his standard of judgment just."—*Albany Argus.*

"His work will be found to contain a great deal of valuable information, many suggestive reflections, and much graphic and interesting descriptions."—*Portland Express.*

The Conversion of the Roman

Empire. The Boyle Lectures for the year 1864. Delivered at the Chapel Royal, Whitehall, by CHARLES MERIVALE, B.D., Rector of Lawford, Chaplain to the Speaker of the House of Commons, author of "A History of the Romans under the Empire." 8vo. 267 pp.

"No man living is better qualified to discuss the subject of this volume, and he has done it with marked ability. He has done it, moreover, in the interest of Christian truth, and manifests thorough appreciation of the spiritual nature and elements of Christianity."—*Evangelist.*

"The author is admirably qualified from his historical studies to connect theology with facts. The subject is a great one, and it is treated with candor, vigor, and abundant command of materials to bring out its salient points."—*Boston Transcript.*

Christian Ballads. By the Right

Rev. A. CLEVELAND COXE, D.D., Bishop of Western New York. Illustrated by John A. Hows. 1 vol., 8vo. 14 full page engravings, and nearly 60 head and tail pieces.

"These ballads have gained for the author an enviable distinction; this work stands almost without a rival."—*Christian Times.*

"Not alone do they breathe a beautiful religious and Christianlike spirit, there is much real and true poetry in them."—*Home Journal.*

Mount Vernon, and other Poems.

By HARVEY RICE. 12mo.

"Fresh and original in style and in thought. * * * Will be read with much satisfaction."—*Cleveland Leader.*

D. APPLETON & CO.'S PUBLICATIONS. 5

The Internal Revenue Laws.

Act approved June 30, 1864, as amended, and the Act amendatory thereof approved March 3, 1865. With copious marginal references, a complete Analytical Index, and Tables of Taxation. Compiled by HORACE DRESSER. 8vo.

"An indispensable book for every citizen."
"An accurate and certainly a very complete and convenient manual."—*Congregationalist.*

Speeches and Occasional Addresses.

By JOHN A. DIX. 2 vols., 8vo. With portrait. Cloth.

"This collection is designed chiefly to make those who are to come after us acquainted with the part I have borne in the national movement during a quarter of a century of extraordinary activity and excitement."—*Extract from Dedication.*

"General Dix has done a good service to American statesmanship and literature by publishing in a collected form the fruits of his ripe experience and manly sagacity."—*New York Tribune.*

The Classification of the Sciences.

To which are added Reasons for Dissenting from the Philosophy of M. COMTE. By HERBERT SPENCER, Author of "Illustrations of Universal Progress," "Education," "First Principles," "Essays: Moral, Political, and Æsthetic," and the "Principles of Psychology." 12mo.

"In a brief, but clear manner, elaborates a plan of classification."—*Hartford Courant.*

"One of the most original and deep thinkers of the age. * * * Will greatly assist all who desire to study Mental Philosophy."—*Philadelphia Press.*

Orlean Lamar, and Other Poems,

by SARAH E. KNOWLES. 12mo. Cloth.

"Not only lively and attractive with fancy, but it has the excellence of being pure, moral, and Christian."—*Religious Herald.*

Lyrical Recreations.

By SAMUEL WARD. Large 12mo. Cloth.

"There is a wealth of beauty which discovers itself the more we linger over the book."—*Journal of Commerce.*

"Its pages bear abundant evidence of taste and culture."—*Springfield Republican.*

Lyra Anglicana; or, A Hymnal

of Sacred Poetry. Selected from the best English writers, and arranged after the order of the Apostles' Creed. By the Rev. GEORGE T. RIDER, M.A.

"As beautiful and valuable a collection of Sacred Poetry as has ever appeared."—*St. Louis Press.*

"Will be found very attractive from the warm devotional tone that pervades it."—*New York Times.*

"Much of the poetry is not found in American reprints."—*Gospel Messenger.*

Lyra Americana; or, Verses of

Praise and Faith, from American Poets. Selected and arranged by the Rev. GEORGE T. RIDER, M.A. 12mo.

"They are collections of the most beautiful and touching poetic expressions of devotion."—*The Chronicle.*

"The collection is purely American; the lyrics are all full of devotion and praise. Unusual taste has been evinced in the selection of the poetry."—*Troy Times.*

On Radiation. The "Rede" Lecture,

delivered in the Senate House before the University of Cambridge, on Tuesday, May 16, 1865, by JOHN TYNDALL, F.R.S., Professor of Natural Philosophy in the Royal Institute and in the Royal School of Mines. Author of "Heat considered as a Mode of Motion." 12mo. Cloth.

Contributions to the Geology

and the Physical Geography of Mexico, including a Geological and Topographical Map, with profiles of some of the principal mining districts. Together with a graphic description of an ascent of the volcano Popocatepetl. Edited by Baron F. W. VON EGLOFFSTEIN. Large 8vo. Illustrated. Cloth.

"The general interest excited on this continent as well as in Europe by late political events in Mexico, where a wide field for mining and land speculation is about to be opened again to foreign industry and foreign capital, has induced me to submit to the public two interesting publications of this highly favored region."—*Extract from Introduction.*

Histoire de Jules Cesar.

Par S. M. I. NAPOLEON III. Tome Premier. 8vo. With Maps and Portrait.

"No work has excited as much attention as the Life of Julius Cæsar, by the Emperor Napoleon, which has been so many years in preparation, involving the expenditure of large sums of money in procuring material and examining localities."—*Miss. Republican.*

"We are glad to see it in this form, because we get a clearer insight into the illustrious author through his own vernacular. The original gives the best spirit of a book, and it is always to be preferred."—*Boston Gazette.*

The Handbook of Dining, or

Corpulency and Leanness Scientifically Considered; comprising the Art of Dining on Correct Principles, Consistent with Easy Digestion, the Avoidance of Corpulency, and the Cure of Leanness. Together with special remarks on the subjects. By BRILLAT-SAVARIN, author of the "Physiologie du Gout." Translated by L. F. SIMPSON. 12mo. Cloth.

"This is a book that almost everybody will wish to read, as almost every one is either too fleshy or too lean, and consequently will desire to see what directions so eminent a writer as Savarin gives to prevent one and cure the other. The volume contains curious facts and suggestions, and some very valuable ones."—*Eastern Argus.*

Freedom of Mind in Willing, or

Every Being that Wills a Creative First Cause. By ROWLAND G. HAZARD. 12mo, pp. 455. Cloth.

"It is a very admirable work; a book for thinkers."—*Boston Gazette.*

"A valuable addition to the literature of the subject; its style is clear and its arguments both strong and well put."—*The Methodist.*

Beatrice. By Julia Kavanagh,

author of "Nathalie," "Adele," "Queen Mab," etc., etc. Three volumes in one. 12mo. Cloth.

"This is one of the best novels published in a long time. The authoress has achieved a reputation second to none in the literary world as a romance writer. This is her last great effort, and it is a remarkably interesting one. The plot is a candid embodiment of great ideas and action."—*Troy Times.*

"The scene is laid in one of the suburbs of London. The insight into certain phases of social life which it gives is curious. The heroine 'Beatrice' is a striking character. The plotting Frenchman 'Gervoise' is also drawn with consummate art. In a word, there is more real sturdy stuff in Beatrice than in a score of the current novels of the day."—*Albany Evening Journal.*

Report of the Council of Hygiene

and Public Health of the Citizens' Association of New York upon the Sanitary Condition of the City. Published with an introductory statement, by order of the Council of the Citizens' Association. Large 8vo, 360 pp. Illustrated with numerous maps, plans, and sketches. Cloth.

"Is devoted to a minute account of the causes of disease, death, and misery, and of the sanitary reforms needful to arrest those evils."—*New York Express.*

"No volume of intenser interest has ever seen the light in this city than this record of the state of things now existing. The investigations have been most thorough."—*New York Paper.*

"The result is no mere collection of statistics, but interesting, deeply interesting rehearsals of facts."—*New York Commercial Advertiser.*

Social Statics; or, The Conditions

Essential to Human Happiness Specified, and the first of them developed. By HERBERT SPENCER. Author of "Illustrations of Progress," "Essays: Moral, Political, and Æsthetic," "Education," "Principles of Biology," "Principles of Psychology," etc. With a notice of the author, and a steel portrait. Large 12mo, 518 pp. Cloth.

"The topics of the book will be found to be treated in a masterly manner. It is a work that thinking men will delight to read, and one which all would profit by reading."—*Eastern Argus.*

"He is a profound and earnest thinker, and possesses the rare faculty of discussing abstract questions in a way to interest every class of readers."—*Chicago Christian Times.*

The Correlation and Conservation

of Forces. A Series of Expositions, by Prof. GROVE, Prof. HELMHOLTZ, Dr. MAYER, Dr. FARADAY, Prof. LIEBIG, and Dr. CARPENTER, with an Introduction and brief Biographical Notices of the chief promoters of the new views, by EDWARD L. YOUMANS, M. D. "The highest law in physical science which our faculties permit us to perceive, the conservation of force." —Dr. Faraday. One thick volume, 12mo, 438 pp. Cloth.

"These papers are invaluable to scientific men and scholars, and should have an extensive reading."—*Troy Daily Times.*

"Their expositions are remarkably free from technicalities, and are written in a style which renders them suited for popular reading."—*Home Journal.*

"Will be read with profound attention by thoughtful men."—*N. Y. Observer.*

Cyclopædia of Commercial and

Business Anecdotes, comprising Interesting Reminiscences and Facts, Remarkable Traits and Humors, and Notable Sayings, Dealings, Experiences, and Witticisms of Merchants, Traders, Bankers, Mercantile Celebrities, Millionnaires, Bargain Makers, etc., etc., in all Ages and Countries. Designed to exhibit, by nearly three thousand illustrative Anecdotes and Incidents, the Piquancies and Pleasantries of Trade, Commerce, and General Business Pursuits. By FRAZER KIRKLAND. Embellished with Portraits and Illustrative Cuts. Large 8vo. 2 vols.

"It is a most complete illustration of the habits of thought, manners, and eccentricities of the leading business men of the world, forcibly illustrated by anecdotes remarkably well told."—*Northwestern Church.*

"Will be found a very readable book, containing many rich and racy anecdotes."—*Bangor Whig.*

"A capital work, well arranged and carefully prepared."—*Hunt's Magazine.*

Essays: Moral, Political, and

Æsthetic. By HERBERT SPENCER, author of "Illustrations of Universal Progress," "First Principles of Philosophy," "Education," "Social Statics," "Elements of Biology," "Elements of Psychology," "Classification of the Sciences," etc., etc. 12mo. Cloth.

"The author is one of the most profound thinkers of the age."—*Eastern Argus.*

"A valuable addition to literature and science. Such works do the world good."—*Boston Gazette.*

Apologia Pro Vita Sua. Being

a Reply to the Pamphlet entitled, "What, then, does Dr. Newman Mean?" "Commit thy way to the Lord, and trust in Him, and He will do it. And He will bring forth thy justice as the light and thy judgment as the noonday." By JOHN HENRY NEWMAN, D. D. Large 12mo, 393 pp. Cloth.

"A more important contribution to polemical literature has rarely been published."—*Philadelphia Press.*

"This is a book of deep and possibly permanent interest."—*Christian Times.*

"It is a work which should be read by all who wish to keep informed in the Church matters of the day."—*Northwestern Church.*

Pelayo.   An Epic of the Olden

Moorish Time, By ELIZABETH T. PORTER BEACH. Illustrated. 12mo.

"I have been charmed to perceive how skilfully the author has availed herself of the materials for poetic embellishment furnished by the history of that romantic period."—*William C. Bryant.*

"It is a story of great interest, told in flowing verse, in which descriptive talent and poetic fervor are not wanting."—*Albany Argus.*

"The plan of the poem is well formed, the details are managed with considerable skill, and the poetry is characterized at once by imagination and feeling."—*Watchman and Reflector.*

At Anchor: A Story of our

Civil War, by an American. 12mo. Cloth.

"This is a story of the war, well written and interesting from the beginning to the close. Those who commence will be sure to read it through."—*Boston Journal.*

"A graceful and readable story of flirting and fighting, and love and loyalty."—*Congregationalist.*

History of the Rise and Influence

of the Spirit of Rationalism in Europe. By W. E. H. LECKY, M. A. 2 vols., small 8vo. Cloth.

"We opened these volumes, never having heard the name of the author, and entirely ignorant of his pretensions to a place in English literature. We closed them with the conviction that Mr. Lecky is one of the most accomplished writers and one of the most ingenious thinkers of the time, and that his book deserves the highest commendation we can bestow upon it.... This book well deserves to be universally read and carefully studied. ..In a word, we hope to see this work take its place among the best literary productions of the age."—*Edinburgh Review.*

An Introduction to the Devotion-

al Study of the Holy Scriptures. By EDWARD MEYRICK GOULBURN, D. D., Prebendary of St. Paul's, Chaplain to the Bishop of Oxford, and one of Her Majesty's Chaplains in Ordinary, Author of "Thoughts on Personal Religion." From the Seventh London Edition. 12mo. Cloth.

"I wish this little Treatise to be regarded as part of a large work ("Thoughts on Personal Religion") which has been more recently published, in which I have attempted to give some suggestions for the performance of religious exercises in general. Among these the study of the Holy Scriptures does not find place, because I have felt it to be of such transcendent importance as to require a separate treatise.'—*Extract from Preface.*

www.ingramcontent.com/pod-product-compliance
Lightning Source LLC
Chambersburg PA
CBHW032011220426
43664CB00006B/210